KV-467-884

SOCIAL CHANGE AND
CULTURAL TRANSFORMATION
IN AUSTRALIA

90 0343560 6

WITHDRAWN
FROM
UNIVERSITY OF PLYMOUTH
LIBRARY SERVICES

5

SOCIAL CHANGE AND CULTURAL TRANSFORMATION IN AUSTRALIA

ADAM JAMROZIK

Faculty of Social Sciences
Flinders University of South Australia
Faculty of Humanities and Social Sciences
University of South Australia

CATHY BOLAND

Cumberland College of Health Sciences
University of Sydney

ROBERT URQUHART

Social Policy Research Centre
University of New South Wales

Published by the Press Syndicate of the University of Cambridge
The Pitt Building, Trumpington Street, Cambridge CB2 IRP, UK
40 West 20th Street, New York, NY 10011–4211, USA
10 Stamford Road, Oakleigh, Melbourne 3166, Australia

© Cambridge University Press 1995
First published 1995

Printed in Hong Kong by Colorcraft

National Library of Australia cataloguing-in-publication data

Jamrozik, Adam.
Social change and cultural transformation in Australia.
Bibliography.
Includes index.
1. Multiculturalism – Australia. 2. Social change – Australia.
3. Australia – Social conditions – 1945– . 4. Australia –
Ethnic relations. I Boland, Cathy. II. Urquhart, Robert,
1961– . III. Title.
305.800994

Library of Congress cataloguing-in-publication data

Jamrozik, Adam.
Social change and cultural transformation in Australia/Adam
Jamrozik, Cathy Boland, Robert Urquhart.
Includes bibliographical references and index.
1. Social change – Australia. 2. Australia – Social conditions–.
I. Boland, Cathy, 1951–. II. Urquhart, Robert, 1961–.
III. Title.
HM101.J255 1995

303.4'0994–dc20   94–32830
                                                        CIP

A catalogue record for this book is available from the British Library.

ISBN 0 521 41462 8 Hardback

UNIVERSITY OF PLYMOUTH

Item No.	900 343560 6
Date	- 6 JAN 1998 S
Class No.	303.40994 JAM
Contl. No.	0521414628

LIBRARY SERVICES

Contents

Tables

Figures

Abbreviations

ABS	Australian Bureau of Statistics
ACMA	Advisory Council on Multicultural Affairs
AEAC	Australian Ethnic Affairs Council
AIMA	Australian Institute of Multicultural Affairs
BIR	Bureau of Immigration Research
CAAIP	Committee to Advise on Australia's Immigration Policies
DEET	Department of Education, Employment and Training
NACSAR	National Advisory Committee on Skills Recognition
NESB	Non-English-speaking background
OMA	Office of Multicultural Affairs
ROMAMPAS	Review of Migrant and Multicultural Programs and Services
SBS	Special Broadcasting Service

Preface and Acknowledgements

Australia is a country of immigrants. It is also a country of contradictions. From the time the post-war immigration program began in the late 1940s Australian society has been undergoing a process of social and cultural change, while at the same time preserving the homogeneity of its cultural inheritance from Britain and the stability of its 'core' social institutions: the Westminster system of government modified to a federal structure, the legal system, models of professional organisations and a host of other institutions inherited from the colonial era. While most of these institutions have functioned reasonably well for many decades, the resistance to change embedded in them has been weighing increasingly heavily as a kind of 'historical baggage', inhibiting the development of an Australian identity which would more adequately reflect the country's internal social and cultural reality and be more appropriate to relations with the neighbouring countries of the region.

To this day many Anglo-Australians have not been able to accept unequivocally that their country is in the Asia-Pacific region, not in Europe or a part of Britain. These attitudes of uncertainty and confusion have also been reflected in government policies relating to the cultural diversity of Australian society: multiculturalism has been accepted as a policy for some years but, at best, the concept means a tolerance of the cultural diversity of Australia's ethnic communities, provided the Anglo core of the power and class structures remains unaffected. Behind the rhetoric of change and the policy of access and equity there is a resistance to change in the attitudes and vested interests embedded in the institutional power structures of a class society. Whatever cultural transformation has occurred has been a transformation from below, that is, from the cities and mainly working-class suburbs in which immigrants from non-English-speaking countries have found their place in the host society. As a result, Australia is now a society with a multicultural population, regulated and governed by a monocultural power structure.

We argue in the book that unless the monocultural character of the power structure is diluted so that it more adequately reflects the multicultural nature of its population, Australia will not be able to function efficiently as a socially cohesive, industrialised high-technology society. Furthermore, without a cultural transformation Australia will not be able to develop an identity as a nation in its own right, and will run the risk of failing to make a place of significance for itself in the Asia-Pacific region and in the world.

The idea for this book came about when we, the authors, worked together as a research team at the Social Policy Research Centre, University of New South Wales. For reasons beyond our control we have since found ourselves to be in three different institutions. This unexpected separation has caused a delay in the completion of the book and necessitated some re-allocation of tasks among the co-authors. All three authors have contributed ideas and research work, but the final writing has been completed by Adam Jamrozik. The delay has had some positive results because we have been able to take into account some of the changes that have taken place on the Australian political scene in the early 1990s, culminating in the dramatic results of the 1993 Federal elections.

The book has been written from a broad sociological perspective, within an original theoretical and methodological framework, and contains some arguments and conclusions which we hope readers may find interesting and perhaps surprising.

In our analysis of social change and cultural transformation in Australia we have drawn on the work of many people who have examined some of these issues over the past two decades or more. We gratefully acknowledge their contributions and we owe them deep gratitude because we have benefited greatly from their insights. We trust that we have recorded their observations and interpretations as they intended to convey them and we hope that this book will add to the knowledge of the important issues they have addressed before us.

A number of friends and erstwhile work colleagues have also contributed to our work in many ways. We want to record specifically our thanks to Penny Anagnostou, Lothar Bringmann, Jacklyn Comer, Diana Encel, Ruth Errey, Dympna Kava, Loucas Nicolaou, Lynda Pawley, Lynn Sitsky, Donald Stewart, and Michael Wearing. Our special thanks go to Eveline Tindale for reviewing the typescript and for very useful comments and suggestions. We also want to express our thanks to Phillipa McGuinness and Robin Derricourt of Cambridge University Press for their assistance and patience. We hope that interest in the issues of social change and cultural transformation in Australia which the book will generate in its readers will be their reward.

Adam Jamrozik, Cathy Boland, Robert Urquhart

CHAPTER 1

Introduction

Two of the most frequent opening statements made in public speeches and conference papers addressing social issues in Australia are: 'We live in times of rapid social change'; and 'We are a multicultural society'. These assertions are usually received as axiomatic and with enthusiasm by receptive audiences; but at certain other times and in other places that acceptance is likely to be less enthusiastic, especially in the case of the second statement. Indeed, that statement might be, and often is, categorically rejected.

In this book we examine these two assertions by looking at Australian society in a time perspective of close to half a century, from the late 1940s when the mass immigration program began to the early 1990s, with some references to earlier years where this is relevant to the issues we set out to analyse. We consider the nature of social change as a multi-dimensional phenomenon by looking at empirical evidence of changes in the population, in the structure of the family, in the structure of industry and occupations, and in other related indicators of change in the socio-economic structure. As to the assertion that Australia is a multicultural society, we seek to identify those aspects and the population strata of Australian society in which cultural diversity is evident, and those areas of social activity and the population strata where such diversity is less visible or appears to be non-existent. We aim to identify the reasons for any such differences and relate these differences to the class nature and class divisions of Australian society. We consider that the class characteristics of Australian society constitute an integral part of the cultural inheritance from Britain and are maintained in an essentially unchanged form in what we here term the 'core' institutions; by this we mean institutions such as the government and its public

1

administration, the legal system, the education system, professional bodies, organised Christian churches, business organisations and the trade unions.

While focusing on the issues of social change and cultural transformation in Australian society, we raise the question as to what extent the Australian experience might be unique and to what extent that experience has been a reflection of social changes and cultural transformations taking place in other parts of the globe. The question is important, for by viewing the Australian experience in a global perspective we achieve some insight into past and current events which provide an indication of future directions and the options Australian society may have to face.

This introductory chapter outlines the content of the book, the theoretical framework of its arguments, the sources of information and the methods of study used in the collection and analysis of the data. The first chapter introduces the argument, which is further developed in various chapters of the book, that among the many influences on the culture of any society the social stratification of that society will be one of the most important factors; and, further, in Western industrialised societies such social stratification is based on, and is the reflection of, their class structure. The cultures of these societies will then be influenced or mediated by that class structure and differentiated along socio-economic and class lines. For this reason we consider that it is important to perceive and analyse culture and cultural transformation in these societies by using the concept of class as the guiding heuristic in the analysis and interpretation of data.

Our concept of class follows broadly a Marxian/Weberian synthesis, in which class is perceived as an overarching higher-order construct and a basic social division, transcending and overriding, either entirely or to varying degrees, other societal divisions such as gender, religion or ethnicity. Furthermore, we apply this concept of class to Richard Titmuss's (1963) concept of comparative advantage in the '*command over resources through time*', which he used in his analyses of social and economic inequality. The use of this concept enables us to identify the differential access to, and control over, society's resources by various groups and strata of the population. By 'resources' we mean economic, social and cultural resources as well as political power, in both the public and the private sector. Interpreted and applied in such a perspective, the concept of 'command over resources through time' allows for the perception of society as a system of social relations in a comprehensive sense, without pushing the concept of social relations to the Marxian abstraction of 'relations of production'. It also allows for the retention of the Weberian view of social class, status and party as three sources of societal power. In applying the concept of class in this wider and more flexible perspective, we aim to venture beyond the conventional usage of that concept, attempting to generate hypotheses which may facilitate the perception and interpretation of social change and cultural transformation as two interrelated social phenomena.

Conceptual Issues

The existence and nature of social phenomena has been one of the problematic areas in the social sciences, arguments among scholars and disciplines revolving mainly around the relevance of positivist methods in studies of such phenomena which are, essentially, processes rather than things and intrinsically different in their nature from physical objects. We do not wish to enter this debate here except to note, with due emphasis, that the existence and nature of social phenomena depend very much on the way such phenomena are perceived and interpreted. In turn, perceptions and interpretations of social phenomena are based on and are influenced by certain assumptions and concepts which may, or may not, be clearly formulated; often they remain unstated and are 'taken for granted' as common-sense and self-evident knowledge.

Like most concepts in the social sciences and in sociology particularly, concepts related to social structure, social change and culture are not universally agreed upon and uniformly shared: such phenomena are diversely perceived, defined and interpreted, reflecting differences in the guiding theoretical concepts and normative stances used by social scientists, researchers and analysts. The appropriateness and validity of concepts formulated by some writers are thus often questioned by others. For, example, it has been argued by some writers (eg Jakubowicz 1981) that the concept of ethnicity is not a valid concept in social analysis, although in the 'real' world ethnicity as an identifiable attribute of a person or of a social group is commonly accepted and recognised by observers and members of a given social group itself (Nicolaou 1991). Similarly, the appropriateness of the concept of class to the study of contemporary 'post-modern' societies is questioned by some writers on the grounds that other social divisions – such as sex/gender, ethnicity or religion – are the main divisions in such societies. On the other hand, other scholars maintain that social divisions based on class are still fundamental divisions, although the nature of class relations might have changed. For example, Beilharz *et al.* express the view that 'the end of class society is not in sight, at least not from any reasonable perspective' (1992:4). We agree with this statement, for if the class nature of a society can be ascertained by the application of the concept of 'command over resources through time', then the trends towards greater inequality which have been observed in industrialised societies over recent decades suggest an entrenchment of class characteristics in these societies rather than their demise, and Australia is no exception.

In our perspective on Australia as a class society we focus attention on the large and internally-differentiated social stratum of academics, media commentators, public administrators, professionals, and people of related occupations, collectively referred to in the sociological literature as 'the New Class' (Gouldner 1979) or 'the new middle class' (Abercrombie and Urry 1983; Wright 1985). This focus is important because the members of the new middle class occupy key positions of power and influence in the core social institutions which control access to many of society's resources. Furthermore, the new middle class, through a wide range of activities – research, teaching, publishing, policy advice and policy formulation, the administering and delivering of services – engages in 'mental production', that is, it authoritatively defines the nature of the society and its culture, that is, the nature of social reality. It is possible, indeed likely, that any such definitions, being based on perceptions and interpretations of social phenomena from the class position of the definers, will not be the same as the social reality experienced by others in their everyday lives, especially by people in other classes. It is thus unlikely that any social change and cultural transformation that might have occurred in Australia since the late 1940s has occurred uniformly, or has been perceived uniformly, throughout the entire class structure.

In effect, in any society there will always be two kinds of social reality existing, as it were, side by side at any given time: the social reality experienced by people in the course of their everyday life; and the one authoritatively defined by the people who are part of the dominant power structure. The two kinds of social reality may or may not be identical; they rarely are identical, however, because the former is experienced and the latter is only observed and interpreted, and both are mediated through the class position of those who observe and interpret social reality and those who experience it. In this book we attempt to identify both kinds and any differences between them, and then consider the significance of such differences.

The phenomena identified and discussed in this book are examined in the framework of four related concepts which are of the utmost relevance to the analysis of contemporary Western industrialised societies: class; social change; culture; and cultural transformation. In social analyses each of these concepts is the subject of widely differing definitions and interpretations. For example, class structure has been conventionally presented as a structure of inequality based on vertical socio-economic stratification and power differentials in social relations, but it is now argued by some writers (eg Kreckel 1989) that this vertical metaphor is no longer appropriate for the analysis of Western

industrialised societies. Instead, Kreckel suggests, a concept of 'centre'
and 'periphery' now serves better to explain the structure of inequality
and social stratification in these societies. He acknowledges, however,
that it is likely that the vertical metaphor will continue to be the perspective in which people will see the social world because that metaphor
is well embedded both in language and in people's consciousness
(1989:152). Indeed, as Ossowski observed some years ago (1963), in the
perceptions of social structures, in the interpretations of social phenomena, and in expressions of values the vertical metaphor was established
in antiquity and was reinforced in early Christianity. To this day, the
good, the powerful, the rich, the beautiful, the healthy, are all meta-
phorically perceived to be 'on top', and so is the dominant social class.

Similarly, in explaining social change, social scientists have used a range
of theories, attempting to establish causative links with other social
phenomena, ranging from production technology (Marx), to divisions of
labour (Durkheim), to religion (Weber). On this issue, we note particularly the observation made by Tenbruck on the significance of the difference between objective and perceived social change. Tenbruck argues:

> There is a deplorable tendency in sociology to equate social change narrowly
> with objective alterations. However, even radical changes of social conditions
> depend for their social effect on when and how they are being perceived.
> Conversely, social change may occur under stable conditions if people come
> to see, for whatever reason, their situation in a new light.   (1989:16)

If perceptions of social phenomena are mediated by the perceiver's
position in the class structure, then to Tenbruck's comment on the
significance of when and how changes in social conditions are perceived
it is necessary also to add *who* perceives them. This is one of the
questions we ask in this book.

The concept of culture also presents a picture of a wide diversity. In
simple terms, the culture of a society may be defined as 'the whole way
of life'; such definitions have been put forward in many writings on
culture, even if not always expressed exactly in these words. In the
sociological literature the concept of culture tends to be broad rather
than narrow in the inclusion of aspects of social life. For example,
Andrew Milner defines culture as

> that entire range of institutions, artefacts and practices which make up our
> symbolic universe. The term thus embraces art and religion, science and
> sport, education and leisure and so on.   (1991:3)

It is interesting to note that this definition, although broad and
inclusive, does not mention matters of an economic or political nature,
although on reading Milner's arguments it is clear that those matters are

included in the 'and so on'. The definition also speaks of a 'symbolic universe' and does not say whether, or to what extent, that symbolic universe is mythical or is reflected in social reality which may be ascertained objectively. Nevertheless, Milner argues (echoing Karl Marx in his *German Ideology*) that a feature of modern definitions of culture is the 'dominance of a distinctively capitalist mode of production' which includes cultural production (1991:4).

A similar 'looseness' seems to be unavoidable in definitions of cultural change or cultural transformation. Milner justifies this by arguing that 'cultural transformation, unlike material transformation, cannot be determined (that is, known) with the precision of natural science' (1991:44). It is apposite to add here that all social phenomena are of that nature, and attempts to define such phenomena with great precision are not likely to be useful or fruitful.

In our perspective on the changes which have occurred in Australian society since the late 1940s, cultural transformation has been mediated by the class structure. At the level of everyday life in working-class suburbs cultural transformation has been to a certain extent a two-way process, a kind of a dialectical process which affects both the newcomer and the native, transforming the perspectives, attitudes and even social conduct of both, although not necessarily to the same extent or in the same direction. Among the middle classes, the process of cultural trans-formation has been minimal, affecting mainly some forms of social activity, and in the 'core' social institutions the transformation has been virtually absent. How these differences have arisen is discussed in various chapters of the book, but especially in Chapters 8 and 9.

Methods of Study, Hypotheses and Sources of Data

The four issues addressed in this study – social structure, social change, culture and cultural transformation – are appropriate areas for socio-logical endeavour but are also of interest to other disciplines. Culture especially – its concepts and meanings – has been a field of interest pursued by anthropologists, artists, art critics, and people from many other professions and disciplines. We thus extend our perspective into areas which have not been the exclusive domain of sociologists and also to some aspects of society and culture which have not been studied much either by sociologists or by researchers in other disciplines. We examine and analyse empirical data on the relevant aspects of Australian society and then compare them with other writers' accounts of the four concepts mentioned above. Our analysis aims to show how and to what extent these perceptions and interpretations are reflected in the empirical evidence. Furthermore, we attempt to relate the authoritative perspectives and interpretations of these analysts to the common everyday experiences of the population at large. We thus include in our analysis the perceptions, interpretations and actions of a range of social actors, and in doing this we look at the processes of social change and cultural transformation which take place in the operation of Australia's formal core social institutions such as the education system, political institutions, public administration and professional bodies, as well as in the informal encounters and interactions of everyday life.

It is in everyday life that people create and experience their social reality (Berger and Luckmann 1971). It may be argued that the concept of 'everyday life' lacks precision and for this reason it may not be a very useful concept to use in the analysis of the phenomena we have set out to examine. However, everyday life itself is not an orderly and precise experience, but, as Featherstone argues, 'everyday life is the life-world which provides the ultimate ground from which spring all our concep- tualisations, definitions and narratives' (1992:160). It is in everyday life that routine, repetitive tasks and interactions are experienced before they are reflected upon, given a meaning, are conceptualised and en- dowed with certain values. It is through the experience of everyday life that people develop their view of the world around them and con- sciously locate themselves within it. It is also through this experience that, in encounters with one another, people develop their culture which gives them an identity as a community. The process of cultural formation is thus similar to the process of class formation, both taking place through social interaction in the course of everyday living (Thompson 1968).

As the title of the book indicates, our analysis focuses especially on two social phenomena – social change and cultural transformation. Why these two dimensions? The brief answer is simply this: the processes of social change and cultural transformation occur simultaneously, although not necessarily at the same rate or speed, or with the same force. How do these two processes interact and with what effects and outcomes? Does social change affect all strata and classes of society, and does cultural transformation occur equally in all strata and classes? Which aspects of social life are affected? Is there a resistance to these processes and, if so, where does it occur and what forces are at play? These are some of the questions and issues we seek to explore here.

From our observations of the changes that have taken place in Australian society since the late 1940s we have formed the view, or a hypothesis, that cultural transformation occurs as a *transformation from below*, that is, it begins as a social reality experienced by people through their everyday activities and encounters with others (Berger and Luckmann 1971). Because we accept the clear evidence of the fact that the inflow of immigrants from a wide range of ethnic and cultural backgrounds has been the main factor in any cultural transformation that has occurred in Australia, we emphasise the role of working-class people (the working class being broadly defined) as social actors in this transformation. For many years from the start of the immigration program most newcomers settled almost exclusively in working-class suburbs where they came to experience face-to-face encounters with the local population. It was through these encounters and interactions, in the workplace and in the neighbourhood, that the transformation began as a two-way process, the newcomers and the locals influencing each other reciprocally and finding common ground in certain views and interests. In the higher social strata or classes, contacts with immigrants were only transient; immigrants might have been seen at work, on the city streets, in shops, or in newspaper photographs, but they certainly did not live next door.

To this day that situation prevails albeit in a less exclusive way. As will be seen in the chapters that follow, the higher one looks on the socio-economic scale, the less cultural transformation is visible, and in the core social institutions the inherited Anglo-Celtic or, more precisely, Anglo-Saxon monoculture reigns undisturbed. This monoculture, being the dominant culture, acts as a formidable force of stability and resistance to outside influence. Unlike the cultural encounters that take place in the context of everyday social activities which are conducive to a degree of cultural transformation as a two-way process, any encounters between people from different cultures that might take place in the monocultural environment of the core institutions will entail unequal power relationships and consequently will be conducted on the terms of those institutions. In effect, such encounters become encounters between different social classes. Cultural division becomes class division because in the core institutions cultural differences are perceived in class terms, the institutions being the 'core' of the dominant class. On the basis of this observation, we maintain that cultural transformation is mediated through the class structure, resulting in different degrees of transformation in different social classes.

Related to the issue of class-mediated cultural transformation is also the issue of resistance to cultural influences. At times this resistance extends to fear of other cultures or even to open antagonism and conflict, particularly when these cultures are perceived and interpreted as incompatible and based on racial differences. Within the perspective of Australian history, we perceive this issue to have been contrived by the colonial powers and the dominant classes, with the aim of maintaining their own position of privilege and controlling the subordinate classes by pointing to 'the dangers from outside'. As will be seen in the chapters

that follow, there is a remarkable similarity between some of the
arguments and projected fear of other races in the early years of this
century and those found in the late 1980s. Although the language used
in such arguments might now be more discreet, inferences of 'racial
contamination' are often quite clear. Racial differences are presented in
class terms, being clearly based on a notion of the superiority or
inferiority of certain social groups, communities or nations. As Benedict
Anderson expresses it:

> The dreams of racism actually have their origins in ideologies of *class*, rather
> than in those of nation; above all in claims to divinity among rulers and to
> 'blue' or 'white' blood and 'breeding' among aristocracies.   (1983: 136)

In reading about resistance to immigration or multiculturalism in the
daily press, in magazines, or even in the so-called learned journals, it is
important to ask 'Who says so?' Considering this question does not mean
engaging in the pursuit of a conspiracy theory but rather pointing to the
contradiction between the statements purportedly reporting or
reflecting 'public opinion' and the social reality of life in the towns and
suburbs in which immigrants have lived now for close on half a century,
without open conflicts or race riots. It is for this reason that we use
verbatim comments published in the mass media, so as to consider the
significance of 'who says so?' and perhaps also 'why?'

It has to be noted at this point that Australia today is a place of
paradox: the bulk of its population of European origin, but located in
the Asia-Pacific region, or Oceania; populated by large and culturally
diverse immigrant minorities and their descendants, but entirely monocultural in its political institutions and social and economic cultural
mainstream; seemingly developed industrially and economically, but
backward in its productive capacity and experiencing a repetitive economic malaise; once considered to be a 'social laboratory', but in comparison with the industrialised countries of western Europe now
regarded as a laggard in social policies and social development (Castles
1985). How these contrasts and paradoxes developed and continue to
exist are the questions considered in this book.

Since the late 1940s Australia has been experiencing the processes of
social and cultural change, while at the same time sustaining the
homogeneity of its British cultural heritage. Australia has retained the
Westminster system of government, awkwardly modified into a federal
structure; it has the English language, tertiary education and professions
modelled on the English system, the adversarial legal system, and a host
of other traditions, including if not an imitation of the English class
structure, at least some of its features. The stability of its core institutions

has been remarkable. While most of these institutions might be perceived to have functioned reasonably well for many decades, the resistance to change embedded in them, which we see as a function of the colonial inheritance, has been inhibiting the development of an Australian identity and culture which would be more appropriate to the current social and economic conditions and to the region in which Australia is located. Even the debate on a republican form of government and independence from the British Crown has risen and ebbed from time to time without producing much change. Opinions in favour of a republic might have increased in the early 1990s but so have the voices in defence of the British monarchy, raising fears of political instability and social divisions if the monarchy were to be abandoned.

This cultural inheritance continues to exert a powerful hegemonic influence over education, socialisation, politics and the Australian view of the world. As a result, in a country inhabited by well over one hundred ethnic groups, the majority of the Anglo-Australian population remains rigidly monocultural; in a country where a multitude of languages is spoken every day, Anglo-Australians remain monolingual; among a multitude and diversity of religions, the expression 'we are a Christian country' is frequently heard and each day of parliamentary sittings the session begins with a Christian prayer.

Thus, from one perspective Australia has ostensibly changed and is now seen as a multicultural society; from another perspective, it has all the marks of an English colonial outpost, rigidly adhering to the inherited traditions (language, customs, laws, system of government – and a dose of xenophobia) effectively resisting social change and other cultural influences. The resistance to cultural change creates disaffection and disenchantment among immigrants who encounter various forms of antagonism and discrimination, at times in overt forms but nowadays often in more subtle forms; not so much in everyday community life but in encounters with officialdom. Many still meet formal and attitudinal barriers to practising their profession or trade. Non-Christian communities encounter difficulties in obtaining approval for erecting their houses of worship. The economic ills of the country are often explained in terms of 'too many migrants'. From a national point of view these attitudes result in great economic and cultural loss to the country: a waste of the knowledge, skill and talents of immigrants. Such attitudes also lead to a brain drain through the departure of the more skilled and highly educated immigrants who become disillusioned with their experience in the host country.

The argument we put forward here is that behind the rhetoric of change, multiculturalism and 'access and equity' policy there is an inherent and institutionalised resistance to change embedded in social attitudes and in the vested interests of the power structures. We aim to examine why and how, in the face of the extensive multicultural influences present in the country for some decades, the core institutions of Australian society have remained basically unchanged and mono-cultural. What forces are at play in these processes of change and resistance to change?

The 'core' and 'periphery' metaphor appears to be an appropriate concept for this analysis: the monocultural core of social institutions surrounded by forms of ethnic and cultural diversity. We aim to identify some of the social forces located in the core which oppose cultural transformation, and to provide some reasons and explanations as to why such resistance continues despite the rhetoric of change which is frequently heard. It is further argued that unless these core institutions become more open to enrichment by the cultures which are at present on the periphery, Australia will continue to neglect the human resources available in the community. It will thus find it very difficult to raise its economic performance to the level and quality necessary to sustain an adequate standard of living and quality of life and will be unable to develop an identity which can be recognised and accepted by other countries, especially by those of its own region. Furthermore, without cultural transformation Australia is clearly running the risk of losing its place of significance in the region – culturally, politically and economic-ally – and hence the risk of regressing to the status of a so-called third world country. In the past important economic opportunities and human resources have been wasted in Australia because of this resistance to change, and without change the future of this society does not look very promising, either in economic terms or in social and political terms.

The data on which the analysis in this book is based have been drawn from a wide range of sources, such as the population census, research reports and direct observations of everyday life. We have also drawn extensively on analyses of issues and commentaries by academics and others which have been published in the daily or weekly press. We consider that the mass media play an important role in identifying public issues, placing them on the agenda for public debate and influencing public opinion as well as government policy. Newspapers particularly have been used extensively for this purpose, and many social and economic commentators, politicians and other public figures have used this medium to air their views – and their prejudices. The study thus has a strong empirical basis consisting of quantitative and qualita-tive data about Australian society. The book also has a wider frame of reference, attempting to relate the Australian experience of social change and cultural transformation to other societies with similar experiences. Has the Australian experience in these areas been unique, or has it been similar to the experience of other societies in the contemporary world? To the extent that one can generalise from Australian experience, will the concepts and theories of social change and cultural transformation receive new attention and possible reformulation? We consider that in these turbulent times on the world stage a study of these processes is particularly apposite.

As for terminology, we tend to use the term *immigrant* rather than *migrant*, except, of course, when quoting other people. In our view, the former describes more appropriately the people who come to Australia as permanent settlers; the latter, although it has been in general usage in Australia, suggests a transient population. We also speak of *ethnicity*, while being aware that the term is not precise and is ascribed a diversity of meanings (Nicolaou 1991:15–16). In common usage 'ethnicity' may mean nationality, race, religious affiliation or a mixture of all of these. However, terms or names acquire meaning through usage, and 'ethnicity' is one such term: people are seen, and see themselves, as Greeks, Italians, Poles, Vietnamese, or Chinese, even if they have never lived in Greece, Italy, Poland, Vietnam, or China. Jews have retained their ethnic and cultural identity without a country of their own for two thousand years. In Australia, the term 'ethnic' is erroneously applied to people of non-English-speaking background (NESBs), as distinct from people of English-speaking background (ESBs), as if the latter did not have an ethnic identity. This distinction, too, is often a misnomer for other reasons because many people from, say, Hong Kong, Malaysia, India or South Africa have been brought up speaking English. Thus, in the conventional usage, 'ethnic' or NESB really means a person who is not 'white', or not of Anglo-Saxon or Anglo-Celtic background. The distinction has its own strange logic: for example, a person born in Australia whose grandparents emigrated from, say, Italy is an 'ethnic', but a new immigrant from, say, England or Scotland, is not. The former is still likely to be referred to as an 'ethnic Italian'; the latter might be 'English' or 'Scottish' but not an 'ethnic'.

In the pursuit of distinguishing people by their real or assumed origins, the person referred to as an 'Australian' becomes rather mythical. Nevertheless, there is a small majority of the population that constitutes what may be called, at this stage at least, 'the mainstream', even if that majority is itself 'ethnically diverse', much smaller than it is believed to be by some, and continuously diminishing both through immigration and intermarriage. For this reason, although we do not find the term entirely satisfactory, in referring to people of the Australian cultural mainstream we speak of *Anglo-Australians*; and in a historical perspective we refer to the *Anglo-Celtic*, *Anglo-Saxon*, or *British* or *English* inheritance, whichever term appeared to be the most appropriate in a particular case. The usage of these terms has varied widely, both in the literature and in common everyday discussions, and differences of opinion on the correct usage are likely to remain. In particular, the use of Anglo-Celtic as a term indicating homogeneity in the Australian English-speaking population has been questioned on the grounds that it conceals an important distinction and also certain historical facts. As Price points out, 'Anglo-Celtic society has never been uniformly English', either in Britain or in Australia. In Britain, many Irish, Scottish and Welsh persons 'resented the historic practice of treating them as inferior kinds of Englishmen and fought hard to preserve their languages and customs' (1985:43). Now, Price says:

> It is a strange touch of historic irony that when such persons migrate to Australia they find a system of so-called multicultural equality which denies their historic ethnicity and lumps them in with the dominant English group under the category of 'non-ethnic'. (*ibid.*)

Charles Price is not the only person expressing this view. Sneja Gunew finds the term Anglo-Celtic 'totally unacceptable unless used with extreme caution and unless internal divisions [within the population described by that term] are indicated' (1990:101). Castles *et al.* consider the term to be 'an ill-conceived monstrosity, which can only partially paper the gulf', particularly between the English and the Irish (1988:8). These criticisms are warranted, as they point to the assimilationist tendencies which have been characteristic of certain attitudes and practices among Anglo-Australians, attitudes and practices which classify together people of diverse ethnic, cultural or national groups, either through ignorance or for the sake of convenience.

It is necessary to emphasise at this point that most people living in Australia today are immigrants or descendants of immigrants. There is only one section of the population which by its ancestry has the right to call itself 'Australian'. We follow the established usage in referring to these Australians as Aborigines and Torres Strait Islanders, although we are aware that in some areas of Australia Aborigines now refer to themselves as Koories (or Nungas), while using their more specific tribal identities in most parts of the country.

The eleven chapters of the book, fall broadly, but not discretely, into three parts. This arrangement has been arrived at as a way of examining the processes of social change and cultural transformation in Australia, while at the same time looking at Australia in the context of the industrialised societies of the Western 'free market' or capitalist system. The aim of this perspective is to identify common features of these processes in such societies and so propose some theoretical propositions and hypotheses which may be generalised from the Australian situation.

The first part consists of this introductory chapter and Chapter 2, which attempts to identify some of the important issues of culture and social change in class societies. Various perspectives on culture and class structure are examined, seeking to establish a theoretical and empirical context for the analysis of the Australian situation.

The next seven chapters (Chapters 3–9) present an empirical analysis of Australian society. Chapter 3 gives an overview of social changes which have occurred in Australia from the late 1940s to the early 1990s, adding references from earlier periods. Chapter 4 examines the immigration program since the late 1940s and the cultural diversity of the Australian population which has emerged from the inflow of people from all parts of the globe over this time. The evolution of the concept of multiculturalism is analysed in Chapter 5, which identifies its antecedents, contested views and attitudes towards the concept, as well as the methods of implementing the concept in federal and to a lesser degree in state policies.

The interplay of cultural diversity with the existing class inequality in Australian society is examined in Chapter 6. The problematic nature of this interplay is revealed by the position of immigrants in the structure of the labour market, in the differential acceptance of cultural influences in various social strata, as well as in the differences between the rhetoric of multiculturalism and its differentiated acceptance and accommodation in the class structure. The problematic nature of multiculturalism is further examined in Chapter 7 by looking at the issues and tensions in Australian society arising from the diversity of religious beliefs in a country which has been traditionally regarded as Christian.

Chapter 8 attempts to identify the effects of cultural diversity and raises the question as to what extent cultural transformation has occurred in Australian society. It looks at certain areas of social life and economic activity in which the contribution of immigrants has been particularly marked and which has produced positive effects for the whole society. This aspect is further elaborated in Chapter 9 where the focus of the analysis shifts to the identification of the sources of resistance to cultural change. Particular attention is given here to the role played by the core institutions in any processes of change and resistance to change. The use of the mass media – especially the daily press but also radio and television – by critics of immigration and multiculturalism is especially noted as an activity which often appears to be aimed at influencing public opinion rather than at reflecting such opinion, as these commentators tend to claim.

In the final two chapters attempts are made to arrive at empirical and theoretical generalisations from the examination of the Australian experience analysed in the earlier chapters. Chapter 10 raises the question of the choices Australia faces in the direction of its future policy on immigration, multiculturalism and its place in the world community. It presents these choices as part of the Australian search for a new identity in approaching the next century and one hundred years of its existence, defined in its Constitution as a 'self-governing colony'. While the term, 'self-governing colony' is undoubtedly archaic, the fact that it is still in the Constitution conveys the notion of dependence in our view. The task undertaken in Chapter 11 is to draw appropriate conclusions from the study and then to formulate relevant theoretical propositions through bringing together theories of class, social change and culture.

CHAPTER 2

Social Change and Culture in Contemporary Societies

Contemporary societies are changing societies. This attribute is present equally in the industrialised or 'advanced' Western societies and in the societies of the 'underdeveloped' or 'developing third world'. The use of quotation marks is deliberate, to demonstrate that all these terms imply certain systems of economic production which are perceived in the language of economics as stages of progress on the path towards the 'advanced' stage. While these terms may be regarded as essentially descriptive, they also convey certain cultural values, namely that 'development' and 'advanced state' are seen as 'good things'. Social change and culture are thus two related social phenomena; they are causally linked and both serve as defining characteristics of societies.

In this chapter we provide a brief overview of certain characteristics of social change and culture in the global perspective, with the aim of establishing a context for the examination of these two phenomena in Australian society. The overview covers certain political, economic and cultural aspects in world societies today and certain events which, we think, have implications for Australian society and its current and future social and cultural development.

Social Change on the Global Scale

Social change is a multi-dimensional process which rarely proceeds at the same rate or to the same extent in all its dimensions. Nor is it an 'all-or-nothing' process: while no contemporary society is entirely static at any given time in its structure and culture, neither does any one society undergo a complete change in all its aspects over a short or even over a long period of time. The rate of change may be fast or slow, but the processes of change and those of continuity parallel each other, one or the other being at times more prominent. The extent and rate of change also tend to differ among various socio-economic strata and classes. More often than not, it will be the upper and the middle classes that seem to adopt new ways, while the working class and the village people (in Europe) or those in small country towns (such as in Australia) would tend to remain 'traditional' or 'conservative'. This observation, however, may be misleading, as the 'new ways' may be confined to such visible aspects of social life as dress fashion, food preference, or a holiday resort for a season; but behind these changes, or seasonal fads, the continuity of attitudes, values and interests remains solid and undisturbed. In some aspects there may be an integration of the 'local' with the 'imported', or of the 'old' with the 'new'. For example, the impact of the 'global' mass culture projected by the media may affect some aspects of a distinct national, ethnic, or regional culture.

In the economic sphere the changes which have occurred in the industrialised countries over the later part of the current century have been of considerable magnitude, affecting all aspects of economic production and sectors of industry, with corresponding positive or negative effects on the economies of localities, regions, or even entire countries and their populations. In the technical language of economics these changes have been interpreted as processes of 'restructuring'. The debates and analyses of these processes have been conducted in a rather narrow conceptual framework, confined to the systems and methods of economic production and distribution of goods and services. This perspective excludes from consideration some important aspects of social change which are inherently related to economic production and which are thus affected by any change in that area. As argued by Hoggett,

> ... whilst restructuring begins in the economic sphere, narrowly defined, to be successful it must also extend to the socio-institutional sphere (i.e. those institutions concerned with international finance, trade, redistribution, the nation state, the welfare state, the family, etc.).   (1990:1)

Such comprehensive, all-embracing change has certainly taken place in some parts of the globe. The changes which have occurred so rapidly (and unexpectedly) in the countries of eastern Europe and in the countries which were part of the Soviet Union only a few years ago are examples of restructuring which extends to all aspects of social, economic and political life. Yet it is not a case of entirely new structures replacing the existing ones; rather, the changes have meant an introduction of new structures and new mechanisms but also a return to traditional values, attitudes and institutions, including traditional animosities and conflicts. The search for cultural continuity, or rebirth, is evident in the assertion of political independence, ethnic identity, language and religion. It is the traditional core social institutions – the family, the church, private property – that play the key role in the cultural revival and lead to the re-emergence of earlier patterns of social stratification and class divisions.

On a macro-scale the outcome is a fragmentation of the once-powerful Soviet empire: an empire formerly held together by an imposed ideology and force, now replaced by a large number of smaller units based on ethnic identity, language, religion, and economic interests. On a micro-scale the change means a shift from the earlier community-oriented life styles, which were both imposed and encouraged, to individualisation, private property, and a greater focus on family-centred rather than community-centred activities. The transition is painful economically as well as socially, as the discarded values and ideologies are discredited while the new ones do not provide the promised benefits and rewards, at least not for everyone. The new system means new ways of doing things, a new world outlook and new values in human relationships; indeed, a new culture which most people now living in those countries have never experienced except perhaps through their parents' memories and through the media and 'travellers' tales from strange lands'.

In contrast, the countries of western Europe for some years now have been seeking greater unity, attempting to accommodate national interests to a common interest. Under an umbrella of agreements and voluntarily imposed higher political and administrative authority, which can override the authorities of the sovereign member-states, the European Community has found a common purpose in many areas of economic activity. It is progressively extending this commonality into the legal system, legislative provisions concerned with industrial conditions and human rights, and projecting the inclusion of political institutions in due course as well. This search for unity within diversity might be driven by common economic interest and protection against 'outsiders' from other continents, but the significance of the search goes well beyond economics. This is the first time that the culturally diverse countries of Europe have sought such unity by voluntary agreements; the main feature of previous efforts to unify Europe – the Roman Empire, the Holy Roman Empire of Charlemagne, and the brief period of Napoleon's Empire – was a search for unity by conquest and domination. Beneath this new search for unity of economic interests, it seems, is a search for a common cultural heritage and related common values which transcend language differences, traditional enmities and the particular economic interests of member-states.

Thus, on the global scale, social change proceeds in two seemingly opposite directions. On the one hand there is a growth of *universality and commonality*, if not uniformity, typifying the image of the 'global village' of Marshall McLuhan, evident in the growing similarity of patterns of industrial production and patterns of consumption of material goods and services, but also extending into the field of art, music and other cultural pursuits. On the other hand, social, ethnic and national movements lead to greater *fragmentation*, evident in the loosening or even destruction of political and economic systems, supplanted by new or revived nation-states, or ethnic-states, or even new versions of theocratic states.

How does one explain these two ostensibly divergent developments? Each movement, it seems, is fuelled by the pursuit of certain values which are not always manifestly explicit but which nevertheless underpin observed movements and activities. Economic development and progress towards a higher and higher standard of living is one such value, pursued through industrialisation, technological innovation and commitment to the growth of the gross national product. Counterposed to this is the search for, or restoration of, ethnic and cultural identity, which may not necessarily be compatible with an efficient pursuit of economic growth. Another development is the pursuit of 'quality of life' objectives, which are increasingly found to be at odds with the pursuit of a higher standard of living as measured by the volume of material consumption. Concern about air and water pollution, about the 'rat race' of modern economic life, about the exhaustion of non-renewable resources, about the degradation of the environment – all these concerns are in conflict with the dominant value of economic 'progress' measured in material terms.

Viewed in a historical perspective, the twentieth century has been a century of revolutionary changes. On the American continent and in the Pacific the remnants of the once-powerful Spanish empire were replaced by the hegemony of the United States. In Europe, the century began with revolutionary movements against capitalism in 1905 and 1917, and the establishment of a state-socialist system in one of the largest countries on the globe. This was followed later by crude and gross aberrations in the political systems in other European countries through the imposition of the power of fascism and nazism, which led to the world explosion into war and resulted in the death of millions – on battlefields and in the Holocaust of systematic extermination. The end of hostilities did not bring peace but a division of the world into two opposing powers, two opposing ideologies and two opposing political systems and cultures, engaging each other in a game of a 'cold' war but maintaining and strengthening 'hot' war readiness with instruments of destruction threatening to explode into a nuclear apocalypse. Now, the revolutionary events have turned, as it were, full circle, returning much of the world to one dominant ideology and one dominant economic system – and to new political, ethnic and religious fragmentations and conflicts in many parts of the globe.

In the 'third world' the former dominance of European colonial powers has been replaced by a multitude of new states in which political independence has failed to produce political and social stability, democratic regimes, or economic independence and viability. On the contrary, political independence has meant for many of these societies a substitution of one oppression by another, tribal warfare and increased economic exploitation. Under the name of 'development' their economies have been drawn closer than ever before into the global market economy. The transition from earlier subsistence economies, which were compatible with local social systems and cultures, to economies supplying commodities to the industrialised world has led to a growing impoverishment and dependence on that industrialised first world. This integration of former subsistence economies into the world market has also led to a division of labour on a global scale, the mode of economic production in the industrialised countries now reaching the 'post-industrial' stage. However, the concept of post-industrialism is rather a misnomer, for at least two reasons. First, industrial production in the 'advanced' economies has not disappeared; rather, it has shifted to a higher technological mode (Williams 1983:93), requiring high capital investment in machinery and a skilled labour force to operate it. Second, methods in manufacturing industries engaged in mass production based on relatively simple routine operation, and in 'dirty' industries, have not changed significantly but the industries have been shifted to the industrialising countries with cheap labour.

A significant outcome of these developments has been a mass movement of populations across established national borders and even across continents. Hunger, oppression, ethnic, political or religious power struggles, a demand for labour in some countries and unemployment in others, or simply a search for different and better living conditions – these are reasons for masses of people having been on the move, giving rise to tensions and open conflicts in the not always welcoming host countries. Castles (1984:1) notes that during the post-war period an estimated 30 million persons entered Western European countries as workers or worker dependants, constituting 'one of the greatest migratory movements in human history'. Some of these immigrants came as political refugees, some came from former colonies, and others were brought in as 'guest workers' from the less affluent countries of Europe and other places; others entered or were brought in illegally by enterprising employers. Whether legal or illegal, the immigrants became an integral part of the labour force, filling jobs which local workers were unwilling to do, and often filling those jobs at extremely low wages and in poor working conditions.

Immigrant workers were welcome during the period of labour shortage, but as economic conditions worsened and unemployment increased they were being induced or coerced to return to their own countries. Many of them did so but many more stayed and later became subjected to discrimination, racist antagonism and even physical violence. Indeed, racism in Europe has become widespread 'in all countries of immigration' (Castles 1984:5). Expressions of racism also became increasingly violent, especially in Germany where earlier guest workers had been actively sought and laws on the admission of refugees were comparatively lenient. Violence increased dramatically following German reunification, as the new national unity and an economic downturn seemed to revive the old nazi dream of racial purity. Racism became politically significant in Europe before German reunification, as new political parties with a variety of 'national front' labels and neo-fascist or neo-nazi philosophies and slogans were formed and began to attract support from voters by portraying immigrants as a threat to jobs, a threat to national identity and culture, even as a threat to European Christian civilisation. As Castles records in his study, the worst threat is claimed to come from Islamic immigrants, 'who are supposedly out to avenge the defeat of the Turks before the gates of Vienna in 1683, by destroying Europe's Christian civilisation' (1984:39).

At the same time, the immigrants have become an important element in the changing class structure in the countries of Western Europe. By taking up jobs at the lowest level of the labour market immigrants 'have allowed many indigenous workers to move out of unskilled jobs and to achieve real social promotion' (Castles and Kosack 1985:478). Secondly, as immigrants are almost exclusively employed in manual labour, they have become part of the working class, although they are not readily accepted by local fellow-workers, being perceived as competitors for increasingly scarce jobs. Nevertheless, with significant numbers of immigrants the working class has become 'multi-ethnic', unlike the middle classes which have retained their relative ethnic purity. As Castles notes in relation to western Europe, 'immigrant workers entered the labour market at the bottom and tended to stay there. This situation was duplicated in the housing market and access to social facilities' (1984:7). In the commercial sector immigrants' influence may be noticed only in the service sector, such as small business enterprises, restaurants and personal services (Waldinger *et al.* 1990). The effect of immigration on social and political institutions in the host countries has been minimal.

The population movement into western Europe still continues and in recent years it has acquired new forms. With the demise of the Soviet Union and socialist regimes in eastern Europe, borders were opened and people could move west more freely; on working holidays, on barter business, or with the intention of staying for a longer time. People from Asia and Africa enter illegally with the assistance of 'black traders' who extract exorbitant charges for passage but accept no responsibility for outcomes. Those who manage to enter remain as illegal immigrants, working in the worst and lowest paid jobs, and living in fear of racist violence. They provide a flexible, casual and easily expendable labour force, thus constituting 'the very basis on which post-industrial society is run'(Sivanandan 1988). A similar situation exists in the United States where illegal immigrants from across the southern border number many thousands, if not millions, of illegal workers. In all these countries the economy now functions on the principles of a dual labour market: a 'core' of industries engaged in high technology production, and a 'periphery' of low-skill, low-paid jobs performed by local and immigrant (often illegal) labour.

The effect of political and economic changes and mass population movements that followed and still continue – has been a growing inequality on a global scale between the affluent and the poor countries, now referred to as the 'North/South divide'. Inequality has also increased within the borders of societies, in both the industrialised countries and in the 'developing' or 'undeveloped' countries. The growing gap between the affluent and the poor countries replicates, as it were, the processes of growing inequality within national borders. In fact, the dominant ideology of free markets, technological innovation and globalisation of commerce and industry has given rise to what may appropriately be called the world-wide culture of inequality. On all accounts, both types of inequality have now become, more than ever before, the outstanding feature of the contemporary world. Indeed, while poverty in the 'third world' economies remains endemic, in the affluent industrialised countries the emergence and growth of the new 'underclass' has also acquired the characteristics of a permanent fixture of the social structure (Nathan 1987, Magnet 1987). It seems that in the industrialised countries the dominant ideology of the capitalist 'free market' economy can maintain its viability and provide a reasonable standard of living for the majority of their populations, but only by excluding the lower social strata of their own population from the mainstream of social and economic life, and by exploiting poorer countries and subjugating their economies to the priorities of the industrialised countries' economic system.

The Dominance of Economic Thinking

The increasing problems of the world economy present something of a paradox: increasing affluence accompanied by increasing poverty. These problems have been growing in times when the governments of most countries, industrialised or developing, have been committed to policies of economic growth. It is also rather ironic that the situation has worsened as the influence of economists in world affairs has increased. Their influence has extended well beyond the areas and issues which may be considered to be appropriate to the economic domain; it has affected the perceptions and interpretations of social and political issues in all areas of social life and has become the dominant influence on economic and social policy. Moreover this influence has come from one particular school of thought, which came to be known as economic rationalism, the salient feature of which has been the elevation of the market to the status of a god-like creature of superior wisdom and omniscience. Economic rationalism became the dominant creed of economics in the 1980s, having displaced Keynesian theory and the prominence that theory gave to a mixed economy functioning on the basis of an uneasy alliance between the market and the state. It became the dominant influence on governments' policies in many industrialised countries, particularly in Britain, the United States and to a considerable extent in Australia. The disciples of economic rationalism now exert considerable influence also in the so-called 'new democracies' of eastern Europe and in Russia.

The influence of economic rationalism has been pervasive and of considerable significance for a number of reasons, some of which are mentioned below: the list is certainly not exhaustive.

First, economic rationalism is entirely embedded in and congruent with the ideology of capitalism; it is therefore politically acceptable and useful to governments operating within the global capitalist system. Its influence was strengthened by the demise of socialist regimes in Europe and in the Soviet Union, and by the acceptance of market principles in communist China. As a result, there is at present no ideology of comparable strength competing with the ideology of the 'free' market and guiding economic activities in any country, with the exception of Cuba and North Korea (and both these countries are now economically weak and under pressure to change).

Second, although economic rationalism is ideologically embedded and thus value-laden, its disciples, like economists in general, claim their theory to be 'scientific', that is, objective, value-free, and based on axiomatic assumptions. Other social sciences such as sociology are criticised or dismissed by economic rationalists as theoretically and methodologically 'soft' and value-laden. The adherents of economic rationalism refute any demonstration of the failure of their theory by asserting that it has not yet been properly or fully tried in any country. In their views, wherever economic rationalism has been adopted in the policy of economic management, political or social considerations have always 'contaminated' it, hindering its full implementation.

Third, economic rationalism became politically powerful because its disciples operate and control the two most powerful economic institutions in the world which control and allocate funds on a world-wide scale: the International Monetary Fund and the World Bank. The influence of economic rationalism is therefore global, as funds are allocated to governments and private enterprises, mainly those in developing countries, on strict conditions of compliance with economic rationalist principles.

Fourth, economic rationalism has been useful to governments as a legitimising argument for allocating resources in ways that are politically helpful to the party in power, or for reducing public expenditure on the grounds that 'the country cannot afford it'. In the class societies of the capitalist 'free' market system, economic rationalism thus became an influential ideology for legitimising social and economic inequality.

The globalisation of the world economy has allowed the free market perspective to permeate every single country, even Sweden which for many years was perceived as a model of an economy performing well in a social-democratic system, with a high level of government control of economic activities and social policies characterised by a high level of redistributive income transfers. Sweden came under increasing pressure to adopt free market principles; this pressure was said to be due to 'the unexpected influence of conservative academic, governmental and international economists' (Vandenberg and Dow 1991).

How significant has been the influence of economic rationalism, and what have been the effects of this influence? The importance of economics in the management of material resources cannot be denied, but the proponents of economic rationalism have endeavoured to elevate the assumptions underlying their theory to a dominant value, subjugating other values. What Giddens (1987:45) called the 'omniscience of the market' became the basic principle on which business and government decisions were to be made and which the 'rational economic man' would accept, because such a person always acted in his (what about her?) perceived self-interest. In the perspective of such economic reductionism all human behaviour – work, leisure, personal relations, religious belief and so on – can be interpreted in terms of the perception of self-interest: 'the famous homo economicus is a rational self-interested instrumental maximiser with fixed preferences' (Hirsch *et al.* 1987:332). It follows, then, that the value of all social products, activities and pursuits, indeed the whole culture of a society, can be expressed in economic terms and evaluated by economic indices and equations. As a result, important social and cultural aspects and activities can be devalued by economic reductionism, or eliminated entirely from the calculus. As Smith points out:

> The tendency for economics and economic solutions to loom so large in modern social and political thought, carries with it a danger of insensitivity to less amenable and perhaps more subtle cultural needs.   (1981:171)

As the world entered the 1990s, doubts began to appear about the value of economic and social policies guided by economic rationalism. The countries of eastern Europe which had experienced one-party socialist regimes for many decades have endeavoured to adopt free market principles in the management of their economies but are making only slow progress in economic recovery. The Soviet Union fell apart and its largest component, the Russian Federation, entered a period of political turmoil and economic deterioration, threatened with complete economic collapse and political chaos. The gap between the affluent industrialised countries and the 'third world' continued to widen, but the affluent countries had their own serious problems, such as endemic high rates of unemployment and growing inequality, which continued to defy solutions. While economic rationalists persisted with their claims that these were unavoidable sacrifices on the road to economic paradise, some of them were also inferring, albeit with some reluctance, that the sacrifices demanded of a minority of the population might be the necessary price to pay for the affluence of the majority. It was the growing suspicion that the latter rather than the former condition was the real outcome of economic rationalism that made an increasing number of people think that perhaps the promise of economic rationalism was a myth and a search for other solutions to the world's problems was necessary. So far, no such solution has appeared on the political or economic horizon, except for the tentative steps taken by some governments, which suggests that faith in the 'invisible hand' of the free market has waned and failing economies might need some 'visible' intervention by appropriate government action.

Social Class and Culture

Industrialised societies of the Western world, being part of the capitalist economic and social order, are, by definition, class societies. This means, first and foremost, that the characteristic feature of their social structure is inequality, which pervades all social relations, encompassing economic production and consumption, the political and legal systems, and everyday social encounters and activities. It means, further, that relations of gender, age, ethnicity and even religion take place within, and are affected – if not entirely determined – by the class structure and class relations. In other words, class inequality is the dominant feature of these societies' culture.

The concept of class and studies of class structures have been one of the main fields of sociological exploration. It is to be expected that with this level of interest and volume of work there will also be a diversity of views, concepts and interpretations, as well as scholarly disagreements, disputes and conflicts. Indeed, the schools of thought range from one extreme where class structure is seen to be the fundamental characteristic of all societies in the capitalist system, to the other extreme where the concept of social class is seen to be an outdated concept, no longer applicable to the structures of 'post-industrial' societies.

It needs to be noted at this point that for both Marx and Weber the concept of class had economic as well as cultural connotations. Human beings were seen by these two theorists as creative beings, producing material goods as well as cultural symbols, ideas and values. For Marx, human beings developed their consciousness through their daily productive activities and were thereby able to locate themselves, their social being, in a social structure and view themselves and the world around them accordingly (Tucker 1978:4). Weber also saw human beings as aware of themselves and of the social world around them, and with their actions consciously affirming or denying certain values (Smith 1976:100).

In the theoretical perspective of this book we assert the importance and relevance of the concept of class to the understanding of the structure of contemporary societies in the industrialised world. We acknowledge other sources of division in these societies, such as social status, age, sex/gender, ethnicity, religion or sexual preferences, but we see these divisions and corresponding interests as existing *within* the class structure, perhaps at times acting as mediating elements in intra- or inter-class tensions and conflicts, but not challenging the class structure itself. Briefly, in simple terms, in our perspective a class society is one in which access to society's resources – economic, social, political – and the relationships among its population are unequal, being determined by a differentiated 'command over resources through time' (Titmuss 1963). The class structure of such a society is therefore multidimensional, entailing economic, social and political differentiations and divisions, the common factor of these features being inequality. Such a structure also encompasses cultural differentiations and divisions which are evident in life-styles as well as in attitudes and values held by the different classes of the society's population.

However, despite any such differences, what is commonly referred to as a society's culture is usually the so-called *dominant culture* which is embedded in its economic system, in its political institutions, in the legal and education systems and in the professions whose members administer and control these institutions and systems. Counterposed to the dominant culture is the *everyday culture* which is observable in people's everyday activities and which differs from one class to another, although some common features, such as certain leisure pursuits or consumption patterns, may transcend class differences. Nevertheless, class differences are clearly observable in the cultural differences of life-styles, as differential access to material resources leads to the pursuit of, and access to, different cultural experiences and products (Eder 1989:132).

Everyday culture tends to have 'traditional' continuity of characteristics, that is characteristics transferred from one generation to another through the institution of the family, the workplace and the proximate social environment. The means of transfer include oral history, customs, traditions, directly observable examples of social conduct, traditional authority, or moral coercion. The transferred culture does not, however, remain static; through social encounters and interaction in the course of everyday activities people modify and re-make their culture (Thompson 1968). However, in the contemporary world everyday culture has become negatively affected and eroded by the *mass culture* projected by the mass media, especially television, leading to a degree of imitation of the projected conduct, attitudes and values. It is this imitation that superficially masks class differences and serves to create an illusion of social and economic equality. This mass culture is an *exploitative culture*, projected and disseminated by business interests, political interests, ideological or religious interests, and dominant class interests. It is a powerful mechanism, serving to disempower people from maintaining and cultivating their own culture.

The impact of the culture projected by the media is not uniform in strength and influence on all socio-economic strata and classes in society. The more affluent, more educated middle classes have greater ability to be more selective in the acceptance of values projected through the media. They are able to discern, accept or reject, or interpret and modify what they hear, read or see. By contrast, the lower socio-economic strata, the working class, do not have the same resources; in comparison with the images projected by the media their own traditional culture and values are made to appear implicitly inferior. The result then is either an effort to imitate the projected attitudes and values, or alienation from the mainstream of society.

These generalisations, however, need to be qualified. The power of the mass media is undoubtedly great, but with growing access to higher education people are learning to be more discerning and less susceptible to accepting uncritically what they see, read or hear. Furthermore, if the media continue to project attitudes and life-styles vastly different from those of a particular social class of viewers, listeners or readers, the messages are likely to be rejected as irrelevant.

The projected cultural characteristics of contemporary industrialised societies tend to convey images of stability and permanence, but these societies are not static. At any given time and in varied degrees societies change, both in their social structures and in their cultural characteristics. Nevertheless, while any such changes may affect some aspects of a society's culture, the elements which are deeply embedded in its social institutions and in the beliefs, values and modes of conduct in everyday life counteract, slow down and even entirely negate the forces of change. Social change is never total, and cultural continuity may thus be observed even in societies undergoing rapid technological and social change.

One of the common features of change in all industrialised and industrialising societies has been the rapid growth of a social stratum identified and referred to in sociological and political science literature as the 'new middle class' or the 'New Class' (Gouldner 1979, Wright 1985, Jamrozik 1991a). The growth of this class has also meant cultural change in these societies, as it is this class that has become the cultural leader and producer, its 'products' and the values they represent being reflected in literature, films, television and radio, and in the mass media generally. More important still is the role the new middle class plays in education, health and human services as a whole. In effect, the new middle class plays a significant part in authoritatively defining the nature of social reality: at the level of theoretical discourse, in political debate, and in the exercise of their knowledge-power in public administration and in the provision of social services such as education, health and welfare.

In examining the cultural characteristics of class societies, this chapter considers the role of the new middle class in the processes of social and cultural change. In subsequent chapters the role of the new middle class in Australia is examined in relation to social change and the stability of the established social, economic and political order in encounters with the cultural influences of immigrant communities. It will then be shown how the influence of this class is evident in public debates on social issues, including the issues of cultural transformation.

The Meaning of Culture

Culture is a kind of an umbrella term which covers diverse meanings. There is, however, broad agreement among sociologists and anthropologists that the concept of culture embraces what may be called 'the way of life', as defined by Milner (see Chapter 1). For another example, we have Clifford Geertz's definition of culture as:

> ... an historically transmitted pattern of meanings embodied in symbols, a system of inherited conceptions expressed in symbolic forms by means of which men communicate, perpetuate, and develop their knowledge about and attitudes towards life.   (1975:89)

Similarly, Raymond Williams puts forward a definition of culture as a 'description of a particular way of life, which expresses certain meanings and values not only in art and learning but also in institutions and ordinary behaviour' (1981:43). He argues that a social definition of culture enables the inclusion of certain elements of the way of life 'which other definitions do not include', such as:

> the organisation of production, the structure of the family, the structure of institutions which express or govern social relationships, the characteristic forms through which members of the society communicate.   (1981:44)

However, Williams adds, culture may also be defined as an 'ideal', in terms of certain absolute or universal values; or as a 'documentary', in which 'human thought and experience are variously recorded'. Furthermore, Williams sees the need to distinguish three levels of culture: *lived culture*, of a specific time and place and accessible only to those living in that time and place; *recorded culture*, that is, the culture of a particular period; and *culture of the selective tradition*, connecting the lived and the recorded culture. It is very important, Williams points out, to understand especially the operation of the culture of the selective tradition, because what is selected at the time from a range of elements becomes a reflection of the values and emphases of a given period, which will not necessarily be later confirmed (1981:49–50).

In Australia, Michael Liffman observes that, all too often, popular understanding of culture is superficial, stereotyping, and serves to divide people of different communities rather than improve their understanding of one another. In Liffman's perspective:

> Culture, in the important sense, relates to the deep aspects of individual and group life. It deals with attitudes, values and assumptions about such universals as birth, death, pain, understanding of sex and family roles, of faith, divinity, luck, future, progress, misfortune and the like. In this sense it is a deep and not easily understood facet of individual and group life.   (1981:7)

There is a broad agreement in these definitions of culture, with certain emphases on one aspect or another and with some differences in emphases on the social nature of culture. There is also an agreement that cultural meanings and values are to be found in the social institutions which govern social relationships, such as the organisations of production, the family, systems of education, law and politics. Thus, being embedded in these institutions, a society's culture is the embodiment of its social structure and the expression of its values. It follows, then, that the culture of the industrialised societies of the capitalist Western world would reflect the class structure of these societies. The implicit, if not always explicit dominant cultural value in these societies would be the value of inequality (Williams 1983; Eder 1989; Aronowitz 1992).

It needs to be acknowledged, however, that all cultures, and especially the cultures of contemporary Western societies are multidimensional, being composed of a number of cultures which are reflected in those societies' symbols, activities, and in social attitudes and the conduct of various classes of the population. For example, first, there is what may be called the *dead culture*, exemplified by monuments and documents of a world which no longer exists, but one in which the contemporary world sees and seeks its ancestry: the pyramids of Egypt, the Gothic cathedrals of medieval Europe, the Latin language, the gods of Ancient Greece and the mythologies of the 'golden ages' of a distant past. Although belonging to societies long gone, dead culture is part of the historical inheritance which is reflected in social values, systems of government, laws, art and general knowledge. In this sense, the dead culture is very much alive in the contemporary culture. Second, there is the *culture of art and literature* – the culture of the muses – which also draws on past creative works such as music, painting and literature, but augments past works with new contributions from contemporary artists, writers, composers, theatre and film performers, and so on. Third, there is the *culture of the political and economic systems*, reflected in the glass-marble-and-concrete skyscrapers of the cities, in the rituals of political and business institutions and courts of law: it is the culture of the dominant power structure and in industrialised societies within the capitalist system this means *class culture*, or *class-mediated culture*. Then there is *everyday culture* which may be observed in social intercourse in the market place, in the work place, in sporting and recreational activities, as well as in family relations and in social relations generally.

There is also *international culture*, based on proclaimed, if not always pursued, democratic values, the United Nations Charter of Human Rights and international political and business conventions. Another international culture is the *elite culture*, or *haute culture*, of high fashion, conspicuous consumption, the display of wealth and invention of fads or trends: the culture of Gucci, Chanel and Dior, of Concorde travel and first nights on Broadway. Like 'haute couture' or 'haute cuisine', 'haute culture' is exclusive, the metaphor of height serving to maintain and reaffirm among the rich and the very rich belief in their superiority of character and distinctiveness from the people 'down there'. Counterposed to this 'haute culture' is *popular culture*, which is significantly influenced by the *internationalised American culture*, propagated through transnational business organisations: the culture of Coca-Cola, Kentucky-Fried, McDonalds, Pizza Hut, rock n' roll video clips, jeans, and 'family shows' on television during the day and 'sex and violence' in the evening.

The growth of this international culture is facilitated by the advances in communication media and by political and related economic interests. The transnational nature of large business corporations has given rise to a growing interdependence in the world economy. It is one of the wonders, or paradoxes, of the currently observed trends of events on the global scene that this growing economic interdependence of the world economy is paralleled by intensified movements towards assertion of national, ethnic and cultural identities. These two clearly opposing trends seem to demonstrate that interdependence of economic interests is not incompatible with the diversity of national interests or with the diversity of cultures. This is illustrated in a rather perceptive observation of Raymond Williams':

> There was this Englishman who worked in the London office of a multinational corporation based in the United States. He drove home one evening in his Japanese car. His wife, who worked in a firm which imported German kitchen equipment, was already at home. Her small Italian car was often quicker through the traffic. After a meal which included New Zealand lamb, Californian carrots, Mexican honey, French cheese and Spanish wine, they settled down to watch a program on their television set, which had been made in Finland. The program was a retrospective celebration of the war to recapture Falkland Islands. As they watched it, they felt warmly patriotic, and very proud to be British.   (1983:177)

Thus in the contemporary world there is a *global* culture of trade, commerce and politics, facilitated and maintained by the mass media, and *local* cultures which give an identity to nations, states and their populations. Each society is known by its *representative* culture, which becomes synonymous with the society itself because it represents its prevalent or dominant life-style, ways of acting, attitudes and values. As observed by Tenbruck:

> Representative culture includes those beliefs, understandings, images, ideas, ideologies, etc. which influence social actions, either because they are being actively shared, or because they are being passively acknowledged as valid, right, good, or the like.   (1989: 32)

However, Tenbruck cautions, in order to understand the nature of representative culture we need to

> ... probe into the dynamic and productive constitution of representative culture, locate the typical origins of the dominant ideas, trace the lines and networks of their spread and reception, study the links between representative culture, political organisation, social institutions, groups, and associations.
> (1989:33)

We need to note, too, that within a nation or state there is rarely, if ever, a uniformity of culture. In addition to local, ethnic, or religious diversities, there are likely to be also cultural differences related to the socio-economic and class structure of the society. In such societies, as we have said, the culture which represents the society internally and to the outside world is the culture of the dominant class. However, the question 'which class is the dominant class in a society?' does not necessarily lead to a clear-cut answer. Is it always the case, as Marx argued in *German Ideology*, that the class which controls economic production also controls mental production, that is, the cultural expression of the society? Is it perhaps more appropriate to consider and acknowledge the existence of a form of 'alliance' – a form of power sharing – between the *economically dominant* class – the owners and controllers of capital – and the class which is intellectually and *culturally dominant*, that is, the new middle class?

The new middle class, or the intellectuals within it, are the authoritative interpreters of social reality. As Tenbruck argues, in all societies there is a cultural division of labour, and 'the ubiquitous cultural division of labour points to the social role of the intellectuals ... who are entrusted with the social task of interpreting the orders of reality, including the order of society' (1989:25). However, Tenbruck points out that counterposed to the authoritative intepretations of culture there is also the culture of everyday life.

> It is an attempt to reclaim lived reality against the artificial constructs, complex abstractions, and aggregate data of a social science that indulges in the cult of facts. It is also an attempt to save one's identity from the inexorable stream of incoherent impressions, informations, and sensations to which we are being exposed in modern culture.   (1989:31)

In relation to the issues examined in this book, the difference between representative culture and the culture of everyday life is of utmost significance. As will be seen in the chapters that follow, some of the authoritative perceptions and interpretations of social change and cultural transformation in Australia appear to be rather different from those the empirical evidence seems to indicate. This difference between authoritative interpretations and empirical evidence suggests that the representative culture reflects Australian society through the class-mediated perception of the 'interpreters' of social reality, that is, mainly, if not exclusively, the members of the new middle class.

Social Change, Culture and the New Middle Class

In essence, social change means change in social relationships: change in the way people relate to one another, the way they treat one another. Depending on the theoretical perspective one follows, social relationships may be seen to be determined by the structure of class, status, or party (political organisation), as argued by Weber (1968); or the relationships may be seen to be determined, in essence, by the relations of production, as argued by Marx (Tucker 1978). At a certain level of abstraction, therefore, all social relationships may be perceived and interpreted as power relationships. In the everyday encounters between or among individuals or groups, power distribution may be equal or unequal, but on a broad societal level the distribution of power is usually unequal because access to society's resources is unequal. This observation certainly applies to industrialised societies in the capitalist economic system, that is, societies differentiated internally by the class structure in which certain classes, or a class, will be dominant.

In sociological analyses of social structures, especially in those conducted in the Marxian theoretical perspective, the dominant class is deemed to be the class of the owners and controllers of production. Whatever views might be held on the relevance of this theory to contemporary industrialised societies, it is beyond argument that the ownership and control of capital remains the powerful force throughout the world. Indeed, capital is the only truly international and trans-national force, unimpeded by national boundaries, political systems or diverse cultures. Internationalisation of capital ownership and control, and the corresponding globalisation of the economy, have been the two most significant changes to have occurred over the past few decades.

However, as noted earlier, the most significant change in the social structures of industrialised societies has been the growth of the social stratum identified in a vast number of sociological analyses as the New Class, or the new middle class (eg, Mills 1951, Gouldner 1979, Konrad and Szelenyi 1979, Abercrombie and Urry 1983, Wright 1985, Jamrozik 1991a). Some analysts refer to this stratum as the service class, the professional class, the technocratic-managerial class, or the professional-managerial class (J. and B. Ehrenreich 1979); others (eg, Dahrendorf 1959) have acknowledged the existence of such a social stratum but perceive it as lacking the characteristics of a class. Notwithstanding the diversity of definitions or terminology, there is a common factor in all these analyses, namely, the acknowledgement of the emergence and growth of this class as a significant social change factor in industrialised societies. Indeed, Esping-Andersen echoes these views when he asserts that '... the rise of the new middle-strata categories constitutes one of the most profound changes in the class structure of advanced societies' (1985:29).

In relation to the issues examined in this book the emergence and growth of the new middle class is of utmost significance, insofar as one of the most important functions the new middle class performs is providing the authoritative definition of social reality. The new middle class creates, records, reproduces and disseminates knowledge. Indeed, some writers (eg, Bauman 1987) refer specifically to the intellectuals, not explicitly as a class but as a group of people who perform the function of authoritative interpreters and translators of the dominant culture and power in contemporary 'post-modern' societies whose dominant feature is consumption rather than production. Gouldner sees the new middle class as performing the role of 'interpreter' by being active in two related areas of social organisation: the 'cultural apparatus' – the knowledge-producing industry, academia, research, and so on; and the 'consciousness industry' – the mass media (1990:306–16). The power of this class is derived from its members' specialised know-ledge, obtained through study in recognised autonomous institutions of higher learning, and then used authoritatively with societal sanction in a wide range of social, economic and political activities. In sum, the new middle class is composed of the producers, controllers and dissemina-tors of society's culture, and its power is derived from the ownership of specialised knowledge which has been defined as *cultural capital* (Bourdieu 1984).

In contemporary industrialised and now post-industrial, post-modern societies cultural capital is as important as and, at times, more important than material capital: knowledge-power vies for dominance with finance-power, or is in its service and rewarded by it; or, as may be observed at times, the two share power with each other. Is it possible, then, that the knowledge-power of the new middle class could become a challenge to finance-power, a challenge of cultural capital to material capital? While this possibility cannot be excluded from eventuating at some time in the future, there are no signs of this at present. The knowledge-power of the new middle class may present what at times appears to be a cultural challenge to the material production/consumption culture of capital-ism, but that challenge remains at the level of rhetoric and is not reflected in practice. On the contrary, the new middle class serves to strengthen the power of capital by searching for and developing new cultural goods and life-styles, thus extending the scope for the production of new goods and services by capitalist enterprises. Through these activities the members of the new middle class become the 'cultural intermediaries' of capitalism. As observed by Featherstone:

> The new cultural intermediaries can be found in market-oriented consumer cultural occupations – the media, advertising, design, fashion, etc. – and in state-funded and private helping professions, counselling, educational and therapy occupations.   (1989:154)

Bauman argues that the intellectuals have been 'seduced' by the attraction and power of the market place and, having become interpreters of the market ideology, their role is to seduce others into what has now become a 'consumer culture' (1987:163). As with the advance in production technology the need for human labour in industries engaged in material production decreases, capital seeks to engage consumers rather than workers (1987: 180). Efforts expended in that direction are intensive: advertising and the frequent introduction of 'new and better' products now constitute the so-called normal experience of everyday life. However, the decreasing need for human labour creates a growing army of unemployed who are incapable of performing the consumer role. Their desire to be consumers has to be, therefore, repressed. This becomes another important function for the interpreters because 'repression is needed to undo the harm to social order caused by indiscriminate seduction ... The poor must hence be constituted, by law and by practice, as a separate category, to which different rules apply' (Bauman 1987:183). In his more recent analysis Bauman observes:

> The most conspicuous social division under postmodern conditions is one between *seduction* and *repression*: between the choice and the lack of choice, between the capacity for self-constitution and the denial of such capacity, between autonomously conceived self-definitions and imposed categorisations experienced as constraining and incapacitating.   (1992:198)

In exercising the dual function of seduction into consumer culture on the one hand, and repression of desire to participate in that culture on the other, the cultural interpreters, or cultural intermediaries, play an important role in the maintenance and control of the social order. This means, in effect, the maintenance of social divisions that are characteristic of a class society in the 'post-modern' era in which the relations of consumption have replaced to a large extent the relations of production of the earlier period. As will be seen in the chapters that follow, the observations by Gouldner, Bauman and others about the new middle class in industrialised societies apply equally to the new middle class in Australia. As Australian society has grown in the size of its population and ethnic diversity, and as it has passed through various stages of industrialisation to a stage of economic uncertainty, the new middle class of professionals has become increasingly prominent in a wide range of activity both in the private and the public sector of the economy. While the intellectual nature of these activities and functions may vary, their significance in the processes of social change and cultural transformation – or in the maintenance of social stability and cultural continuity – has undoubtedly been profound.

CHAPTER 3

Social Change and Culture in Australia

All societies have their histories; all societies also have their myths. Histories and myths are important because they give a meaning to the present and sometimes point the way to the future. However, histories and myths may also become chains, confining people's thinking to the past, to 'the good old times' or to 'the golden age'; restricting or even blinding people's visions to the changing world around them, and preventing them, as individuals and as a society, to effect the cultural transformation necessary to live their lives to their full potential.

In this chapter we begin to look at the processes of social change and cultural transformation in the context of Australian society. We illustrate these processes by examining data on immigration since the late 1940s, the changing size and structure of the population, the family unit, industry and the composition of the labour force, and corresponding life-styles and cultural expressions. We also include brief comments on internal and external politics, focusing especially on the issue of Australian relations with neighbouring countries. Subsequent chapters elaborate further on these aspects of Australian society. Except for brief references to earlier historical periods, the chapter focuses on the period beginning in the late 1940s when the post-war immigration program was first introduced in Australia.

Most statistical data here relate to the more recent period, from the mid-1960s to the early 1990s. The reason for this is twofold: the acceleration in the rate of change in the structure of Australian industries and related social and economic effects began in the 1960s; and the Australian Bureau of Statistics (ABS) has produced consistent data for that period, especially data on the changes in the structure of Australian industries and corresponding changes in the employed labour force.

As the analysis in this chapter will show, Australian industries and the class structure of Australian society have changed dramatically over this period. Australian society of the 1990s certainly appears to be different from the one of three decades earlier; yet in some aspects it has retained a remarkable continuity which extends back to the early years of the century and beyond.

Early and Recent History

Australia, as we know it that is, a society which was established in 1788 on this large continent by conquest of its original inhabitants, was established as a colony of Britain; moreover, it was established as a *penal* colony. As Russel Ward comments, 'for nearly the first half-century of its existence White Australia was, primarily, an extensive gaol', and 'up to 1840 practically every employer of labour was *ipso facto* a gaoler' (1966:15, 37). The early pioneers, Ward argues, need to be seen in that light, that is, in the social context of their time. The early conditions of colonisation were an important factor in the development of certain social attitudes and social mores. The 160 000 men and women transported to Australia from 1788 to 1868 'ensured that the aura, or "stain" of convictism would be firmly registered on the consciousness of Australians and other observers' (Eddy 1991:25). Subsequent events, such as the gold rush of the 1850s, led to social conflicts and racial intolerance, aimed primarily at Chinese gold diggers but later extended to other ethnic groups of non-English-speaking background. By the time of Federation (1901), antagonistic attitudes towards people of non-Anglo-Celtic backgrounds were clearly established, being especially directed at all 'non-whites' whose entry to the country was from then on prohibited under what became known as the 'White Australia' policy enshrined in the *Immigration Restriction Act* of 1901.

The colour of the skin was very important. In 1902, William Pember Reeves, the first New Zealand Minister for Labour, writing in *State Experiments in Australia and New Zealand* on the policies of 'exclusion of aliens and undesirables', was proudly stating that:

> Alone amongst the chief divisions of the Empire the Commonwealth [of Australia] and New Zealand are not split up by any race fissures. None of their cities are babbles of tongues – none of their streets are filled with dark faces... With extraordinary good fortune Australia and New Zealand contain neither prolific tribes of aborigines nor alien elements too large to be absorbed in the main British stock ... There are black Australian natives, but they are wild men who can neither resist nor mingle with the white race; they simply die out before its march, or flee into the desert, and even in the desert their numbers dwindle.   (1902:325–6)

The antagonistic attitude of Reeves extended to all ethnic groups, except the 'Teutonic settlers' from Northern Europe who were thought to 'blend quickly and completely' with the English or British population, and the only evidence of their origins were 'a few non-English names and a rather larger allowance than usual of blue eyes and flaxen hair in certain neighbourhoods'. The main problems of the colonies Reeves saw were in the inflow of 'coloured aliens' who were 'yellow, brown and black' and in the 'European practice of shooting moral and physical rubbish into young countries as though these were made to be treated like waste plots of ground in the environs of the cities where sanitary arrangements were primitive' (1902:326–7). As for Chinese immigrants, Reeves agreed that people regarded them to be 'industrious, peaceful and frugal people, with a civilisation, a learning, and education of their own', but he did not think these characteristics would make Chinese people any more suitable settlers because, he argued, 'a man may be industrious, and yet be dirty, miserly, a shirker of social duty, and a danger to public health'. In reply to the public knowledge that Chinese immigrants committed few crimes, Reeves argued that 'a man may be a very undesirable citizen without infringing the criminal law' (1902: 354). From Reeves's extensive and elaborate arguments it is clear that Chinese immigrants were unwelcome because they were prepared to work hard under difficult conditions, live frugally, save money, and take their savings with them if they went back to their own country: they con- stituted, it seems, unfair competition.

As Reeves had been a government official in New Zealand and was well acquainted with the laws of the Australian colonies and those of the new Commonwealth, it may be assumed that he presented the 'official' view on these matters, expressing the prevailing opinion of the domi- nant social class. It is a matter of documented knowledge that the print media, such as the *Bulletin*, reflected and disseminated that view, which suggests that the people in power actively propagated fear and hate of non-white populations because they were concerned lest the working class conclude that the dangers of being swamped by 'coloured aliens' were somewhat exaggerated. As Jordan records, when the Immigration Restriction Bill was being debated in the new Federal parliament, the *Bulletin* wrote that the purpose of the Bill was to 'keep out paupers, diseased persons and, above all, 800 000 000 closely adjacent niggers ... [so as] to maintain the purity of the Anglo-Saxon type ... the best and strongest and most intellectual on this earth' (1989:3).

The concern with 'British stock' created many problems for the authorities in deciding who was British and who was not, as there were people who came to Australia from various British colonies and called themselves 'British', although they were not quite 'white'. 'Non-white' persons were not admitted even if they were British subjects. Some of them who were admitted as British subjects were later refused entitlement to age pensions because they were not 'natural-born British subjects'. This discrimination in the *Social Security Act* was removed only in 1947, although Australian Aborigines had to wait another twenty years before they became recognised as citizens (Jordan 1989:49).

To this day, the notion of 'British stock' appears to remain deeply embedded in the Anglo-Australian psyche, at least in the portrayal of the so-called typical Australian in some literature and history text books, and certainly in the images projected by the mass media. While there has always been an assertion of an Australian identity different from Britain, cultural affinity and identification with Britain, or more specifically England, has remained strong. Richard White comments that the very idea of an Australian national identity was a product of European history: 'men like Charles Darwin and Rudyard Kipling have contributed as much to what it means to be Australian as Arthur Streeton or Henry Lawson' (1981:ix).

Indeed, what it is to be Australian is still determined by the British or English 'connection'. To this day immigrants are categorised into those of English-speaking-background (ESBs) and those of non-English-speaking background (NESBs), with different attitudes and different legal conditions applied to each group. Until 1984 immigrants from Britain enjoyed full citizenship rights and those who were registered on electoral rolls then are still entitled to vote in federal and state elections without their having to take up Australian citizenship (Australian Electoral Commission 1992). They are also allowed to occupy permanent positions in the public service, which immigrants from non-English-speaking backgrounds cannot do without taking up Australian citizenship. Further differences in attitudes, if not in law, toward the latter category (the NESBs) are based on their skin colour.

In the political sphere, although Australia became a 'self-governing colony' in 1901 and developed distinct characteristics in social attitudes, it also remained 'more British than the Motherland or any other sister Dominion' (Atkinson 1920: 1). At the time of Federation, Australians 'saw themselves as British first, then as Victorians, South Australians and so on and only gradually became accustomed to being "Australians"' (Eddy 1991: 26). Nor was the new 'self-governing colony' a sovereign state. Its Constitution was (and still is) an act of the British Parliament and its own laws could be invalidated by that parliament; its highest court of law was the English Privy Council and individual citizens and State governments were able to appeal directly to it. As Australia remained part of the British Empire, people in Britain continued to regard it as a 'self-governing colony', and its citizens remained 'British subjects'. In the colonial days

Australians fought British Empire wars under the British flag, in South Africa and Sudan, and later did so in many places during the Great War. With a few exceptions and until the 1960s, the Governor-General and governors appointed by the states were always retired British generals or businessmen, and so were many politicians. In international relations the dependence on Britain was complete. Before World War II Australia had no Department of Foreign Affairs and no ambassadors abroad; Britain handled all its external affairs. Internationally Australia was regarded as, and in effect it was, a British colony – one of the red areas on the world map. As noted by J. D. B. Miller,

> The men who governed Australia in the 1920s and 30s were mostly British and Protestant in origin; they and their parties, the Nationalists, Country and United Australia parties, delighted in their Britishness and proclaimed their undying loyalty to the flag and throne.   (1989:232)

The first 'Australian citizenship' certificate was issued in 1949 to the then Prime Minister J. B. (Ben) Chifley. For a brief period at that time Australians were able to obtain an *Australian* passport, but with the change of the party in power in 1949 this soon reverted to a *British* passport. It was not until the 1960s that *Australian* passports were restored and it was only in the 1966 Census that Australians were allowed to describe themselves as 'Australians' rather than 'British subjects' (Grassby 1984: 158).

For a long time a similar dependence existed in the economic sphere and in the development of industry; this dependence was a significant cause of technological retardation, which also had negative effects on cultural and social development. Examining Australia's economic and industrial performance in a historical perspective, Stephen Hill comments that from the early colonial days Australia was marginal to the industrialised world and was 'a nation crouched in mendicant cringe to the technological fashion leaders of international capitalism'. Hill observes:

> ... Australia's colonialist posture throughout the nineteenth century fundamentally flawed the subsequent development of the nation: its economy was based on successful primary product service to Britain; its sparse technological knowledge resources were developed from manpower crumbs dropped from Britain's industrial table, its models of science and ideologies of training emanated from Britain's imperialism.   (1988:239)

Notwithstanding its dependence on Britain, Australia was seen to have achieved a relatively high standard of living early in the twentieth century and was also regarded as a pioneer in industrial and social legislation (Kewley 1973, Castles 1985, Graycar and Jamrozik 1993).

However, as argued convincingly by White, the belief propagated even prior to Federation that Australia was a 'workingman's paradise' served to preserve the social order and to reconcile the working class to an unequal distribution of wealth (1981:44–5). If it was a 'paradise' it was so for only a small minority of the skilled workforce and at the cost of the exploitation of others. Active promotion of national 'Australian' enthusiasm and patriotism in the early years of Federation served the purpose of protecting the interests of local manufacturers from outside competition. Promotion of patriotism was also class-based; it 'promoted national unity at a time when sections of the labour movement were increasingly militant and class-conscious. National loyalties were encouraged by the middle class: class loyalties were condemned as divisive and un-Australian' (1981:113–14). The projected image of national unity and denial of class divisions was aimed at preserving the interests of the bourgeoisie. Added to this was the projection of threats from outside, a method of maintaining social order and control that has been used effectively since then and (as will be shown in later chapters) is still attempted today. As White observes:

> Protection, not only of local labour and industry from foreign competition, but also of the nation generally from foreign aggression and assaults on its unity or its racial and moral purity became a dominant feature of Australian society.   (1981:114)

After the first decade of Federation, which became noted for some innovative social and industrial legislation – a minimum 'basic' wage (1907), old age and invalid pensions (1909), maternity benefits (1911) – Australia entered a long period of relative stability and slow economic development, later severely interrupted by the Great Depression.

A significant period of social and economic change began in the 1940s. The main sources of this can be found in the changing nature of the economy and in the mass immigration program initiated in the late 1940s. Immigrants' influence has affected many aspects of Australian society, but the first and most important effect of their presence was in the economic sphere. The ensuing changes in the structure of industries have been accompanied by changes in the occupational structure of the labour market and these, in turn, became a significant factor in the changing class structure.

Changes in the occupational structure of employment occurred in two distinct phases. Initially, in the first two post-war decades, there was a growth of employment in manufacturing, with a corresponding growth of manual occupations, giving rise to a growing and increasingly differentiated and fairly affluent working class. That growth stalled around the mid-1960s and employment in manufacturing began to decrease; at first only in relative terms compared to the growth of total employment, but then in absolute terms, with the effect that after periodic fluctuations the number of people employed in the manufacturing industries was lower in 1992 than in 1966, although total employment over that period had grown by 59 per cent (see Table 3.5).

The social and economic significance of the changes in the structure of industries and occupations are discussed below. The effects of immigration on the economy and social and cultural life in Australia are examined in subsequent chapters.

Population

The first census of the population in the post-war period, held in 1947, recorded the population of Australia as 7 579 400. By 1991 the population had grown to 16 849 500, a growth by a factor of 2.22 (Table 3.1). The rate of growth over this period had progressively slowed down: in the first 19 years (1947–1966) the population grew by 51.8 per cent; in the following 20 years (1966–1986) by 35.6 per cent; and in the subsequent 5 years (1986–1991) by 8.0 per cent. A number of factors accounted for this decrease in the rate of growth: a declining fertility rate, fewer children per family, a decrease in the marriage rate and an increase in the rate of divorce (Borowski and Shu 1992).

The decreasing rate of growth and a longer average life-span has resulted in an ageing population structure: people 65 years of age or above accounting in 1991 for 11.3 per cent of the total population, compared to 8.0 per cent in 1947. This ageing process is likely to continue into the foreseeable future, but in comparison with the population of other industrialised countries Australia will remain a relatively 'young' country for many decades.

Since the late 1940s, apart from the natural increase through births, the Australian population has increased through immigration. As may be ascertained from the data in Table 3.2, over 5 million people entered Australia from 1947 to 1991 as permanent settlers. Taking into account permanent departures, it may be estimated that over this period immigrants accounted for the increase of over 3 million persons, or about 35 per cent of the total increase in population. As a result, certain population characteristics have also changed: while 90.2 per cent of the population in 1947 was born in Australia, by 1986 this proportion had decreased to 77.6 per cent (Table 3.3). When the second generation (the children of immigrants) is taken into account, four out of ten persons living in Australia in the early 1990s are either overseas-born or are the children of one or both parents born overseas.

Table 3.1 *Changes in Age Structure, Australia, 1947–1991*

Age group (years)	1947 '000	1947 %	1966 '000	1966 %	1986 '000	1986 %	1991 '000	1991 %	Increase 1947–92 '000	Increase 1947–92 Ratio
Total population	*7579.4*	*100.0*	*11 508.2*	*100.0*	*15 602.2*	*100.0*	*16 849.5*	*100.0*	*9270.1*	*2.22*
0–14	1899.1	25.1	3 392.5	29.5	3 636.8	23.3	3 727.4	22.1	1828.3	1.96
15–24	1204.6	15.9	1 902.1	16.5	2 598.9	16.7	2 685.3	15.9	1480.7	2.23
25–44	2253.7	29.7	2 971.7	25.8	4 752.7	30.5	5 290.6	31.4	3036.9	2.35
45–64	1611.9	21.3	2 297.7	20.0	2 967.0	19.0	3 245.1	19.3	1633.2	2.01
65 and +	610.1	8.0	986.4	8.6	1 646.7	10.6	1 900.9	11.3	1290.8	3.12

Source: Australian Bureau of Statistics, Census data

Table 3.2: *Population, Australia: Permanent Arrivals, Departures, Net Gain,*
1947–1991

Year	Arrivals	Departures	Net gain	Mean net gain per annum
1947–1959	1448.8	n/a	n/a	—
1960–1966	808.4	112.1	696.3	99.5
1967–1971	807.0	170.8	636.2	127.2
1972–1976	494.7	188.0	306.7	61.3
1977–1981	402.7	114.6	288.1	57.6
1982–1986	450.0	108.5	341.5	68.3
1987–1991	645.3	212.0	524.3	104.9

n/a = not available.
Source: Borowski, A. and Shu, J. (1992), *Australia's Population Trends and*
          Prospects 1991, Melbourne, Bureau of Immigration Research

Most Australians live in family settings (94 per cent of the population in 1986) but the characteristics of the family have been changing. The trend has been towards fewer families with dependent children, more one-parent families, and more persons living alone. As shown in Table 3.4, between 1974 and 1986 the proportion of two-parent families (legally married or de facto) decreased slightly over that period from 89.3 per cent to 86.0 per cent of all family units. A similar decrease occurred in the proportion of two-parent families with dependent children, but these families still accounted for the majority of two-parent families in 1986. The increase in the proportion of married couples without dependent children has been due partly to the growth of the older population (see Table 3.1), many of whom are retired couples who would have had dependent children in their earlier years. Older people also account for the increase in the number of persons living alone: of the 961 200 such persons in 1986 (6.2% of the population), 40 per cent were at least 65 years old.

A significant change in family structure has been the growth of one-parent families. This type of family increased both in numbers and as the proportion of families with dependent children, from 9.2 per cent in 1974 to 14.9 per cent in 1986. It needs to be noted, however, that a great majority of one-parent families have a 'transitional' character, the parent being separated or divorced from her or his partner and likely to re-marry or re-establish a new household in a relatively short period of time. Nevertheless, whatever the reasons for its emergence and growth, or its character, the one-parent family unit has now become a significant element in Australian society: it is an indication of the diminishing stability in the institution of the family, which has social and economic

Table 3.3: *Birthplace of Population, Australia, 1947–1986*

Birthplace	1947 '000	1947 %	1966 '000	1966 %	1986 '000	1986 %	Increase 1947-86 '000	Increase 1947-86 Ratio
Total population	*7579.4*	*100.0*	*11550.5*	*100.0*	*15602.2*	*100.0*	*8022.8*	*2.06*
Australia	6835.2	90.2	9419.5	81.5	12110.5	77.6	5275.3	1.77
New Zealand	43.6	0.6	52.5	0.5	211.7	1.4	168.1	4.86
UK & Ireland	541.3	7.1	908.7	7.9	1127.2	7.2	585.9	2.08
Other English-speaking countries	16.2	0.2	35.6	0.3	99.9	0.6	83.7	6.17
Southern Europe	57.5	0.8	548.2	4.7	638.2	4.1	580.7	11.10
Other Europe	52.8	0.7	436.6	3.8	456.4	2.9	403.6	8.64
Asia	24.1	0.3	101.4	0.9	536.2	3.4	512.1	22.25
South America	1.2	0.0	2.6	0.0	46.7	0.3	45.5	38.92
Other countries	6.5	0.1	44.9	0.4	131.2	0.8	124.7	20.18
Not stated	1.0	0.0	5.0	0.0	244.2	1.6	—	—

Note: Southern Europe: Greece, Italy, Malta, Spain, Yugoslavia
Other Europe: France, Germany, Netherlands, Poland, Scandinavian countries
Asia: Lebanon, China and Hong Kong, India and Sri Lanka, Malaysia, Vietnam
Source: ABS (1991), *Multicultural Australia*, Cat. No. 2505.0

implications of considerable magnitude. The economic viability of the one-parent family varies according to that parent's class position and his or her ability to obtain employment in the labour market, which often corresponds to that class position. However, notwithstanding class and socio-economic differences, the economic viability of one-parent families is rather precarious in comparison to those with two income-earners, especially those in the professional and related fields. Thus, while the two-earner family has been a factor in upward class mobility, the one-parent family is likely to be a factor in class mobility in the opposite direction, especially if social mobility is considered in an inter-generational perspective.

Two family characteristics are of particular relevance to the issues examined in this book: one is the birthplace of parents; the second is the increase in families with two incomes earned from employment. Concerning the first characteristic, the inflow of immigrants has given rise to intermarriage of Australian-born and overseas-born persons. In the 1986 census, of all recorded couple families 61.3 per cent showed both partners born in Australia, in 15.8 per cent one partner was born in Australia and the other overseas, and in 21.1 per cent both partners

Table 3.4: *Australian Families, 1974 and 1986*

Family composition	1974[1]			1986[2]		
	'000	%	%	'000	%	%
All families	*3470.1*	–		*100.0*	*4158.0*	–
100.0						
Two-parent families	3098.7	100.0	89.3	3575.1	100.0	86.0
– with dependent						
children	1805.4	58.3		1854.0	51.9	-
– no dependent						
children	1293.3	41.7		1721.1	48.1	
One-parent families						
with dependent						
children	183.2	–	5.3	324.2	–	7.8
All families, no						
dependent						
children	188.2	–	5.4	258.8	–	6.2
All families with						
dependent children	1988.6	100.0	(57.3)[a]	2178.2	100.0	(52.4)[a]
– Two-parent families	1805.4	90.8		1854.0	85.1	
– One-parent families	183.2	9.2		324.2	14.9	

Note: [a] Per cent of all families.
Sources: [1] ABS (1980), *Social Indicators No. 3*, Cat. No. 4101.0
[2] ABS (1989), *Australian Families and Households, Census 86*,
Cat. No. 2506.0

were overseas-born (in 1.8 per cent of families one or both partners did not record the place of birth) (ABS 1991, Cat. No. 2505.0). As the second and now third generation of immigrants reach maturity, inter-marriage of Australian-born persons of different ethnic backgrounds will increase, adding further to the mixed ethnicity of the Australian population.

As to the other characteristic, the two-earner family, the labour force data recorded by the Australian Bureau of Statistics (ABS) indicate that in 1992 (August) in 47 per cent of couple families both partners were employed. However, when older retired couples were excluded from the calculation the proportion of two-earner families rose to 60 per cent, and 56 per cent of these were couples with dependent children (ABS 1992, Catalogue No. 6203.0). This certainly was not the case in the earlier decades when two-earner families accounted for a small minority of two-parent families (the 1954 census recorded a participation rate in the labour force by married women of 12.6 per cent). The significance of this change for the social structure of Australian society is discussed later in this chapter.

Industry and the Labour Force

On the industrial scene Australia in the 1990s is a vastly different place from the one it was in the 1960s and certainly more different from the place it was in the 1940s. In the field of employment the change has been multidimensional, entailing shifts of employment from industries engaged in material production to service and 'management' industries and from manual to non-manual occupations, a change in the sex/ gender composition of the labour force, and a significant growth of unemployment. As shown in Table 3.5, from 1966 to 1992 the rate of growth in the labour force exceeded the rate of growth in the popula- tion by a factor of 1.11, but employment lagged behind, recording growth by a factor of 0.87, resulting in the rise in unemployment by a factor of 15.56. Even more telling was the increase in the average length of unemployment: from 3.0 weeks to 48.2 weeks, a growth factor of 17.07, indicating an increasing entrenchment of unemployment among certain sections of the labour force.

The change in the gender composition of the labour force has been one of the most significant aspects of social change, affecting relationships between the sexes, family structure, and the distribution of individual and, more particularly, family incomes. Between 1966 and 1992 employment of women increased at a rate more than twice the rate of increase in total employment and four times the rate of increase in the employment of men, rising from 30.2 per cent to 42.3 per cent of all employed persons. Most of this increase came through the rise in the employment of married women, from 15.8 per cent to 26.3 per cent of the employed labour force. The cumulative effect of these changes on the socio-economic stratifica- tion and class structure of Australian society has been profound.

In the structure of industry there has been a clear shift in employment from industries of material production to the 'management industries', that is, industries engaged in the management of material and human resources: finance, property and business services; public administra- tion; and community services. A smaller numerical and percentage in- crease occurred in the service sector of recreation and personal services. In effect, of the total increase in employment of 2 855 400 persons over this period (1966–92), 1 790 100 persons, or 62.7 per cent, found employment in the three sectors of the management industries, most of them in community services. Another 343.4 thousand persons, or 12.0 per cent of the total increase in employment, went to the recreation and personal services sector. In contrast, employment in industries engaged in material production remained entirely static, and in manufacturing there were 126 300 fewer persons employed in 1992 than in 1966, a decrease of 10.2 per cent.

Table 3.5: *Changes in Employment, Australia, 1966–1992: Industry Sectors*

Industry sector	1966 '000	%	1992 '000	%	Change 1966–1992 '000	%	Ratio[1]
Population							
15 years+	*8180.3*	*100.0*	*13722.2*	*100.0*	*5541.9*	*67.7*	*0.00*
Labour force	4902.5	59.5	8585.7	62.6	3683.2	75.1	1.11
Participation							
rate	—	59.9	—	62.3	—	4.0	1.04
Employed	4823.9	98.4	7679.3	89.4	2855.4	59.2	0.8
Unemployed	78.6	1.6	906.4	10.6	827.8	1053.2	15.56
Average duration							
of unemployment							
(weeks)	3.0	—	51.2	—	48.2	1606.7	17.07
Employed: all							
industries	*4823.9*	*100.0*	*7679.3*	*100.0*	*2855.4*	*59.2*	*0.00*
Men	3365.6	69.8	4433.4	57.7	1067.8	31.7	0.54
Women	1458.2	30.2	3245.8	42.3	1787.6	122.6	2.07
Married women	761.2	15.8	2016.9	26.3	1255.7	165.0	2.79
Material production	*2222.6*	*46.1*	*2228.1*	*29.0*	*5.5*	*0.2*	*0.00*
Agriculture and							
related	429.6	8.9	398.0	5.2	−31.6	−7.4	—
Mining	58.0	1.2	91.6	1.2	33.6	57.9	0.98
Manufacturing	1232.5	25.5	1106.2	14.4	−126.3	−10.2	—
Electricity, gas,							
water	96.5	2.0	105.4	1.4	8.9	9.2	0.16
Construction	406.5	8.4	526.9	6.9	120.4	29.6	0.50
Distribution services	*1368.9*	*28.4*	*2085.3*	*27.2*	*716.2*	*52.3*	*0.88*
Wholesale and							
retail trade	993.5	20.6	1594.7	20.8	601.2	60.5	1.02
Transport and							
storage	270.0	5.6	375.0	4.9	105.0	38.9	0.66
Communications	105.4	2.2	115.6	1.5	10.2	9.7	0.16
Management							
industries	*945.4*	*19.6*	*2735.5*	*35.6*	*1790.1*	*189.3*	*3.20*
Finance, property,							
business services	294.4	6.1	898.8	11.7	604.4	205.3	3.47
Public							
administration	165.0	3.4	346.2	4.5	181.2	109.8	1.85
Community							
services	486.0	10.1	1490.5	19.4	1004.5	206.7	3.49
Recreation, personal							
services	*287.0*	*5.9*	*630.4*	*8.2*	*343.4*	*119.7*	*2.02*

Note: [1]   Ratio of the growth in the labour force, employment and
            unemployment related to the growth population 15 years
            and over. Ratio of the growth of various sectors of industry
            related to the growth of total employment.
Sources: ABS (1987), *The Labour Force, Australia, Historical Summary, 1966–1984*,
            Cat. No. 6204.0.
            ABS (1992), *The Labour Force, Australia, August 1992*, Cat. No. 6203.0.

Over the whole period from 1966 to 1992 all sectors of industry, except agriculture and other primary industries and manufacturing industries, recorded a growth in employment in absolute numbers. However, in *relative ratios* to the growth in total employment, employment in some sectors of industry has been expanding while in others it has been shrinking. The use of relative measurements is important, as employment in an industry or occupation may be growing in absolute numbers while shrinking in relation to other industries or occupations. The application of this concept, first developed in an earlier study (Jamrozik and Hoey 1982), allows comparisons of trends and various dimensions in relative terms, both quantitative and qualitative. Furthermore, because this concept takes into account a number of dimensions in relation to one another, it facilitates identification of those changes in the labour market which are causally linked to changes in the social structure.

Comparison of data at two points of time separated by 26 years indicates the extent of change over the period but does not tell us much about what had occurred in the intervening years. Some of this information is provided in Table 3.6 where the changes in population, labour force, employment and unemployment are shown for a number of years between 1966 and 1992. The years 1972, 1975 and 1983 were years when the party in power in the federal government changed; 1989 was the year when the growth of employment in the 1980s reached its peak and was then rather suddenly followed by recession and rapidly rising unemployment. While the trends recorded for each of these periods cannot be interpreted as being due entirely to the policies of the government of the day, the data suggest that those policies might have been among the causative factors of these trends. For example, distinct differences are easily noticeable between the periods 1975–1983 (Conservative Coalition government) and 1983–1989 (Labor government). In effect, the period 1983–1989 was something of a departure from the overall trend for the entire period 1966–1992: this was the only period when unemployment actually decreased and employment increased above the rate of increase in the labour force, and there was also some growth in employment in the industries of material production. However, of all sectors it was the management industries that showed a sustained growth in employment throughout the whole period, even during the three years of recession after 1989.

Parallel with the shifts in employment among various sectors of industry was an equally significant shift in the occupational structure of employment, from manual to non-manual occupations. Because the Australian Bureau of Statistics changed its classification system for occupations in 1986, it is not possible to provide here comparable data for the whole period 1966–1992. However, as shown in Table 3.7, even in

Table 3.6: *Population, Labour Force, Employment and Unemployment, Australia, 1966–1992*
(N = '000)

Population/Labour force/Employment/ Unemployment		1966	1972	1975	1983	1989	1992	Change 1966–92
Population								
15 years +	N	*8180.3*	*9379.2*	*9935.9*	*11 606.2*	*13 075.4*	*13 722.2*	*5541.9*
– Increase over								
period	%	–	14.7	5.9	16.8	12.7	4.9	67.7
Labour force	N	4902.5	5753.9	67119.7	6 927.9	8 197.0	8 585.7	3683.2
– Increase over								
period	%	–	17.4	6.4	13.2	18.3	4.7	75.1
Employed	N	4823.9	5609.7	5841.3	6 241.1	7 727.6	7 679.3	2855.4
– Increase over								
period	%	–	16.3	4.1	6.8	23.8	-0.6	59.2
Unemployed	N	78.6	144.0	278.4	686.8	469.4	906.4	827.8
– Increase over								
period	%	–	89.6	93.3	146.7	–31.7	93.1	1053.2
All employed	N	*4823.9*	*5609.9*	*5841.3*	*6 241.1*	*7 727.6*	*7 679.3*	*2855.4*
– Increase over								
period	%	–	16.3	4.1	6.8	23.8	–0.6	59.2
Material production	N	2222.6	2417.9	2356.4	2 162.0	2 462.4	2 228.1	5.5
– Of all								
employed	%	46.1	43.1	40.3	34.6	31.9	29.0	–17.1*
– Increase over								
period	%	–	8.8	–2.5	–8.2	13.9	–9.5	0.2
Distribution services	N	1368.9	1571.5	1612.3	1 722.6	2 154.2.	2 085.3	716.4
– Of all								
employed	%	28.4	28.0	27.6	27.6	27.9	27.2	–1.2*
– Increase over								
period	%	–	14.8	26.0	6.8	25.1	–3.2	52.3
Management industries	N	954.4	1271.0	1501.2	1 965.8	2 556.1	2 735.5	1790.1
– Of all								
employed	%	19.6	22.7	25.7	31.5	33.1	35.6	16.0*
– Increase over								
period	%	–	34.4	18.1	30.9	30.0	7.0	189.3
Recreation, personal services	N	287.0	349.7	371.5	390.8	554.7	630.4	343.4
– Of all								
employed	%	5.9	6.2	6.4	6.3	7.2	8.2	2.3*
– Increase over								
period	%	–	21.8	6.2	5.2	41.9	13.6	119.7

Note: * Percentage points.
Sources: ABS (1987), *The Labour Force Australia, Historical Summary 1966–1984.*
Cat. No. 6204.0.
ABS (1989–1992), *The Labour Force Australia, August 1989, 1992,*
Cat. No. 6203.0

Table 3.7: *Changes in Occupation Structure of Employment, Australia 1986–1992*

Occupation	1986 '000	%	1992 '000	%	Change 1986–92 '000	%
All employed persons	*6885.7*	*100.0*	*7679.3*	*100.0*	*793.6*	*11.5*
Management and professions	*1985.2*	*28.8*	*2398.7*	*31.2*	*413.5*	*20.8*
Managers and administrators	756.0	11.0	869.5	11.3	113.5	15.0
Professionals	825.5	12.0	1063.6	13.8	238.1	28.8
Para-professionals	403.7	5.9	465.6	6.1	61.9	15.3
Clerks, sales, personal services	*2138.2*	*31.1*	*2453.0*	*31.9*	*314.8*	*14.7*
Clerks	1190.9	17.3	1279.7	16.7	88.8	7.5
Sales, personal services	947.3	13.8	1173.3	15.3	226.0	23.9
Trades, plant operators, drivers	*1698.8*	*24.7*	*1696.8*	*22.1*	*−2.0*	*−0.1*
Tradespersons	1154.2	16.8	1149.6	15.0	−4.6	−0.4
Plant operators, drivers	544.6	7.9	547.2	7.1	2.6	0.5
Labourers and related	*1063.6*	*15.4*	*1130.9*	*14.7*	*67.3*	*6.3*

Source: ABS (1986, 1992), *The Labour Force Australia, August 1986–1992,*
        Cat. No. 6203.0

the short period from 1986 to 1992 the rate of employment for managers, administrators, professionals and para-professionals rose almost twice as fast as total employment, accounting in 1992 for close to one-third (31.2%) of all employed persons. By comparison, in 1966 the broadly equivalent occupational categories (managers, executives, professionals and technical workers) accounted for only 16.6 per cent of all employed persons. The change over this period clearly indicates a rapid rate of professionalisation of the labour force, and indications are that with the restructuring of industry which gathered pace in the late 1980s the rate of professionalisation has been accelerating.

As noted earlier, the third feature of the employment structure has been a changing gender composition of employed persons. This change has occurred not only within industries but also within occupations, and the shift towards the employment of women has been most prominent in the expanding industries and occupations. Thus, while accounting for 42.3 per cent of all employed persons in 1992, women accounted for 56.6 per cent of employed persons in the management industries and for an equal percentage of those employed in the recreation and personal service industries. (Table 3.8).

Table 3.8: *Persons Employed, Australia, August 1992: Gender Composition*

Industry/occupation	All employed (1) '000	%	Men (2) '000	%	Women (3) '000	%	% of (1)
All employed	*7679.3*	*100.0*	*4433.4*	*100.0*	*3245.8*	*100.0*	*42.3*
Industry:							
Material production	*2228.1*	*29.0*	*1720.1*	*38.8*	*508.1*	*15.7*	*22.8*
Agriculture, land related	398.0	5.2	280.4	6.3	117.7	3.6	29.6
Mining	91.6	1.2	82.8	1.9	8.7	0.3	9.5
Manufacturing	1106.2	14.4	807.0	18.2	299.2	9.2	27.0
Electricity, gas water	105.4	1.4	91.2	2.1	14.3	0.4	13.6
Construction	526.9	6.9	458.7	10.3	68.2	2.1	12.9
Distribution services	*2085.3*	*27.2*	*1248.9*	*28.2*	*836.4*	*24.8*	*40.1*
Wholesale and retail trade	1594.7	20.8	867.3	19.6	727.4	22.4	45.6
Transport and storage	375.0	4.9	301.8	6.8	73.2	2.3	19.5
Communications	115.6	1.5	79.8	1.8	35.8	1.1	31.0
Management industries	*2735.5*	*35.6*	*1186.1*	*26.8*	*1549.3*	*47.7*	*56.6*
Finance, property, business services	898.8	11.7	459.0	10.4	439.7	13.5	50.6
Public administration	346.2	4.5	217.6	4.9	128.6	4.0	37.1
Community services	1490.5	19.4	509.5	11.5	981.0	30.2	65.8
Recreation, personal services	*630.4*	*8.2*	*278.3*	*6.3*	*352.1*	*10.8*	*55.9*
Occupation:							
Management and professionals	*2398.7*	*31.2*	*1511.9*	*34.1*	*886.8*	*27.3*	*37.0*
Managers and administrators	869.5	11.3	651.2	14.7	218.3	6.7	25.1
Professionals	1063.6	13.8	612.4	13.8	451.2	13.9	42.4
Para-professionals	456.6	6.1	248.3	5.6	217.3	6.7	46.7
Clerks, sales, personal services	*1173.3*	*15.3*	*404.7*	*9.1*	*768.6*	*23.6*	*65.5*
Clerks	1279.7	16.7	287.7	6.5	991.9	30.6	77.5
Sales, personal services	1173.3	15.3	404.7	9.1	768.6	23.6	65.5
Trades, plant operators, drivers	*1696.8*	*22.1*	*1500.8*	*33.9*	*196.0*	*6.0*	*11.6*
Tradespersons	1149.6	15.0	1030.8	23.3	118.8	3.6	10.3
Plant operators, drivers	547.2	7.1	470.0	10.6	77.2	2.4	14.1
Labourers and related	*1130.9*	*14.7*	*728.2*	*16.4*	*402.6*	*12.4*	*35.6*

Source: ABS (1992), *The Labour Force, Australia, August 1992*, Cat. No. 6203.0

The cumulative effect of the shifts in these three dimensions – *gender, industry, occupation* – has been an increasing concentration of women in that section of the labour market where the *expanding* sectors of industry provided employment for the *expanding* occupations. In contrast, the highest concentration of men has remained in those sections of the labour market where *both* the sectors of industry and the occupations have been *shrinking*. As shown in Table 3.9, in August 1992, 34.7 per cent of all employed persons were employed in the *expanding/expanding* sector of the labour market (cell A) and the majority of the employed persons in that sector were women (59.6%), a much higher percentage than the percentage of women in the entire employed labour force (42.3%). This sector of the labour market accounted for nearly one-half (49.1%) of all employed women, compared with 24.2 per cent of all employed men. At the other extreme, the *shrinking/shrinking* sector of the labour market (cell D) accounted for 27.7 per cent of all employed persons and the composition was 86.4 per cent men and 13.6 per cent women, accounting for 41.4 per cent of all employed men but only for 8.9 per cent of all employed women.

The data in Table 3.9 indicate a trend in the changing structure of the labour market which confirms a high degree of continuity of the trends identified in the study mentioned earlier (Jamrozik and Hoey 1982). The data show clearly that the change in the occupational structure of employment has proceeded at a faster rate than the shifts of employment from one sector of industry to another, indicating that the nature of employment has been changing in most industries, although not at the same pace in all sectors. It is also clear that the majority of women who entered the labour force have found employment in the expanding occupations and expanding industries, thus taking up a major share of the new jobs. As most of these expanding occupations have been in the professional and para-professional areas, and the majority of employed women are married (62 per cent in August 1992), the increase of two-earner families has been particularly prominent among the managerial and professional population strata – the new middle class.

Education and Employment

Paralleling the professionalisation of the labour force, there has been a significant rise in educational attainment levels. This change also has been multi-dimensional, entailing the number and proportion of people with post-school qualifications, the levels of such qualifications, and the gender composition of the groups with post-school qualifications.

Historically, interest in education in Australia was mostly limited to compulsory schooling to the age of 15 years. As a result, relatively few young

Table 3.9: *Configurations of Expanding and Shrinking Industries and Occupations: Employed Persons, Australia, August 1992*

	Occupations								
	Expanding (+)			Shrinking (−)			All employed (+ −)		
Industries	'000	%1	%2	'000	%1	%2	'000	%1	%2
	A(+ +)			(B+ −)			AB(+ +) + (+ −)		
Expanding (+)									
Persons	2665.5	100.0	34.7	700.8	100.0	9.1	3366.3	100.0	43.8
Men	1072.3	40.4	24.2	392.3	56.0	8.8	1464.6	43.5	33.0
Women	1593.2	59.6	49.1	308.5	44.0	9.5	1901.7	56.5	58.6
	C(− +)			(D − −)			CD (− +) + (− −)		
Shrinking (−)									
Persons	2186.4	100.0	28.5	2126.5	100.01	27.7	4312.9	100.0	56.2
Men	1132.1	51.8	25.5	1836.7	86.4	41.4	2968.8	68.8	67.0
Women	1054.3	48.2	32.5	289.8	13.6	8.9	1344.1	31.2	41.4
	AC (+ +) + (− +)			BD (+ −) + (− −)			Total ABCD		
All employed (+ −)									
Persons	4851.9	100.0	63.2	2827.3	100.0	36.8	7679.3	—	100.0
Men	2204.4	45.4	49.7	2229.0	78.8	50.3	4433.4	—	57.7
Women	2647.5	54.6	81.6	598.3	21.2	18.4	3245.8	—	42.3

Note: %1 = per cent in column
%2 = per cent of total employed
Source: ABS (1992), *The Labour Force, Australia, August 1992.* Cat. No. 6203.0

people would stay at school to the final year, even fewer would complete secondary education (matriculation or Higher School Certificate) and only a small number of those who did so would proceed to tertiary education. From the 1960s onwards the situation has been changing rather dramatically, especially in the 1980s. In 1969 only slightly more than a quarter of young people (27.5%) attended school to the final year; by 1991 that proportion had risen to 71.3 per cent (these percentages are average school retention rates for all young people attending school in Australia, ignoring differences between the states and considerable differences between public and private schools) (ABS 1992, Cat. No. 4221.0).

The increase in the population with post-school education was even greater. As shown in Table 3.10, in 1969 only 20 per cent of the population had some post-school qualifications, and fewer than three per cent (2.7%) held a tertiary degree. In 1992, 42 per cent of the population had some post-school qualifications and the number of degree holders had risen to 9.4 per cent, 3.5 times the 1969 percentage. The increase in educational attainment was particularly prominent among women: over three times the percentage increase in post-school qualifications, from 11.6 per cent to 36.5 per cent; and over six times the percentage increase in degree holders, from 1.3 per cent to 8.0 per cent.

Table 3.10: *Educational Attainment of Population, Australia, 1969 and 1992*

	All persons ('000)	All with qualifi- cations %	With post-school qualifications			Without post- school qualifi- cations %
			Degree %	Trade %	Certificate diploma other %	
1969[1]						
Persons	6440.2	20.2	2.7	8.9	8.7	79.7
• Men	3260.8	28.7	4.0	16.0	8.7	71.3
• Women	3179.4	11.6	1.3	1.6	8.6	88.4
1992[2]						
Persons	12 155.2[3]	41.8	9.4	13.3	19.1	53.4
• Men	6 113.6[3]	46.9	10.8	23.7	12.4	48.2
• Women	6 041.6[3]	36.5	8.0	2.8	25.7	58.6

Note: [1]   Data for 1969 relate to population 20 to 64 years
        [2]   Data for 1992 relate to population 15 to 69 years
        [3]   Includes 590.6 thousand persons (4.9%) still at school
             (298 400 men; 292 800 women)
Source: a)   ABS (1984), *Social Indicators No. 4*, Cat. No. 4101.0
         b)   ABS (1992), *Labour Force Status and Educational Attainment,*
             February 1992, Cat. No. 6235.0

With the changing field of economic production, technological innovation and changing organisation of work, educational qualifications
became an important factor in a person's access to employment, a career
structure in a professional occupation with relative security of tenure,
good income and fringe benefits. The significance of educational
qualifications, especially of a university degree, is clearly evident from
the data in Table 3.11. Persons with post-school qualifications consistently record higher participation rates in the labour force, higher
frequency of full-time employment, and lower rates of unemployment.
Similar differences are consistently recorded in the occupational structure: of all occupations, professional employees of both sexes record the
lowest part-time employment rates and unemployment rates, in each
case only about half the rates for labourers and related workers (ABS
1993, August, Catalogue No. 6203.0). These differences and corresponding inequalities in the labour market tend not to be revealed in the data
on employment, part-time employment and unemployment published
in research monographs which provide only averages for the entire
labour force (see Saunders 1993, for example).
   Of economic and social significance is the high concentration of
persons with tertiary degrees in the expanding sectors of industry,

Table 3.11: *Educational Attainment and Labour Force Status, Persons 15–69 Years, Australia, February 1992*

Labour force status		All persons	With post-school qualifications				Without post-school qualifications
			All with qualifications	Degree	Trade	Certificate diploma other	
All persons	*'000*	*12 155.2*	*5076.5*	*1139.5*	*1620.2*	*2272.8*	*6485.2*
	%	*100.0*	*100.0*	*100.0*	*100.0*	*100.0*	*100.0*
In labour force	'000	8 557.2	4174.8	1010.0	1359.4	1772.1	4196.0
Participation rate	%	70.4	82.2	88.6	83.9	78.0	64.7
Employed	'000	7 571.1	3830.2	950.5	1240.8	1610.2	3559.5
	%[1]	88.5	91.7	94.1	91.3	90.9	84.8
Full-time	'000	5 873.7	3160.5	813.5	1140.8	1183.6	2711.5
	%[2]	77.6	82.5	85.6	91.9	73.5	76.2
Part-time	'000	1 697.4	669.6	137.0	100.0	426.6	887.9
	%[2]	22.4	17.5	14.4	8.1	26.5	24.9
Unemployed	'000	986.1	344.6	59.4	118.6	161.9	596.6
	%[1]	11.5	8.3	5.9	8.7	9.1	14.2
Not in labour force	'000	3 589.0	901.8	129.5	260.8	500.7	2289.2
	%	29.6	17.8	11.4	16.1	22.0	35.3

Notes: *   Includes persons with other (not stated here) qualifications
         [1]   Per cent of the labour force
         [2]   Per cent of all employed
Source: ABS (1992), *Labour Force Status and Educational Attainment Australia, February 1992.* Cat. No. 6235.0

particularly in the management industries: as shown in Table 3.12, in February 1992 over 70 per cent of all employed degree holders were employed in those industries. In comparison, the shrinking sectors of industry which are engaged in material production (agriculture and other primary; mining; manufacturing; electricity, gas and water supply; construction) accounted for only 12.4 per cent of employed degree holders. Educational qualifications thus constitute another dimension in the quantitative and qualitative structural changes in the labour market, adding to the cumulative effects of a growing division between expanding and shrinking industries and occupations.

Education, Employment and Social Class

What kind of social effects have emerged from the changes in education and employment discussed in this chapter? It has been evident for some

Table 3.12: *Educational Attainment of Employed Persons 15–69 Years, Australia, February 1992*

Industry groups[1]	All employed persons[a]	All with qualifi- cations[b]	With post-school qualifications			Without post- school qualifi- cations
			Degree	Trade	Certificate diploma	
All industries						
'000	*7571.1*	*3830.2*	*950.5*	*1240.8*	*1610.2*	*3599.5*
%	*100.0*	*50.6*	*12.6*	*16.4*	*21.3*	*47.5*
Material production						
'000	2206.3	1054.8	118.1	618.3	310.2	1135.2
% in group	100.0	47.8	5.4	28.0	14.1	51.5
% of all employed	29.1	27.5	12.4	49.8	19.3	31.5
Distribution services						
'000	2103.5	822.6	116.6	360.7	337.0	1176.9
% in group	100.0	39.1	5.5	17.1	16.0	55.9
% of all employed	27.8	21.5	12.3	29.1	20.9	32.7
Management industries						
'000	2643.7	1681.7	672.0	156.0	843.7	956.9
% in group	100.0	63.6	25.4	5.9	31.9	36.2
% of all employed	34.9	43.9	70.7	12.6	52.4	26.6
Recreation, personal services						
'000	617.6	271.1	43.9	105.8	119.4	330.5
% in group	100.0	43.9	7.1	17.1	19.3	53.5
% of all employed	8.2	7.1	4.6	8.5	7.4	9.2

Note: [1] Classification of industries as shown in Tables 3.5 and 3.8
[a] Includes persons still at school
[b] Includes persons with other (not defined here) post-school qualifications

Source: ABS (1992), *Labour Force Status and Educational Attainment, February 1992, Australia*, Cat. No. 6235.0

years that the trends in the structure of employment which began to appear in the 1960s would lead to growing inequality in Australian society. However, neither at the time when the potential effect of these trends became apparent (Jamrozik and Hoey 1982), nor when the trends accelerated in the 1980s did this issue attract much attention in social and economic research. Only in the late 1980s and early 1990s, when the evidence became overwhelmingly clear (Jamrozik, 1991a), did belated acknowledgement of growing inequality begin to appear. The 1990 ABS survey of income distribution showed clearly that the gap between incomes in the highest decile of income earners and those of income earners in the lowest three deciles had widened over the previous decade. In the highest decile 70 per cent of income earners (both sexes) were managers, administrators, professionals and para-professional persons (ABS 1992, Cat. No. 6546.0).

An important factor in this growing inequality has been the emergence and growth of the two-income family in the high income range. The two-income family among high income earners engaged in professional occupations in the public or private sector of the economy is now a 'norm', leading to life-styles for these people which are in many ways similar to those of the earlier middle-class bourgeoisie, with domestic servants (usually immigrant women or students) now increasingly accepted as an essential part of the household. If there are young children, they are cared for in centres subsidised by the state and/or by the employer, or they are in the hands of a nanny (Horin 1992b). At the other end of the scale is the one-income or one-and-half-income family, the man holding onto increasingly tenuous manual employment in an industry which continues to shed labour, and the woman providing the second income from a part-time, often casual job in a service industry or as a domestic servant in a household of a professional family. For many at this end of the scale unemployment has now become the norm.

As would be expected, these structural changes in the labour market have produced significant changes in the class structure of Australian society. With the decrease of employment in industries of material production the working class has shrunk and the fastest-growing social stratum has been the new middle class of professional, para-professional and related white-collar occupations composed of both men and women. While there are within this class considerable differences in occupations and corresponding incomes, as well as beliefs and political attitudes, the class as a whole constitutes an important and politically significant social stratum, with some common characteristics and common interests. It is also this class that plays an important role in the processes of cultural continuity and change in Australian society. Although its members are exposed to cultural influences from other societies, through education, literature and travel, their prevailing attitudes to the non-Anglo cultures entering Australia through immigration are at best ambivalent and more often rather negative or even antagonistic. These issues are discussed later, especially in Chapter 9.

More than ever before, Australia in the post-war years has developed the characteristics of a class society. The class structure does not fit the image of a dichotomy of capital and labour, because interposed between the two is now the large new middle class whose position of economic advantage and social power is derived from its 'cultural capital' of knowledge and professional expertise, the latter sanctioned by society and often legally protected. The possession of this cultural capital facilitates access to social power and material resources or economic capital, it leads to the development of class consciousness and the corresponding class interests. Possession of cultural capital and the corresponding rewards obtained in the labour market tend to be seen as a validation of individual effort, thus legitimising inequality in terms of individual achievement (Eder 1989:127). With the increase in the number of women in professional and related occupations inequality through such individual achievement has occurred in both sexes and the high rate of class homogamy in the professional class maintains the family as the basis of the class structure (Jones 1987, Jamrozik 1991a, Horin 1992a).

The legitimation of growing inequality in Australian society is achieved by explanations which centre around structural changes in the labour market, but the growth of the new middle class, *as a class*, and its position of advantage in the class structure tends to be either ignored or denied. Beilharz *et al.* (1992) explain the lack of attention given to this class in social analyses by way of what may be called theoretical blinkers. They say:

> Probably the role of the [new] middle class has been taken insufficiently seriously because those who view Australia as a class society most frequently view Australian history as a tussle between two major classes: ruling versus working class. The [new] middle class fails to show up on this grid. (1992:4)

The advantage which the new middle class enjoys in contemporary Australian society, its 'command over resources through time', tends to be perceived and justified in cultural terms, that is as the result of individual achievements of its members and as the value of of their contribution to society, thus implicitly ascribing to them certain moral qualities. It is symptomatic of this approach to the legitimation of inequality that the population at the bottom of the socio-economic scale – the human residue of the market economy – is now referred to as the new 'underclass'. The concept of the 'underclass' came into increasingly frequent usage in the 1980s (Crisp 1990), and the people so categorised, although their position might be acknowledged as an outcome of the changes in the labour market and government policies, are often perceived as a class of people somehow morally or intellectually 'deficient' – or both – or socially 'inadequate', unable or unwilling to change and encouraged to maintain their 'irresponsible' lifestyles by public income support and welfare services. The inequality generated by the changing class structure of Australian society is thus legitimised in cultural terms rather than in solely economic terms.

The position of the new middle class in the class structure of Australian society and the role this class plays in the power structure of society are crucial factors in understanding the processes of social change and cultural transformation in this country. Increasingly, the members of the new middle class are the dominant actors in these processes. The articulate, educated professionals who occupy positions of power and influence in the management industries – finance, property and business services; public administration; and community services (health, education, welfare, law, and so on) – are now the 'guardians' of the core institutions and of the interests these institutions represent. Outwardly, the new middle class may be adopting, rather willingly, it often seems, changing patterns of attitudes and behaviour, but with its growing size, affluence and influence, it has increasingly become a conservative force, enhancing and preserving its class interests.

Furthermore, as they become more affluent, the members of the new middle class tend to adopt the values of the 'old' middle class – acquisitiveness of material possessions, an affluent though perhaps at times 'artistically bohemian' life-style, and a critical, even contemptuous and antagonistic view of other classes, especially of the working class and its life-style.

Much of the power of the new middle class lies in its members' professional knowledge – recognised by society as 'authoritative' because it has been acquired in the institutions of higher learning – which enables them to authoritatively define social reality. As a result, the way the nature of social issues is perceived by the population depends much on the definitions of such issues by these members of the new middle class, be they commentators and analysts in the mass media, administrators in the public service, advisers and consultants to governments, members of the helping professions, or teachers and researchers in universities and associated research institutions. As has been observed by Beilharz *et al.*:

> This new middle class has perhaps grown faster than any other occupational grouping, and now possesses significant power because of its capacity to claim that it can define and meet human needs.   (1992:65)

In many areas of social life the new middle class, while ostensibly presenting an image of modernity and challenge to the established order, has become a conservative force, developing perceptions of social issues and attitudes to them in terms of its own values and interests, and presenting them authoritatively to the community as 'scientifically objective' values and interpretations of social reality. Nowhere is this role perhaps more evident than in the work of social welfare agencies, especially in the attitudes displayed towards Australian Aborigines. For example, a study of practices in the state welfare department of New South Wales, carried out in the late 1970s by the (now defunct) Family and Children's Services Agency of New South Wales (FACSA), revealed that despite an increasing professionalisation of welfare services and a corresponding sophistication of language used in the official files, the perception of issues evident in the practices and attitudes had not changed much from earlier times (FACSA 1981).

Perusal of case files in any welfare agency, either government or private, would reveal negative perceptions and interpretations of issues concerning the Aboriginal population (Jamrozik 1982). The language might have changed and overt moral criticism might now have been replaced by 'scientific' assessments, but the attitudes remain transparently similar. Nor are such attitudes confined solely to agencies' dealing with the Aboriginal population; immigrants, especially those from a non-English-speaking background (NESBs), do not always fare much better. Indeed, reading some of the psychologists' or social workers' assessments of children's intelligence or of parents' behaviour, the ethnocentrism in value judgements and negativism towards anything perceived as 'foreign' is striking. In schools, if children of immigrants do not do so well, it is their parents who are seen to be at fault because 'they work to get rich quickly and neglect the children'; but if children excel in their school work, the parents are 'pushing them too much to succeed'.

Under the guise of their 'scientific objectivity' these professionals thus express the narrow ethnocentrism of Anglo-Australians, characterised by an apparent inability to conceive of the idea that cultural differences do not necessarily imply superiority or inferiority. In spite of extensive exposure to other cultures, Anglo-Australian professionals and bureaucrats in the public service still have great difficulty in accepting that there can be, and are, different ways of owning things, different laws, different systems of government decision-making, different social, family and kin systems. In professional perceptions and assessments things that are 'different' are also seen to be, implicitly or explicitly, inferior. Such perceptions are applied mainly to immigrants from different cultures who find their place in the lower echelons of the labour force. However, these perceptions are not confined to them; they are extended to the working class in general, including the Anglo-Australian working class. Professional interpretations of differences are thus perceived in cultural terms as well as in class terms. The dominant professional culture becomes also the dominant class culture. It is in this perspective that social change and cultural transformation in Australian society need to be perceived and understood.

Australia in the 1990s

Australian society of the 1990s faces an uncertain future. Its economic development stalled in the 1980s; in fact, it stalled in the mid-1970s and for nearly a decade the economy stood still and unemployment continued to increase (see Table 3.6). The economic recovery recorded in the 1980s showed a promise of change but this later proved to be something of an illusion created by entrepreneurs in speculative investment who developed all sorts of ventures and purchased properties, with funds borrowed mainly from overseas and from gullible local people who were promised high returns for their money. It was a decade when the dominance of economists and economic rationalists reached its peak: economists became expert analysts and advisers on the whole spectrum of economic and social issues, from investment and employment to health, education, welfare and immigration. After the 'crash' of 1987 thousands of people lost their savings, most banks found themselves with huge bad debts, and the economy soon followed with a sharp downturn.

Economic recovery has been slow and uncertain. While there are signs of gradual improvement in economic growth, in productivity and export trade, unemployment remains high and there are no signs of its reduction to any significant degree in the foreseeable future. Overall, over one-fifth of the adult population (16 years and over) relies on government for income support through pensions or benefits, the four largest categories of recipients being age pensioners, unemployed persons, invalid pensioners and sole parents (Graycar and Jamrozik 1993). Despite government income support measures, inequality of individual and particularly of family incomes increased dramatically during the 1980s.

As shown earlier in this chapter, employment in the industries of material production has not grown in absolute numbers since the mid-1960s and employment in manufacturing industries has actually declined by 10 per cent over this period. Furthermore, the educational qualifications of the labour force engaged in material production have remained low despite the overall increase in the educational level of the labour force as a whole. Most persons with tertiary qualifications have found employment in the management industries, in financial institutions, public administration and community services. As will be shown in the next chapter, manual work in manufacturing industries has been performed to a significant extent by immigrant labour.

Rather belatedly, the federal government came to acknowledge in the late 1980s that the economic performance of an industrialised society depends to a significant extent on the quality of its labour force. The solution is now sought in encouraging young people to complete their schooling and continue with some post-school education, preferably in one of the technical fields. The outcome of these initiatives is uncertain, for a number of reasons. First, the number of students in post-secondary and tertiary education has increased considerably but investment in educational facilities has remained inadequate. Although public expenditure on education has increased considerably since the mid-1960s, the system cannot cope with or even absorb the numbers of willing candidates (see Graycar and Jamrozik 1993, Ch. 3). The second reason is the strong emphasis on vocational and 'competency-based' training rather than on a broader educational approach which would enable people to become better prepared for finding a place in a changing labour market. The situation thus presents a paradox in that emphasis on vocational training comes at a time when it is not known which vocational skills may be needed in the near let alone in the more distant future.

The problems experienced by Australian society in the 1990s are not solely economic; they are social, political and, in the broad meaning of the term, cultural. The colonial inheritance, or historical baggage referred to earlier still weighs heavily on the Anglo-Australian psyche, and is especially evident in government policies, in the 'old establishment', as well as in the new middle class. The language and some forms of personal and social conduct or life-style might be 'new' but the attachment to the colonial inheritance is 'old'. It is nearly one hundred years since Federation, and the country clings to the British monarchy, to the British flag and other accoutrements inherited from the 'mother country'. In the late 1960s Donald Horne wrote, 'Australia has remained a province of Britain. It is, in a sense, now also a province of the U.S.A. ... a nation in which most activities are derivative and most new ideas are taken from abroad' (1968:86). In the early 1990s things are perhaps a little different but not much. For example, there might be an acknowledged acceptance of 'multiculturalism', even a proclaimed policy of multiculturalism (discussed below, in Chapter 5), but no Anglo-Australian would regard himself or herself as a 'multicultural' person. The concept is commonly perceived as a division between two distinct population groups: the 'Australians' and the 'multiculturals', similar to the 'us' and 'them' in the class structure. As will be discussed in later chapters, the concept itself came under sustained attack from some quarters in the 1980s.

Certainly, Australian society has changed since the late 1940s and the evidence of change is visible in many areas of social and economic life.

However, change has occurred primarily in those areas of social activity which add to the richness and cultural diversity of social life without disturbing the existing social divisions of the class structure or the economic and political interests which are embedded in that class structure. The core institutions which form the basis of power in society – the political organisation, government bureaucracy, the education system, the professions and their organisations – have remained relatively undisturbed.

The colonial inheritance is an important contributing factor to the country's rather confused world outlook and to the uncertainty about its future. Two hundred years since colonisation of this continent and Australians still have not succeeded in coming to terms with the geographical position of their country. Indeed, Australians refer to the neighbouring Asian countries as 'the Far East'. As expressed by Denis Kenny (1992), 'Australian society and culture were founded as an outpost of the cultural ecology of the Atlantic ... Australia is in the Pacific, but, so far, not of the Pacific'. Australians have remained 'regional fringe dwellers', not really belonging to the region in which they have lived now for generations (Hoffman 1984). This feeling, he continues, is

> ... a state of mind in which Australians regard themselves as being 'cut off' from somebody, something, somewhere ... It is an intimation that Australia is not our home, that we are alien to the region ...   (1984:59)

Neighbouring countries are perceived to hold both a promise and a threat. There might be a recognition of the importance of developing commercial links with 'Asia' and considerable progress in that direction has certainly been made in recent years, but acceptance of cultural differences is still difficult. The need for the shift towards Asia in commerce and politics has been perceived rather belatedly as a necessity now that the countries of Europe and the United States have become competitors on the world market rather than consumers for Australian products. With the end of the cold war Australia has also lost its strategic importance to the super powers, but in the eyes of neighbouring countries it is still perceived as an outpost of Europe or of the United States, rather than as a genuine neighbour. The challenge facing the country is thus the task of reconciling its colonial heritage with the realities of the present times.

There are, however, some indications of change. The federal elections held in March 1993 brought a surprise to most people and a rude shock to some. Against all predictions and odds, the Labor Party retained office and did so with a substantially increased majority. It also did so despite an economic recession and record levels of unemployment, and despite (or perhaps because of?) the Prime Minister's raising the issues of a republic, a new flag, and a higher level of economic and political integration with neighbouring countries. The results suggest a growing gap between the perceptions and interpretations of social reality by political and economic analysts, media commentators and many politicians and the social reality experienced by 'ordinary' or 'average' persons in the course of their everyday lives. The extensive 'post mortem' interpretations of these results provide some interesting insights into the changing political and social climate which appears to be rather conducive to a cultural transformation, an important part of which would be the readiness of Australians, both 'Anglo' and 'ethnic', to jettison the country's colonial inheritance and develop a new identity for their country, more 'at home' in its geographical location and surrounding cultures.

CHAPTER 4

Immigration and Cultural Diversity

Australia, a country which had been one of the distant outposts of the British Empire until the onset of World War II and had maintained its English language, institutions and culture, by the early 1990s had become a country of great cultural diversity. This change was a predictable, if not planned or intended, outcome of the immigration policy initiated in the 1940s. The program, designed in the first place to increase the size of the population but at the same time ensure the preservation of its Anglo-Saxon-Celtic character, had changed over the years producing a stream of immigrants of increasing ethnic and cultural diversity. It needs to be noted, however, that the Anglo-Saxon-Celtic population was itself already culturally diverse, the division between the British and the Irish being particularly strong (Young 1991). The flow of immigrants from non-English-speaking countries led to a new division between those of English-speaking background (ESBs) and 'the others' who were given a succession of names, starting with 'reffos' and 'Balts', followed by 'new Australians', 'new settlers' and finally the NESBs (non-English-speaking background), with one other special collective name, 'Asians'. On recent (early 1990s) estimates there are more than one hundred languages other than English spoken in the country, not counting an even greater number of different Aboriginal languages (Clyne 1991). As to ethnic diversity, the number of identifiable ethnic groups also exceeds one hundred, but an exact number is difficult to ascertain. For example, Price lists sixty-six such groups, plus 'others' (1988:124) (Table 4.1).

Acceptance of this great cultural diversity did not come without concern, anxiety and debate that was at times emotional. The initial fear in some quarters about the dangers of 'dilution of the Anglo-British character' of the population by the inflow of immigrants from eastern and then southern Europe was later replaced by the fear of so-called 'Asian' immigration. In retrospect, considering the fears expressed at each intake of immigrants of a 'new' ethnic group, it is rather surprising that the ever-growing diversity of the population has been accommodated into Australian society with relatively little tension and only rare outbursts of localised ethnic, social, or racial conflict. However, tensions and conflicts are present below the surface and emerge into public view, especially in times of economic downturn. At such times respectable economic analysts and commentators fill columns in the press with their authoritative findings which indicate 'beyond any doubt' that the problems in the economy are due to 'too many migrants', or to 'the wrong kind of migrants'. Negative comments in the media about effects of immigration usually appear at the same time as the 'Asians out' graffiti reflecting these comments appear on the walls of public buildings and toilet blocks in city parklands. Recommendations are then advanced for the benefit of policy makers that to improve the economy the scale of immigration needs to be reduced or its composition changed, or that it has to be stopped entirely (Jamrozik 1991c). Indeed, an analysis of Australian economic performance since the immigration program began would show that at *each* downturn in the economy immigration has always come under the critical spotlight. It is therefore rather difficult not to gain the impression that for many economists, other expert analysts and media commentators immigration has been a useful 'explanation of last resort'. Such arguments are easily proposed because by selecting certain aspects of immigration and omitting others one can demonstrate what one wants to demonstrate. We will return to this issue later in the chapter and later on in the book.

This chapter provides an overview of the Australian immigration program since the 1940s by looking at changes in the demographic and ethnic intake, the position of immigrants in the labour market, changes in policy and attitudes towards immigrants, and immigrants' contribution to the Australian economy. The focus of the chapter is on the difficulties which monocultural Australia has experienced in accepting the cultural diversity brought in by immigrants from various non-English-speaking countries. The effects of immigration on social, economic and cultural life in Australia are discussed in later chapters.

A History of Immigration

That Australia is a country of immigrants is a matter of historical fact. Except for the Aboriginal people – the only true Australians who, as is now well documented, have lived here for at least 40 000 years – all others

Table 4.1: *Ethnic Origins of Australian Population, 1988*

Origins/Region	Groups	Population	%
Total population *100.00*	66*	*16 300 000*	
Anglo-Celtic	5	12 151 950	74.55
West, North Europe	12	1 212 060	7.44
East Europe	15	627 430	3.85
South Europe	7	1 200 090	7.36
West Asia	9	346 780	2.13
South-East Asia	9	200 850	1.23
South Asia	5	97 420	0.60
Other Asia	4	226 710	1.39
Africa	not specified	20 190	0.12
America	not specified	6 320	0.04
Pacific Islands	not specified	40 200	0.25
Aborigines, TSIs**	not specified	163 000	1.00

Notes: *   Does not include 'not specified'
              **   Torres Strait Islanders
Source: C. A. Price (1988), 'The Ethnic Character of Australian Population',
              in J. Jupp (ed.), *The Australian People: An Encyclopedia of the Nation, its*

are immigrants or descendants of immigrants, going back into local ancestry to just over 200 years at the most. From the start of white colonisation, too, the immigrants brought with them considerable cultural and ethnic diversity. Many of the first settlers – the convicts – were Irish, Welsh or Scottish, thus Celtic rather than English; and later in the nineteenth century free settlers and recruited workers came from many places and a variety of cultures. However, from the 1880s Australia pursued a 'consistent and sophisticated racial theory as part of national self-definition' in admitting immigrants, embodied later in the *Immigration Restriction Act* 1901, which became known as the White Australia policy and which continued until the 1960s (Jupp 1991:18).

At the time of Federation the population was mainly 'British': 77 per cent of the total population was born in Australia, 10 per cent was born in England and Wales, 3 per cent in Scotland and 5 per cent in Ireland. Of the remainder, 1 per cent was born in Germany (not necessarily German) and 0.8 per cent was born in China (White 1981:112). The population was, or appeared to be, British, because the earlier large minority ethnic groups (Chinese and Kanakas) had been either expelled or repatriated, and under the provisions of the Constitution the Aboriginal population was not counted (it required approval by the whole population in a referendum to include them, and this was not done until 1967).

For the next 45 years or so immigration remained low, the population barely doubling from 3.7 to 7.5 million between 1901 and 1947. Its 'British', or English, character had been maintained almost unchanged, although small numbers of immigrants from various countries of Europe did settle in Australia in the 1930s. In 1947, 90 per cent of the population was born in Australia and another 7 per cent was born in Britain and Ireland (see Table 3.3). Australia was indeed an outpost of the British Empire, notwithstanding the links established with the United States during the Second World War.

The growth of cultural diversity began with the start of the immigration program in 1947. Initially the aim of the program was twofold: to increase the size of the population, the 'populate or perish' philosophy which entered public consciousness during the Second World War; and, related to this, to build up the economic strength of the country through industrialisation and the associated provision of infrastructure: roads, power and water supply. Immigrants were expected to come mainly from Britain and Ireland, the desired ratio was to be ten to one in favour of English-speaking, white, British subjects. This ratio however, was not achieved: although people from Britain and Ireland accounted for the largest immigrant group, their numbers remained at less than 50 per cent of the total intake. The majority of early immigrants, from 1947 to the early 1950s, came from the post-war refugee camps of western Europe, recruited with the assistance of the International Refugee Organisation, an agency of the United Nations.

Recruiting immigrants from those camps was a decision partly determined by the necessity of reaching optimum numbers of workers, but it also had the unique advantage of procuring at low cost a labour force that could be directed to any work or place and under conditions which would be unacceptable to the local workers or to British immigrants. As Jupp records:

> There was inadequate shipping to transport British immigrants, while refugees could be brought out in barely converted troop carriers. There was insufficient housing for settlement at Australian standards, whereas there were recently emptied army camps waiting to take displaced persons. As there was labour shortage in the cities, continuing demand in rural areas and on outback construction sites could only be met by directing labour, which would have been unacceptable for free British immigrants. (1991:23)

Immigration policies of successive Australian governments were guided by the same principles, with increasing attention being given to the immediate needs of the labour market, and little thought given to longer-term social and demographic implications and outcomes. Combined with the changing sources of immigrant inflow, these policies have produced

Table 4.2: *Comparative Age Structure of Australian-born and Overseas-born Population, Australia, 1989 (percentages)*

Birthplace	Age group (years)				
	0–14	15–24	25–34	55–64	6+
Total population	*22.1*	*16.3*	*41.8*	*8.7*	*11.1*
Born in Australia	26.4	17.9	37.8	7.6	10.3
Born overseas	6.8	11.0	56.0	12.5	13.6
Total Asia	12.8	17.7	56.4	6.9	6.2
Total Europe	3.3	7.1	55.7	16.0	17.9
– Poland	5.9	3.9	37.9	18.5	33.8
– Italy	0.5	2.8	53.3	25.3	18.2
– Greece	1.3	4.0	65.2	19.9	9.6
– Netherlands	2.0	3.3	58.6	18.1	17.8
– UK & Ireland	4.0	9.1	55.0	12.8	19.2
– Germany	2.9	5.2	60.3	18.3	13.3

Sources: P. Whiteford (1991) and ABS

'abnormal' demographic compositions and age structures in various ethnic groups. With the passage of time, as the young immigrants grew old, this policy has led to considerable social costs which are now largely borne by the affected populations. Many of the early immigrants arrived in Australia as single persons and remained so: gender imbalance in the immigration intake and working in the outback regions were not conducive to marrying or establishing families. Now, as these people are old, it is their ethnic communities that have to care for them.

The 'abnormal' age structures of certain immigrant groups – the effects of these policies – are clearly evident in the data presented in Table 4.2. This table is a chronological record of the successive stages of immigrant intake, which started in central Europe, passed through southern Europe and then the Middle East, made some brief excursions to Latin America, and eventually reached the countries of South-East Asia – a kind of historical and colourful multicultural travelogue of Australian policies of recruitment and importation of human resources.

The age structures of various immigrant groups shown in Table 4.2 reflect the time of their arrival in Australia. For example, persons born in Poland – the largest non-English-speaking ethnic group of the earliest post-war arrivals from 1947 to 1951 – show the highest proportion in the 65 years-and-over age group, three times higher than among persons born in Australia. They are followed by other European immigrant groups, all of whom (except those born in Greece, the majority of whom arrived somewhat later) show a high proportion of population in the retirement age group. By comparison, the age structure of immigrants from Asian countries reflects clearly their relatively recent arrival. It is also evident that the trend towards ageing immigrant groups is going to increase in the near future and will continue to do so for some years, as all persons born in Europe show a high proportion of people in the age group 55 to 64 years.

What the statistics in Table 4.2 do not show is the extent to which these imported human resources have been put to their full productive use and potential, or the extent to which they have been wasted. Whatever the successes of the immigration program might have been, both for the immigrants and for the host country, the negative outcome for both has been a great waste of human resources created by early immigration and settlement policies. While there was much talk of importing 'skills', immigrants from non-English-speaking backgrounds recruited at first from the refugee camps in Europe – the 'Displaced Persons' or 'DPs' – and then those from Italy, Greece and Yugoslavia, were confined to manual, menial jobs. Policy rhetoric might have emphasised 'brains' but what was really sought was 'brawn'. A person's educational and occupational background might have been recorded in the recruitment process, but allocations to employment and the corresponding pay and working conditions were made on the basis of two attributes: sex and physical fitness. All men were classified as 'labourers'; all women as 'domestics'. Then, after another medical examination which included a test of physical strength, each person was classified as capable of doing heavy, medium, or light work. There was no freedom to choose employment, because the condition for admission and free passage to Australia was a two-year contract to work in jobs and places decided by the authorities (Kunz 1988). Any change of employment had to be first approved by the authorities, and any change of address had to be notified to the police. Employment opportunities were curtailed by legal and bureaucratic restrictions, the vested interests of the established professions and trades, and not always friendly Anglocentric attitudes of some sections of the native population. Kunz comments that the policy of classifying the immigrant 'Displaced Persons' occupationally as 'labourers' (all men) and 'domestics' (all women) meant that 'even before they were interviewed for work, former public servants, tradesmen, university lecturers, architects, priests, doctors and artists were, as a welcome, told of their future place in Australia' (1988:165). There were no mechanisms available to them for recognition and acceptance of trade or professional qualifications, and no facilities for learning English.

No doubt, there was at the time a demand for skills in Australian industries but, above all, there was a demand for people to do the hard menial tasks in road construction, power and water supply, and general maintenance work. There was also strong opposition from members of professional organisations and trade unions to the recognition and acceptance of immigrants' occupational qualifications, lest the immigrants take 'their' jobs. Kunz notes that of the early immigrants who arrived in Australia as 'Displaced Persons' only about one in four of those who had had fifteen to eighteen years of study and a diploma or degree had eventually succeeded in recapturing their professional status in Australia, and some of those who succeeded had taken twenty years to reach that stage (1988:188). Most of them failed to have their qualifications accepted: some tried but later gave up in the face of insurmountable barriers; others resigned themselves to their newly-ascribed status and to whatever occupation they managed to obtain. The waste of imported knowledge and skills which occurred in those years must be seen as an irredeemable loss to Australian society.

The experience of those early immigrants would later be repeated by succeeding waves of newcomers, notwithstanding the manifest policy of recruiting immigrants with certain occupational skills. The issue of skills as a priority criterion in selecting immigrants has been a subject of debate throughout the duration of the immigration program, but what sorts of skills were sought was not always clear. The policy as stated tended to emphasise a priority for 'skilled' rather than 'unskilled' immigrants, but there seemed to be an unstated policy of bringing in people who would fill the 'unskilled' jobs at the low end of the labour market. This certainly was the case in the earlier phase of the immigration program and continued well into the 1970s. Castles *et al.* observe about that phase:

> The Department of Immigration in many cases deliberately sought out low-skilled workers for recruitment. As newcomers lacking language proficiency, often without industrial experience and qualifications, the migrants provided a source of labour for unskilled and semi-skilled jobs. Often discrimination and non-recognition of qualifications forced even highly-skilled migrants into manual manufacturing jobs.   (1988a:24)

This situation is to this day reflected in the employment statistics which clearly show that immigrants from non-English-speaking backgrounds, of both sexes, are still overrepresented in industries of material production and in manual trades, and are underrepresented in management and in corresponding professional and other non-manual occupations (Table 4.3).

The issue of skills importation continues to be debated but remains largely unresolved. One reason for this has been the perceived value of imported skills, counterposed to the value of improving local skills through training. While some analysts and commentators have emphasised the need to continue the policy of giving priority to skilled immigrants, others have argued that this policy has been a factor in the

Table 4.3: *Employed Persons, Australia, May 1990:*
Industries and Occupations

Industry/ Occupation	Persons			Men			Women		
	All '000	ESB %	NESB %	All '000	ESB %	NESB %	All '000	ESB %	NESB %
All employed	7916.1	11.4	14.3	4638.7	11.5	15.3	3277.3	11.2	12.9
Industries:									
Material production	2428.1	11.5	18.5	1872.2	11.6	17.4	555.9	11.1	22.1
Distribution services	2199.1	10.3	12.8	1323.7	10.7	14.4	875.4	9.6	10.3
Management industries	2697.6	12.6	11.6	1284.4	11.6	11.4	1511.0	12.6	11.0
Recreation, personal services	591.4	9.7	15.4	256.3	10.3	18.7	335.1	9.2	13.0
Occupation:									
Managers and administrators, professionals, para-professionals	2325.4	12.4	12.7	1508.6	12.3	14.1	816.9	12.6	10.0
Clerks, sales, personal services	2547.0	10.9	10.3	752.9	11.5	11.6	1794.1	10.6	9.7
Tradespersons, plant operators, drivers	1807.3	11.8	18.0	1584.8	12.0	16.5	222.5	11.0	28.1
Labourers and related	1236.3	9.8	20.5	792.4	9.0	18.8	443.9	11.3	23.4

Source: ABS (1990), *Employed Persons, Australia, May 1990*, Tables E23, E24 (unpublished data)

government's abrogation of responsibility for developing adequate training programs (Bills 1988: 157). Opinions have also been expressed that employers in Australia have become free loaders, preferring to employ 'ready-made' skilled immigrants rather than providing training opportunities for the existing labour force (Barnett 1990:37).

It may be argued on this point that Australia has been 'free loading' in its attitude to human resources ever since the start of the immigration program. Attitudes to education and training of the labour force, especially those employed in manual occupations, have been ambivalent, to say the least. As shown in Chapter 3, there is a great educational gap between the labour force engaged in material production and the professionals employed in the management industries (Table 3.12). It was not until the 1980s that governments gradually, though rather reluctantly began to realise that for the economy to function and to manage changing technology, education would have to receive much greater attention than had been the case in the past. The federal government began to take some action in that direction but progress has been slow and positive results not startlingly evident, so far. For these policies to be effective a change in public attitudes would have to occur, especially in the attitudes of employers who traditionally, have been negatively disposed towards 'over-educated' young people entering the labour force.

Perceptions of the Value of Immigration

Ever since its inception in 1947 the immigration program has been a subject of public debate which has revolved around three issues: the level of intake as a factor in population growth; the demographic, ethnic and racial composition of the intake and its potential threat to the dominant British character of the country; and the needs of the labour market and the effect on the economy. The last of these issues received increasingly more attention as the economic situation in Australia worsened in the late 1980s. Arguments on this issue also became more elaborate: attempts have been made to measure the effect of immigration on employment and unemployment; on capital inflow and outflow; on investment; on savings and public and private spending on goods and services; on overseas debt; and on the problems of providing services in the large cities where the newcomers tended to settle (Figure 4.1). The economic issue and the other two issues mentioned earlier continue to be debated with varied intensity, with repetitive or 'new' arguments, often advanced as if they were self-evident and had their own ontological validity. As observed by Withers (1990), the debate 'has a very parochial air, with us endlessly rehashing old issues' and, furthermore, there is 'a real danger that well meaning people frustrated at the real problems they perceive, whether of foreign debt or a fragile environment, will all too readily seek a scapegoat solution'.

The danger in some of the arguments lies not only in that many of the 'economic' reasons which are voiced against immigration lack substance or are highly hypothetical, but often they also have xenophobic overtones. For example, the arguments about immigrants' taking jobs away from local workers appear with a monotonous frequency, although there are convincing counter-arguments which demonstrate that immigrants create jobs because of their high demand for goods and services in the initial period of their settlement and through the initiative some of them

Figure 4.1: *Advantages and Disadvantages Claimed on the Issue of the Economics of Immigration, 1990*

Advantages Claimed	Disadvantages Claimed

Economic Growth and Productivity

Advantages Claimed	Disadvantages Claimed
Migrants bring an entrepreneurial culture to Australia. (Sheridan, *Australian* 2–3/6/90) Business migrants, mostly from Asia, bring capital to Australia (12 000 brought around $3 billion in 1988). Asian migrants are political conformists and committed to economic materialism. (Viviani, *Australian* 29/5/90) Immigration will produce the economic goods as long as occupational qualifications are recognised and the social-economic infrastructure is run efficiently. (Stutchbury, *Australian Financial Review* 11/4/90) Immigrants have created as many jobs as they have taken. Immigrants provide a cheap source of labour. Immigrants add entrepreneurial 'drive and energy' to the nation's industries. A cut in immigration would reduce real growth, depress employment, increase inflation and lead to a drop in the current account deficit of $700m a year. (Neales, *AFR*, 25/5/90)	Migrants do not bring enough capital to Australia to compensate for their economic costs and this means more overseas borrowing. (Birrell, *Australian* 20/6/90) 'There is no doubt that the additional capital demands created by our yearly intake of migrants greatly exceed the additional savings generated by them.' (Argy, quoted in Gittins, *Sydney Morning Herald* 11/4/90) Average long term real wages are lower with high levels of immigration. EPAC suggest a cut in immigration intake by 70 000 a year would improve the current account deficit by $3.6 billion. Sydney and Melbourne spiralling housing prices are directly attributable to immigration levels. Migrants brought $2 billion to Australia in 1988 but $11 billion was spent on housing and infrastructure. One immigrant costs Australia $80 000 a year. Migrants add more to demand than supply, are inflationary, necessitate GDP growth, inflate import need by 3 per cent. (Neales, *AFR*, 25/5/90)

The Labour Force

Advantages Claimed	Disadvantages Claimed
There have been substantial skill benefits in areas such as food, design, architecture, literature and the performing arts. (Lipski, *Australian* 31/5/90) There is a substantial skilled migration to Australia and present immigration levels are not historically high relative to population. (Withers, *Australian*, 30/5/90)	Return to the early 1970s and make better use of the existing workforce: cut down on immigration and increase women's participation in the labour force. (Birrell, *Australian* 30/5/90) Too many immigrants destroy the economy as they help to determine the impact on Australia's natural resources. (Toyne, *Australian*, 1/6/90)

Figure 4.1: *(cont.)*

Advantages Claimed	Disadvantages Claimed
Socio-Cultural Costs and Benefits	
Family reunion schemes use a natural institution that is an inexpensive substitute for government services. (Sheridan, *Australian* 2–3/6/90)	The present migration policy, in effect, discriminates against the Australian homeless. This is because new migrants, especially refugees, receive high priority for public housing so that other groups may suffer. (Blainey, *Australian* 2–3/6/90)
Teaching English is a small price to pay when Australia benefits from migrants' skills and trade links with their homeland countries. (Sheridan, *Australian* 28/5/90)	The additional demand for housing and other social infrastructure costs such as higher population growth brought about by immigration has adverse effects on the current account. (Walsh, *AFR*, 8/5/90)
Immigration has helped to make Australia more culturally diverse, more tolerant, and a more optimistic forward-looking society. Economic arguments aside, this is enough to justify migrants' contribution to the national interest. (Lipski, *Australian* 31/5/90)	The major pressure for increases in immigration intake comes from selectively politically active ethnic lobby groups and this contributes to population growth. (Barnett, *Australian* 29/5/90)

display in starting their own small business ventures. A similar lack of substance has been a feature of arguments about immigration as a cause of the growth of foreign debt, lower standards of living and welfare expenditure. As illustrated by the examples in Figure 4.1, for each argument on these issues there is a counter-argument, and some commentators even present both. It needs to be noted that the statements quoted in Figure 4.1 came from the national daily press and were not made by uninformed persons but by well-known and highly regarded journalists and academics. Clearly these diametrically opposite opinions cannot all be valid 'scientific deductions'; at most, they might have been arrived at by the authors' selective observations, seeking to substantiate their subjective values and prejudices.

In times of worsening economic conditions, such as those in the late 1980s and early 1990s, the arguments tend to present immigration and immigrants as a cost rather than a benefit. For example, as noted in Figure 4.1, one commentator has estimated the cost of each immigrant at $80 000. In the atmosphere created by such arguments the economic, social and cultural value of the contribution the immigrants have made to Australian society tends to be overlooked or deprecated and immigration then tends to be perceived as a source of society's ills rather than benefits.

The prevailing perspectives on immigration, especially those of the 'economic' kind, and the methods of research used in this field have always been rather narrow. The use of such narrow economic criteria in various assessments of the value of immigration has been a conceptual and methodological flaw which has led and continues to lead to findings and conclusions of doubtful validity.

Focus on the economic value of immigration has always figured prominently in Australian government policy, but debates on this subject have contained and continue to contain some very simplistic and narrow arguments. Such arguments have served to bolster negative attitudes and prejudices and have been harmful to national cohesion, to the economy, and to national interests.

Analyses based only on the economic value of immigration have viewed the immigrants mainly as a supplementary labour force to the local workforce; some government documents have also tended to see the value of immigration from this perspective (DEET 1989, for example). While such a narrow view undoubtedly reflects fairly common attitudes in economic analyses of immigration policy, it is not one which allows for an assessment of the full potential value of immigration. Such a perspective may be appropriate for countries which experience labour shortages and aim to overcome these by temporary importation of workers who are expected to return to their home countries when they are no longer required, as was the case with the *Gastarbeiter* ('guest workers') in Germany. However, even in the countries of western Europe where such policies were adopted, the outcome has not been satisfactory because 'temporary' workers tend to become permanent settlers (Castles 1984).

Australian immigration policies thus present a fundamental lack of logic, a basic contradiction, in that the policy of seeking permanent settlers has always been driven not by long-term objectives, not even by short-term objectives, but rather by the narrowly-perceived immediate needs of the labour market. As stated in the report of the Committee to Advise on Australia's Immigration Policies (CAAIP):

> Traditionally, immigration has been used as a tap. When employment oppor-tunities were ample the flow of immigrants was turned up. When unemploy-ment rose the tap was turned off.   (1988:37)

Long-term economic and social effects carry little weight in such per-spectives. It is truly remarkable that such perspectives still prevail in various analyses and commentaries as well as in government policies, as the effects of these policies are now very clearly visible in what may be termed the abnormal demographic structure of Australia's overseas-born population (Table 4.1).

Barriers to the Acceptance of Cultural Diversity

An aspect of immigration policy which has always been a source of problems and tensions has been the issue of overseas educational and occupational qualifications. Ever since the inception of the post-war immigration program the emphasis in manifest policy has been on giving priority to skilled immigrants, and the level of skills thus imported has indeed continued to rise throughout the duration of the program. However, relatively little progress has been achieved in enabling these skilled immigrants to practise their skills in the labour market. For example, as late as 1989 a federal government report (DEET 1989:1) acknowledged that about one-third of all immigrants with professional, para-professional and trade qualifications did not have those qualifications recognised, and of the new immigrants two-thirds did not work fully in their former occupations. Of the medical practitioners who immigrate to Australia from non-English-speaking countries and hold qualifications from those countries about three-fifths of those who sit for competency examinations conducted by the Australian Medical Council do not pass. The report commented that in the previous twenty years or so 'there has been much talk but relatively little action' in solving this deeply entrenched problem. It then concluded:

> Given factors such as these, and given the fluctuation of the migration program over the years, it is estimated that the pool of migrants who have wanted to practise their occupation in Australia but have not had their skills recognised is more than 200 000 of all arrivals since 1969.   (DEET 1989:4)

It may be reasonably expected that these estimates by DEET were rather on the conservative side. Furthermore, if 200 000 immigrants arriving since 1969 did not have their skills recognised, how many in that category would there have been since 1947? What have been the economic and social costs of this waste of human resources? The report stated:

> Even allowing for the fact that many people with unrecognised overseas skills *do* manage to move into another part of the skilled work-force, the economic costs to the community in areas such as providing support services and loss of productivity could be estimated in tens, if not hundreds of millions of dollars.
> (DEET 1989:5)

It is thus evident that from the late 1940s to the early 1990s Australia has imported a considerable quantity, quality and diversity of human resources but has not utilised them to the best advantage. The reasons for this failure to utilise fully the imported knowledge and skills are many, and some are examined in various parts of this book. One outstanding reason, which has been prominent since the inception of the program, has been the conservatism inherent in the core institutions of Australian society. This conservatism has been a feature of the organisation of public and private enterprises and has been particularly evident in the resistance of professional associations and trade unions to the acceptance of newcomers. The equivocation on this issue in the policies of successive federal and state governments has been a reflection of these attitudes. To this day, despite the rhetoric of change, the issue of recognition and acceptance of immigrants' qualifications and skills remains a largely unresolved problem. The problem persists mainly in trade and professional organisations, as noted by the New South Wales Committee of Inquiry into the Recognition of Overseas Qualifications:

> In the market place, the resistance to recognising training and experience from abroad manifests itself in a number of ways. Whilst there is a real and necessary concern to maintain standards of practice, there appears to be, in many quarters, a prejudice against the overseas-trained.　　　(1989:19)

The other significant factor in the underutilisation of imported human resources has been the narrow perspective on the value of immigrants' knowledge and skills. Irrespective of any other value that might have been acknowledged by successive governments from time to time, immigrants have been regarded, first and foremost, as a supplementary labour force, to be imported as the need arises, as it were, for immediate consumption or utilisation like any commodity or any other kind of goods or services. As the Minister for Employment, Education and Training once expressed it, 'skilled migration has been, and continues to be, used to help ease labour bottlenecks' (DEET 1987:1–2).

In this narrowly utilitarian, one-dimensional perspective the potential of the imported human resources has been given little, if any, consideration. As shown in the conceptual framework developed in a study of immigrants' contribution to knowledge and skills (Jamrozik *et al.* 1990; see Figure 4.2), appreciation and utilisation of the value of imported human resources depends, first, on the kind and level of knowledge and skills sought, and, second, on the extent to which conditions are created for that knowledge and skills to be transferred to other person or persons, for incorporation into the production process, and for integration into the local culture. Such a perspective would make it possible to view these resources as human capital with full economic, social and cultural potential, not simply as a supplementary 'factor of production' of limited application and usefulness. Unfortunately, such a perspective has been sadly lacking in attitudes towards

Figure 4.2: *Contribution of Knowledge and Skills by Immigrants:*
A Conceptual Framework

Levels of Skills Integration

	(i) Retained by the immigrant	(ii) Transferred to other person(s)	(iii) Incorporated into production process	(iv) Integrated into local culture
L E V E L S	*1. Supplementary:* Skills are imported to fill in the gaps/overcome shortages of particular skills in the resident labour force.			
O F	*2. Complementary:* Skills are imported to enlarge the range of skills within the existing structure of trades and/or professions.			
S K I L L S	*3. Qualitative:* Skills are imported to raise the levels of existing skills, to apply new technologies and methods of production.			
S O U G H T	*4. New Skills:* Skills not present in the labour force are imported to start new industries and open new areas of industrial activity.			

immigrants, especially towards those from non-English-speaking back-grounds. The potential of extending the vision on the value of imported human resources as human and cultural capital has received little consideration. The following statement by the Secretary of the Department of Immigration and Ethnic Affairs in 1983, illustrates this limited perception. The Secretary acknowledged the important contribution made by immigrants to the Australian economy, but in discussing the problems which arise from time to time in adjusting the labour market to the demands of the economy, he said:

> Migrants can fill a valuable role in lubricating the adjustments in the market. They are more mobile and willing to move to where the jobs are than Australians, who may have housing and family commitments. Thus they can often fill shortages more quickly and effectively than Australians.
>
> (Menadue 1983:95)

Considering the fact that this statement was made in 1983, not much seems to have changed in attitudes to immigration since the late 1940s. Immigrants are clearly not looked upon as 'Australians' and they apparently do not have family commitments; therefore, they can be used as 'lubricants' to make the labour market work smoothly.

The recognition of immigrants' educational qualifications and occupational skills as we have said has been an ongoing problem since the late 1940s and one that has been well known and frequently commented on. Processes of skill recognition and acceptance have been kept under scrutiny for decades. Formal means to this end have been adopted, such as the Committee (later Council) for Overseas Professional Qualifications and the *Tradesman's Rights Regulation Act* 1946, but these bodies and legal provisions have been more effective in protecting the exclusivist interests of professions and trades than in facilitating immigrants' admissions to them. In 1983 a Committee of Inquiry into the Recognition of Overseas Qualifications produced a large report with wide-ranging recommendations. In spite of all these efforts ostensibly to solve this problem, little has been achieved; after close to 50 years of the immigration program the problem still exists, attenuated somewhat perhaps but certainly not solved. The new federal bodies established to deal with the problem, the National Office of Overseas Skills Recognition (NOOSR) and the National Advisory Committee on Skills Recognition (NACSAR), began to function only in 1989 and it is difficult at the time of writing to see whether and to what extent there has been any improvement in this area.

In the early period of the immigration program the attitudes of Australian officialdom to professional qualifications from non-English-speaking countries were not only negative but often overtly antagonistic, causing great disappointment, disillusionment, and the departure of many who saw these attitudes as clearly discriminatory and did not want to face the future in the host country under such conditions. As Kunz records:

> ... the departure of one in five of the best educated refugees was a loss which to a large extent nullified the efforts made by the selection teams to secure the 'best types' of immigrants for Australia. It was the result of a series of thoughtless, discriminating and hostile actions which began with the sometimes gross, other times minor, misrepresentations of the recruiting staff. It continued in Australia with the unhelpful, repressive and frequently humiliating attitude of a largely uneducated officialdom which was either unable to understand the value of intellect or resented it, particularly if manifested in the person of a foreigner. Ultimately it culminated in the jealousy shown by Australian professional bodies to their 'colleagues' in need.   (1988:225–6)

How much has the situation on this issue changed since then? Extensive studies (for example, Iredale 1987, 1989, Collins 1988, Castles *et al.* 1989, and many others) acknowledge that efforts have been made to overcome or at least alleviate the problem, but these studies also confirm the observation made by the Department of Employment, Education and Training (DEET) (1989:1) that 'there has been much talk but relatively little action' in this area. Castles *et al.* conclude from their study conducted in the late 1980s that 'major problems exist with regard to recognition of overseas trade qualifications ... Existing arrangements often favour tradespeople from English-speaking countries or Northern Europe to the detriment of those from Southern Europe, Asia or Latin America' (1989: Executive Summary: 11–12).

The seemingly intractable nature of this problem suggests that Australia carries 'historical baggage' – attitudes and practices from the early post-war years, or perhaps even from the early years of Federation – and has not been able to discard it. Another reason has been the more direct matter of self-interest: a powerful force contributing to the intractability of the problem has been the resistance of established trade and professional organisations to the admission of newcomers, as a means of protecting their members' interests. Iredale observes from her study:

> The frequently unstated reason for the existence of occupational regulation is the need to protect the conditions of existing workers. Control over who and how many enter an occupation is exerted on governments and training institutions, as well as on overseas trained applicants. In this way, the exclusiveness and income of the occupational group is protected.   (1989:92)

However motivated, such attitudes and practices have been and continue to be discriminatory. The claims of various professional bodies that they act to protect the community and maintain standards cannot always be justified, but these claims have been effective in 'keeping the foreigners out'. Iredale expresses the view that, whatever the reasons given by professional bodies for their resistant attitudes, a significant reason has been 'a chauvinistic attitude to non-British/non-Australian qualifications' (1989: 104). In the contemporary usage of the term these are clearly 'restrictive trade practices', in some cases stretching the borders of legality. In an earlier study Iredale concluded:

> Governments' endorsement of widespread self-regulation by many professional and other groups enabled the opportunity for discrimination to occur in the past. This discrimination was rarely overt but was systematic.
> (1987:199–200)

Another aspect of the problems encountered by immigrants with the acceptance of their occupational credentials concerns the quality of information they receive before they decide to emigrate to Australia.

Complaints about misinformation have been made frequently by immigrants who claimed that they had been given an assurance by immigration officials that their qualifications would be accepted. Such claims have always been denied but the frequency of complaints suggests that misunderstandings and misinformation have occurred. There have also been instances which suggest that misunderstandings might have been created by information which was clearly not correct, presenting conditions for employment in professions and trades in an unduly favourable light. Kunz illustrates such an instance by the reproduction of a recruitment leaflet issued by the refugee organisation (IRO) in Innsbruck, Austria, in 1949 (in German), which states:

> *Occupational restrictions:*
> basically such *do not* exist in Australia. Any D.P. [Displaced Person] trained for a particular vocation has the assurance that he will be able to work in a corresponding field. This regulation also applies to *medical practitioners.*
> (1988:50–1) (emphasis in the original)

An interesting piece of information indeed, as the medical profession, represented by the Australian Medical Association (until 1962 the *British Medical Association*) has been perhaps the strongest opponent of any acceptance of qualifications in that profession which did not come from Britain, Canada, the United States, or South Africa.

Misinformation issued in 1949 could perhaps be explained and excused on the grounds of serious problems of communication between Australian officials who, for the first time in their lives, went to work in a country where English was not spoken by everyone. Using interpreters whose proficiency in either of the two languages required for the occasion was often only marginally useful did not eliminate problems. As people who went through those early selection processes well remember, the success of an interview often depended not only on an interpreter's competence but also on his or her attitude towards the person interviewed. In the emotionally-charged atmosphere of the early post-war years ethnic differences among prospective immigrants often meant also ethnic animosities and antagonisms when people of diverse national and ethnic groups found themselves in the same boat, proverbial and real. The means of communication in the selection of immigrants in those days were, at best, rather primitive. Eliciting or conveying information on personal histories which the interviewer could not possibly comprehend, and, in return, obtaining or conveying information about a country which was distant and completely unknown to the interviewed person (and to the interpreter as well) could not be effectively achieved by using language limited to a few hundred words.

However, the problem of misinformation was not confined to the early days of the immigration program. Nearly thirty years later, in 1976, the Australian Population and Immigration Council found in a study of a sample of 7500 heads of immigrant families that 46 per cent of those interviewed reported that the information they had received prior to coming to Australia from Australian immigration officials on the question of acceptance of occupational qualifications was wrong (1976:123). Similarly, in a study of Polish immigrants who arrived in Australia in 1980–83 and settled in Sydney, many of the persons interviewed complained that the information they had received prior to departing for Australia about the recognition of occupational qualifications, and about housing, social services and related matters, was misleading and unduly optimistic (Polish Task Force 1983). Even more recently, in 1989, the New South Wales Committee of Inquiry into the Recognition of Overseas Qualifications has stated:

> It is evident to the Committee that many individuals with overseas qualifications are given incorrect information by employers, employment agencies and other service providers about the need to have their qualifications 'recognised' before they can seek employment.   (1989:19–20)

The Committee has further noted that there was in that area a 'preponderance of misinformation and misunderstanding', and the authorities responsible for the recognition and acceptance of overseas qualifications 'could do more to dispel this myth' (1989: 20).

The history of Australian immigration policy and the experience of immigrants thus present something of a paradox: on the one hand, seeking and giving preference to skilled persons has always been the manifest aim of the policy, but the conditions immigrants have faced on arrival have not been conducive to the exercise of their knowledge and skills, either to their own or to their host country's advantage. The frequency of the claims of misinformation has been too great for them to be rejected as not true. Even allowing for optimistic visions of the future which prospective immigrants might create for themselves and thus become predisposed to 'hearing what they want to hear', evidence of misinformation has been consistent over many decades. Therefore, it has to be accepted that, as a general trend, prospective immigrants have been receiving information which clearly suggested much easier acceptance of their occupational credentials and, consequently, much better prospects for practising their profession or trade than was the case in reality.

Why would this be so? The probability of a deliberate conspiracy of Australian officialdom is unlikely. The explanation has to be sought in a number of factors which, together, might have produced a cumulative outcome of misinformation. Factors may be suggested, with appropriate qualifications as to the degree of their probability: some of these factors would be mainly attitudinal, derived from the monocultural nature of the public service; others would be accounted for by the political and/or administrative expediency which might have influenced or entirely determined certain actions of officials at a given time.

First, from the perspective of the narrow monoculturalism of the Australian core institutions, most, if not all, educational qualifications and occupational credentials obtained in non-English-speaking countries have been regarded as inferior. As any immigrant knows, talking about one's qualifications and experience to an Anglo-Australian official would always be met with a response of incredulity: to this day immigrants are seen to have a tendency to exaggerate the quality of their credentials in order to enhance their chances of admission to the country, or to obtain a better job. An attitude thus seems to have developed which allows for the criteria of selection to be met but on the tacit understanding that the difficulties the immigrant might later encounter in having his or her credentials accepted would not matter much because these credentials are probably not as good as their owner has claimed. Furthermore, the responsibility for assessing and accepting educational and occupational qualifications of immigrants after their arrival in Australia is not usually the responsibility of the public service, but of a statutory body in which the relevant profession or trade has the major voice. It seems that a certain degree of bureaucratic 'buck passing' might be at play on this issue.

Second, as illustrated in Figure 4.2, the economic value of immigration – the basis of the immigration policy – has been perceived mainly as a 'supplementary labour force'. From such a perspective, if an immigrant's credentials fit a particular demand they will be accepted; if there is no urgent demand for these skills, it is very likely that the immigrant will accept an inferior position in the field of his or her competence. A person with the credentials of a medical practitioner will accept the job of a medical orderly or a laboratory technician, a qualified nurse becomes a nurse's aide, a social worker becomes an ordinary 'welfare worker' or an 'ethnic aide' in a welfare organisation.

Perceived as a supplementary labour force, immigrants in Australia have also been been perceived as an *expendable* labour force. As shown earlier (Table 4.3), immigrants from non-English-speaking backgrounds are overrepresented in manual occupations and, correspondingly, in industries engaged in material production; and they are, as noted earlier, underrepresented in management, administration and the professions, and in corresponding sectors of industry. The position of NESB immigrants in the labour market is therefore more vulnerable

Table 4.4: *Labour Force, Australia, February 1992: Birthplace, Labour Force Status and Educational Attainment*

Employment status/ Educational attainment	All persons in labour force		Born in Australia		Born outside Australia	
	'000	%	'000	%	'000	%
The labour force	*8557.2*	*100.0*	*6352.0*	*100.0*	*2205.2*	*100.0*
Employed	7571.1	88.5	5670.5	89.3	1900.6	86.2
Unemployed	986.1	11.5	681.5	10.7	304.6	13.8
Employed[1][4]	*7571.1*	*100.0*	*5670.5*	*100.0*	*1900.6*	*100.0*
With post-school qualifications[2]	3830.2	50.6	2793.4	49.3	1036.8	54.6
– Degree	950.5	12.6	647.6	11.4	302.9	15.9
– Trade	1240.8	16.4	900.7	15.9	340.1	17.9
– Certificate, diploma	1610.2	21.3	1221.2	21.5	389.0	20.5
Without post-school qualifications[3]	3599.5	47.5	2751.9	48.5	847.5	44.6
– Attended highest level secondary	1102.5	14.6	846.7	14.9	255.8	13.5
– Did not attend highest level	2471.9	32.6	1891.9	33.4	580.0	30.5
Still at school	141.5	1.9	125.2	2.2	16.2	0.9
Unemployed[1][4]	*986.1*	*11.5*	*681.5*	*10.7*	*304.6*	*13.8*
With post-school qualifications[2]	344.6	8.3	215.6	7.2	129.0	11.1
– Degree	54.9	5.9	29.3	4.3	30.2	9.1
– Trade	118.6	8.7	75.1	7.7	43.5	11.3
– Certificate, diploma	161.9	9.1	108.0	8.1	53.9	12.2
Without post-school qualifications[3]	596.6	14.2	425.3	13.4	171.3	16.8
– Attended highest level secondary	181.4	14.1	129.8	13.3	51.6	16.8
– Did not attend highest level	409.1	14.2	292.7	13.4	116.4	16.7

Notes:
  [1] Includes persons still at school
  [2] Includes persons with other (not stated here) qualifications
  [3] Includes persons who never attended school or whose school attendance could not be determined
  [4] The percentage shown is that for the labour force in each category (employed and unemployed)
Source: ABS (1992), *Labour Force Status and Educational Attainment, Australia, February 1992.* Cat. No. 6235.0

than that of the Australian-born labour force because, as discussed in Chapter 3, they are overrepresented in occupations and industries which have been shrinking for some years (see Table 3.9). This continues to be the situation, although compared with the Australian-born labour force, immigrant workers of both English-speaking and non-English-speaking backgrounds have higher educational qualifications. In times of economic recession immigrants record higher rates of unemployment (Table 4.4), but in times of high demand for labour unemployment rates for immigrants tend to be similar to those of the Australian-born labour force (Jamrozik 1991c).

Outcomes of Attitudes to Cultural Diversity

Faced with the problems of recognition of their occupational credentials, immigrants in Australia have adapted and continue to adapt to these conditions in a variety of ways. As already discussed, many of those unable to work in their profession or trade accept a lower status, lower grade and lower income jobs. Others, determined to regain their occupation and corresponding status, eventually succeed, even if this necessitates taking up new courses of study, at times for a number of years, and at the price of much personal and family sacrifice of time and money. Others again leave Australia, either going back to their home country or to another country.

The movement of population to and from Australia on a permanent and long-term basis indicates that the higher the occupational qualifications of a person the more likely it is that this person will leave Australia. As the data in Table 4.5 show, the net gain of population movement between permanent and long-term arrivals and departures from 1982–83 to 1987–88 was 47.6 per cent of the total arrivals, but the net gain was considerably lower among the 'skilled' persons: those with professional qualifications showing lower net gain than those with trade qualifications, and both showing lower net gain than those in the 'semi-skilled' and 'unskilled' categories. It needs to be noted that the long-term arrivals and departures categories include both immigrants and Australian-born persons. However, data from the Department of Immigration, Local Government and Ethnic Affairs indicate that approximately 70 per cent of permanent and long-term departures consist of overseas-born persons, and within this group persons with professional and technical occupations show a higher rate of departure than those in other categories (DILGEA 1987:33–4). There are also clear indications that in times of economic recession the net gain of permanent and long-term population movement decreases. For example, in the year 1990–91, the net gain was 40.1 per cent, and in the age group 25 to 34 years it was 35.2 per cent (ABS 1991, Cat No. 3101.0).

Table 4.5: *Permanent and Long-Term Movement of Population, Australia, 1982–83 to 1987–88*

Occupational groups	Permanent and long-term arrivals		Permanent and long-term departures		Net immigration gain	
	number	%	number	%	number	%
Total movement	*1 115 900*		*100.0*	*584 880*		*100.0*
530 800		*47.6*				
Workers	516 900	46.3	288 410	49.3	228 490	44.2
Not in the						
workforce	514 960	46.2	259 100	44.3	255 860	49.7
Not stated	83 820	7.5	37 370	6.4	46 450	55.4
Total workers	*516 900*		*100.0*	*282 410*		*100.0*
228 490		*44.2*				
Skilled	346 800	67.1	216 840	75.2	129 960	37.5
– professionals	277 620	53.7	177 030	61.4	100 590	36.2
– trades	69 180	13.4	39 810	13.8	29 370	42.5
Semi-skilled	110 430	21.4	43 030	14.9	67 400	61.6
Unskilled	51 600	10.0	26 980	9.4	24 620	47.7
Not previously employed or						
unemployed	8 110	1.6	1 560	0.5	6 550	80.8

Another form of adaptation to the problem of non-acceptance of occupational credentials has been self-employment. As already observed by Price some years ago, the trend towards self-employment became a feature among some immigrants, particularly those from Italy and Greece (1968:98–102). The desire to establish their own independent businesses stemmed partly from the hostility emanating from the local population, which the immigrants from these countries experienced in the pre-war years. Authors of other studies (for example, Inglis and Strombach 1984) have advanced the same explanation for the trend towards self-employment among immigrants as did Price, adding further that some immigrants were more enterprising than the resident population and were more keenly prepared to venture into self-employment. As Glezer has also commented:

In responding to the opportunities of the economy, ethnic groups brought with them a variety of skills and preferences affecting their participation in business. Among the preferences was a desire to be independently employed. But the skills were frequently a capacity to adapt to the new environment rather than any specific knowledge of an industry. (1988:861)

The trend towards self-employment, which will be discussed in later chapters, was recorded in each wave of new arrivals, such as those from Lebanon, Malaysia, Vietnam or China. As a result, whether due to legal and administrative constraints, their perception of opportunities, their venturesome disposition towards self-employment and independence, or to the cumulative effect of all these factors, immigrants from non-English-speaking backgrounds have brought new knowledge and skills and cultural diversity to those areas of economic activity in which constraints imposed by the host country on their practising a profession or trade were either low or absent.

Immigration and Cultural Diversity in the 1990s

As if to celebrate forty years of the Australian immigration program, the late 1980s became the time for launching a debate about the future of the immigration policy. The debate has continued since then, and at this time (1993) its outcome is still uncertain. It has been a strange debate, for while most participants in it seemed to agree that the program had been of great value to Australia in the past, opinions were sharply divided on the more recent immigrant intake in terms of numbers, demographic and occupational composition, the family reunion program, the number of refugees, and sources of immigrant intake. Arguments put forward were mainly economic arguments, revolving around the capacity of the Australian labour market to absorb the imported labour force, problems of unemployment, the cost of settlement, the country's overseas debt, and a range of related matters. However, from the variety of indirect statements, inferences, anecdotal references to opinions from unspecified sources and concerns about the views of 'the community', which were interwoven with the economic arguments, it was difficult to resist an impression that other concerns were on people's minds, concerns which they were somewhat reluctant to express freely. As will be seen in the chapters to follow, issues of 'social cohesion', 'the Australian character' 'the English language' and 'cultural mix' were in the background of economic arguments, thus suggesting that many of the concerns expressed were not solely about economic issues but about the cultural transformation of Australian society.

The debate began intensively in 1988, after the release of the report produced by the Committee to Advise on Australia's Immigration Policy (CAAIP), which was appointed by the federal government. It was taken up by the print media, especially by the national daily the *Australian*, with participation from journalists, academic researchers, business people and politicians, among others. It constituted the main theme at the 'National Outlook' and other conferences organised by the Bureau of

Immigration Research (BIR), which was established in 1989 on the recommendations in the CAAIP report.

One clear effect of the debate has been a reduction in the immigration intake, from around 140 000 in the late 1980s to 80 000 in 1992. The government decided to decrease the numbers on the grounds of high unemployment rates, although opinions on the relationship between immigration and demand for labour differed widely. Some research bodies held the view that an increase in immigration intake of well above 140 000 would be good for the economy and would increase the demand for labour; others held an entirely opposite view, recommending big reductions (Neales 1990). Arguments about occupational skills also differed widely, as they have done from the start of the immigration program. It is clear that these arguments have not been concerned solely with the issue of 'what kinds of skills were needed in the labour market?', but very much with the issue of 'whose interests would be affected if certain skills were imported?' It is not likely that the answers to these two questions would be compatible with each other. It is interesting to note that in reducing immigration intake in 1992 the government also reduced the proportion of the skilled category from 38 per cent to below 30 per cent (Millet 1992a).

The issue of imported skills has always been one of the main issues in immigration policy, but its problematic nature has never been openly stated. As discussed earlier in this chapter, recognition of occupational qualifications from overseas has been one of the most serious and persistent problems faced by immigrants from non-English-speaking countries. Whatever reasons might have been advanced over the years for the persistence of the problem, the resistance to cultural diversity inherent in the core institutions and the defensive attitudes of trade and – more particularly – professional organisations, aimed at protecting their self-interests, have undoubtedly been the main factors.

However relevant immigration might be to the economy, overseas debt, or population growth and the environment, it has been an interesting coincidence that increasing pressure for debate on these issues in the late 1980s paralleled increasing higher levels of educational and occupational qualifications among the immigrants from non-English-speaking countries. It is not difficult to conclude, therefore, that the issues of economy, national interests, vested group or class interests, and cultural diversity are all closely interwoven and difficult, if not impossible, to separate. Closely related to these issues is also the concept of multiculturalism which is discussed in the next chapter.

CHAPTER 5

The Australian Multicultural Experiment

Immigrants to Australia have come from all parts of the globe, and over the years the cultural characteristics as well as the socio-economic composition of successive immigrant groups have changed. These changes have in turn brought about changes in the composition of the Australian population and, in time, changes in policy responses. Community attitudes and government policies in response to this increasing ethnic and cultural diversity have moved over the years, from assimilation to integration, then to cultural pluralism, to be replaced later by the concept of multiculturalism. Each shift in policy has been an acknowledgement of the ineffectiveness of the policy of the time and each has meant a further acceptance of cultural diversity in Australian society. A more critical view, however, would be that these shifts did not represent any radical policy change but were aimed at only a slowing down of the assimilation processes, not their abandonment. As a result, changes in expressed policies have shown themselves to be rather superficial in practice and effect. Even the much-debated policy of multiculturalism, which was manifestly adopted by the Labor government in the early 1970s, later accepted and further developed by the Coalition government in the late 1970s and actively promoted by the Labor government which came to power in 1983, was translated and reduced in practice to the issues of 'access and equity'. Nowhere has there been any indication, either in the rhetoric or in practice, that multiculturalism would mean a cultural dilution of the character of the Anglo-Australian core of social and political institutions. There might have been much discussion about tolerance of and sensitivity to cultural differences, about 'a fair go' and 'access and equity', but the notion of the institutions themselves becoming 'multicultural' has not entered the debate. Thus, in effect, the manifest policy on multiculturalism means an acceptance of a culturally diverse society but one governed, administered and socialised by mono-cultural institutions.

This chapter provides a critical examination of its antecedents and the introduction of the concept of multiculturalism in Australia. It identifies a range of views and attitudes as well as methods of implementation of the policies in state and federal spheres and then poses a question about its future.

The Antecedents of Multiculturalism

The proximate antecedents of multiculturalism in Australia, that is, the concepts which guided government policies towards immigrants from the late 1940s, were those of *assimilation* and *integration*. However, since colonial days, the composition of the population of Australia has always been multicultural. The history of events which eventually led to the situation of the 1990s has been extensively analysed by such scholars as Martin (1981), Jupp (1984a and b), Collins (1988), Castles *et al.* (1988a), and many others. The literature on the subject of multiculturalism in Australia is indeed quite voluminous and diverse, recorded in numerous books, journal articles and research monographs (see Bibliography). What follows here is only a brief outline of events, which shows that the path to multiculturalism was long and laborious, at times even tortuous. Furthermore, the concept is still widely contested at various levels: in theoretical explorations, in empirical studies, in debates on government policy, and in common-sense views on Australian society. Indeed, in the early 1990s, multiculturalism may officially still be the policy of federal and state governments, it is certainly at the level of rhetoric, but in policy administration it is increasingly difficult to find. Furthermore, argu-ments against the policy multiplied sharply in certain quarters during the late 1980s and the future of the policy is uncertain, notwithstanding the government's assurance of its continuing commitment to the policy (OMA 1993b).

The first cultural division in Australia was between the native inhabit-ants and the invaders of 1788, but the invaders were also from a mixture of cultures, being of English, Irish and Scottish backgrounds, with small numbers of other 'ethnics'. However, apart from the native Australians – the Aborigines – most of the newcomers could be appropriately called Anglo-Saxon or Anglo-Celtic. The division between 'Anglo' and 'Celtic' was very real and in some aspects of social, political and economic life it persists to this day, albeit in a subdued form. From the outset, while the British Crown might have been the colonial power, the dominant culture and ideology, as well as the dominant power, was unequivocally English.

The Celts, many of whom were 'unwilling guests of English justice', and others who came as free settlers, were second-grade citizens (Tatham 1993). With the passage of time the English-Celtic, mostly English-Irish, division became less sharply defined, but differences persisted, especially in religion and politics. As Jupp observes, 'Australians between 1900 and 1950 frequently congratulated themselves on being 99 per cent British, which was never strictly true but became part of the national myth' (1988b:166). Being 'British' in Australia also meant being white, and there could be perhaps no greater insult directed at someone than to suggest that he or she had 'a touch of the tar-brush'.

When the mass immigration program began in the late 1940s, most of the inhabitants (except the Aboriginal people, who were not counted as part of the Australian population until the census of 1971) were English-speaking 'Australians', rather cautious, and often overtly antagonistic towards any 'non-British' ethnic people. As Castles *et al.* comment, at that time:

> Australia was an unusually homogeneous society. A central part of this homogeneity was a persistent culture of racism manifest most prominently in contempt for Aborigines and fear of the 'yellow peril' to Australia's north.
>
> (1988a:1)

The first non-British immigrants were selected for their outward similarity to the local Anglo-Celtic population. The newcomers, who were selected as 'good types' (Kunz 1988:131), were termed 'New Australians' and were expected to assimilate in due course. The process of assimilation was guided by what Jean Martin defined as 'the ideology of settlement', which was shared to a high degree by official and non-official bodies, such as churches, trade unions, employers, and voluntary associations. This ideology consisted of 'a set of beliefs and values on the way in which migrants could and should be incorporated into Australian society'. Martin identified six essential elements of this ideology which guided attitudes towards the newcomers. First, Australians were considered to be 'democratic and individualistic, free of class prejudice and essentially generous-hearted and open-minded towards anyone who shares their central values'. Second, the important characteristic that all immigrants were seen to share was that they were 'lucky to be here'. Third, with the help of certain organisations, such as the state-supported Good Neighbour Council inaugurated at that time, Australian society was thought to be able to incorporate the newcomers 'without undue strain and without undergoing radical change itself'. Fourth, any 'national groups' or any other form of immigrant organisations were seen to be 'unnecessary and a potential threat to this smooth incorporation'. Fifth, it was considered that the process of incorporation would involve individual assimilation and would depend on individual goodwill from both sides. Sixth, 'it would be contrary to the prevailing egalitarian values and detrimental to assimilation for migrants, as migrants, to be given unique privileges or consideration of any kind' (1981:44).

The period of assimilation policies continued up to the mid-1960s and was then gradually replaced by policies of integration. It was not a radical change and it did not come about because the government of the day acquired a new vision of Australian society. The policy of assimilation might have been criticised by some because it was forcing people to deny their own ethnic and cultural inheritance, but such critiques did not carry much weight with the policy makers. Assimilationist pressures were relaxed and the notion of integration became accepted with some reluctance because it became clear to policy makers that assimilation was not working as intended or expected. This was not so much because immigrants did not want to become part of Australian society but rather, it was not working because of the legal constraints imposed on them and because the attitudes of the host population towards them were not very receptive. In policy as well as in public attitudes, immigrants from a non-English speaking background were expected to forget their past, to give up their language and culture, and to assimilate, but only as second-grade citizens.

The term 'integration' did not mean that ethnic and cultural diversity was accepted as a permanent feature of Australian society. Rather, it meant that some aspects of diversity which did not disturb or threaten the dominant culture and social order, such as displays of folklore or ethnic food festivals, would be accepted as colourfully 'exotic' entertainment for the Anglo-Australians, at the same time keeping the immigrants 'happy'. However, this was also a period during which it became evident, through research and everyday observation, that immigrant organisations, far from being a barrier to social cohesion, often acted as a bridge between an immigrant group and the host society. Similarly, the significance of the family in the settlement process became gradually recognised and this recognition led to changes in immigration policy, with more attention being given to the balance of the sexes and family reunion.

Research on school performance by the children of immigrants in the 1960s also showed that many of them had difficulty in coping with school work because of their poor command of the English language. As a result of such findings the federal government in 1970 began to provide funds for special programs of English classes for children. It soon became evident, however, that the States' education systems were unable to take full advantage of that assistance, mainly because of lack of suitable facilities. For example, in the State of Victoria, a survey of the program revealed that more than one-third of the 229 schools with 10 or more immigrant children reported that they had no accommodation available for conducting such programs. Of the schools which began to hold special classes and provided information on accommodation, '46 reported classes being held in the staff-room, 11 in a storeroom, 10 in a hallway, 6 in a sick bay and 6 in a cloak room' (Martin 1981:42).

Policy intentions were thus not complemented by the allocation of appropriate resources. Nevertheless, with the lessening of pressure towards assimilation ethnic communities began to develop their own organisations and group activities: in sport, folklore, arts, and in providing Saturday schools for their children, teaching community languages and maintaining their culture. It was through such activities that immigrant communities aimed to retain their ethnic and cultural identities, and the notion of cultural pluralism began to take root.

The period of multiculturalism was ushered in with the election of the Whitlam Labor government in December 1972 and the appointment of Al Grassby as Minister for Immigration. Although during the three years of that government the intake of immigrants was substantially reduced, due mainly to emerging recessionist trends in the economy, new emphasis was given to services which aimed to facilitate immigrants' settlement. Among the measures introduced were the telephone interpreter service, support for 'ethnic' radio, the establishment of bilingual welfare positions in the public service, a number of inquiries into various aspects of immigration and settlement, and encouragement of teaching community (immigrant) languages in schools. The position of Commissioner for Community Relations was also established in 1974, followed by the passing of the *Racial Discrimination Act* in 1975. Parallel developments in social policy, such as the establishment of a Social Welfare Commission and the introduction of the Australian Assistance Plan by that body, a nation-wide program aimed at encouraging political and social participation, legitimised for the first time in Australian history political participation at the 'grass roots' (Graycar 1979). Ethnic communities were thus able to organise and make their needs and interests known to the public and to the government.

The incoming Coalition (Liberal–Country Party) government in 1975 continued and further developed the policies adopted by its predecessor. The next 15 years also saw a number of committees and reports on the issues of immigration and multicultural policy. The Australian Ethnic Affairs Council (AEAC) was established in 1977, and after a series of conferences and consultations it produced the document entitled *Australia as a Multicultural Society* (AEAC 1977). Another committee,

Review of Post-Arrival Programs and Services for Migrants, was formed
by the government to examine the provision of services for immigrants.
That committee's report, *Migrant Services and Programs* (1978), which
became known as the Galbally Report (after the chairman of the committee), recommended a vast number of measures. The most significant
among the recommendations adopted were the establishment of the
Special Broadcasting Service (SBS), including radio and television, and
the formation of a statutory body, the Australian Institute of Multicultural Affairs (AIMA). The Institute (established in 1979) was to
conduct research on issues of immigration, ethnicity and multiculturalism, disseminate information to the community, and advise the government on relevant matters.

The Galbally committee formulated four guiding principles on which
services and programs of particular interest to ethnic communities were
to be based in future. The principles were:
(a) all members of our society must have equal opportunity to realise
    their full potential and must have equal access to programs and
    services;
(b) every person should be able to maintain his or her culture without
    prejudice or disadvantage and should be encouraged to understand
    and embrace other cultures;
(c) needs of migrants should, in general, be met by programs and
    services available to the whole community but special services and
    programs are necessary at present to ensure equality of access and
    provision; and
(d) services and programs should be designed and operated in full
    consultation with clients, and self-help should be encouraged as
    much as possible with a view to helping migrants to become self-
    reliant quickly. (1978: 4)
Viewed together, the four principles asserted the rights of immigrants to
equal access to society's resources but also acknowledged that during the
process of settlement immigrants might need special services and provisions. These special provisions were envisaged as temporary in character, as their main purpose was to facilitate self-help and independence
in new settlers. The principles reflected the philosophy of self-help
which was pursued by the Coalition government, but in a broad perspective they also acknowledged the legitimacy of the ethnic diversity of
Australian society.

One of the early decisions of the incoming Labor government in 1983
was to establish a Committee of Review of the Australian Institute of
Multicultural Affairs. The Committee produced its report in November
1983, and its findings were extremely critical of the Institute's performance. Substantiating its opinion by submissions from a variety of

community organisations, comments from academic researchers, and findings and opinions of a number of commissioned consultants' reports, the Committee concluded that 'AIMA has been neither effective nor efficient in fulfilling its charter, which was to address itself to the central issues of multiculturalism in Australia'. The main recommendation of the Committee was to abolish the Institute and replace it by 'a new independent statutory authority, designated as a "Commission", located within the portfolio of the Minister for Immigration and Ethnic Affairs'. The Commission was to be accountable to the Parliament through the Minister (Committee of Review of AIMA 1983, Vol.1:1, 65–7).

The recommended commission was not established and the Institute continued to function for some time but under a new directorship. Later, in 1985, the government commissioned another committee to conduct a Review of Migrant and Multicultural Programs and Services (ROMAMPAS). That committee also held wide-ranging consultations, received a large number of submissions, and produced an extensive report with far-reaching recommendations (ROMAMPAS 1986). Following this report, the government closed the Institute of Multicultural Affairs and established in its place an Office of Multicultural Affairs (OMA) located in the Department of the Prime Minister and Cabinet. It also appointed an Advisory Council on Multicultural Affairs (ACMA) consisting of twenty-one members drawn from various community organisations and universities. At its inaugural meeting in 1987, ACMA was asked by the Prime Minister (R. J. L. Hawke) 'to assist in the preparation of a National Agenda for a Multicultural Australia'. A report to that effect, *Towards a National Agenda for a Multicultural Australia: (discussion paper)*, was published by ACMA in 1988. The policy document announcing the National Agenda was published by the government a year later (OMA 1989a).

This was not the end of formal inquiries and reviews on immigration or multiculturalism or both. While the government was focusing attention on multiculturalism and 'access and equity' issues, arguments were developing in the economic area about the value of immigration, in terms of its costs and benefits, the needs of the labour market for certain skills, and unemployment. Responding to these pressures, the government appointed in 1987 another Committee to Advise on Australia's Immigration Policies (CAAIP). The Committee produced its report, *Immigration: a Commitment to Australia*, in May 1988. Although commissioned to advise the government on immigration matters, the Committee saw the policy on immigration and that on multiculturalism to be closely related, and made observations and recommendations in those terms (CAAIP 1988). One significant outcome of that report was the establishment of another 'independent' body, the Bureau of

Immigration Research (BIR), attached to the Department of Immigration, Local Government and Ethnic Affairs. The Bureau received a substantial budget allocation to conduct in-house and commissioned research, and hold conferences and seminars. Since then the BIR has become the main research body on immigration matters directly funded by the government, and in its research agenda and dissemination of data and opinions through its reports and national conferences it has become a forum for debate on immigration and multiculturalism.

Multiculturalism as Government Policy

The concept of Australia as a multicultural society first appeared in government policy documents in 1972, and for the next fifteen years it was a subject of public debate and of diverse interpretations. It was only in the late 1980s that the federal government undertook the task of developing what was termed a 'National Agenda for a Multicultural Australia', based on an explicitly formulated and defined policy. After extensive public consultations and commissioning a large number of 'policy option papers' (Jupp, ed. 1989), the government, through OMA, published a series of documents aimed at defining the concept of multiculturalism and its implementation through government policy. Each government department was required to follow with its own document, explaining how the policy would be implemented in that particular area of public administration.

In the main document, *National Agenda for a Multicultural Australia* (OMA 1989a), the term 'multicultural' was defined as 'simply a term which describes the cultural and ethnic diversity of contemporary Australia'. The policy of multiculturalism meant 'government measures designed to respond to that diversity'. The policy was not concerned with the selection of immigrants but with 'managing the consequences of cultural diversity in the interests of the individual and society as a whole'. There were three dimensions of multicultural policy:

• cultural identity: the right of all Australians, within carefully defined limits, to express and share their individual cultural heritage, including their language and religion;
• social justice: the right of all Australians to equality of treatment and opportunity, and the removal of barriers of race, ethnicity, culture, religion, language, gender or place of birth; and
• economic efficiency: the need to maintain, develop and utilise effectively the skills and talents of all Australians, regardless of background.

The document also defined some limits to Australian multiculturalism, summarised as follows:

- multicultural policies are based upon the premise that all Australians should have an overriding and unifying commitment to Australia, to its interests and future first and foremost;
- multicultural policies require all Australians to accept the basic structures and principles of Australian society – the Constitution and the rule of law, tolerance and equality, Parliamentary democracy, freedom of speech and religion, English as the national language and equality of the sexes; and
- multicultural policies impose obligations as well as conferring rights: the right to express one's own culture and beliefs involves a reciprocal responsibility to accept the right of others to express their views and values. (OMA 1989a:vii)

The underlying principles of the agenda were expressed in eight specific goals which had been proposed by the Advisory Council on Multicultural Affairs (ACMA 1988):

1. All Australians should have a commitment to Australia and share responsibility for furthering our national interests.
2. All Australians should be able to enjoy the basic right of freedom from discrimination on the basis of race, ethnicity, religion or culture.
3. All Australians should enjoy equal life chances and have equitable access to and an equitable share of the resources which governments manage on behalf of the community.
4. All Australians should have the opportunity fully to participate in society and in the decisions which directly affect them.
5. All Australians should be able to develop and make use of their potential for Australia's economic and social development.
6. All Australians should have the opportunity to acquire and develop proficiency in English and languages other than English, and to develop cross-cultural understanding.
7. All Australians should be able to develop and share their cultural heritage.
8. Australian institutions should acknowledge, reflect and respond to the cultural diversity of the Australian community. (OMA 1989a: 1)

The National Agenda was to serve as a policy framework within which a wide range of programs and activities would be carried out. The most significant among these were to be: a strategy to improve processes for recognising overseas qualifications and expansion of courses for bridging training; a major community relations campaign; an improved access and equity strategy; legislation to make the existing Special Broadcasting Service an independent body and extension of its facilities to regional cities; additional resources for English language courses; reviews of law and administrative decision-making; and an investigation of the desirability of a Multiculturalism Act for Australia (OMA 1989a: ix–x). The document also explained the meaning of the principles underlying the aims and objectives of the Agenda, such as participation, basic rights, social justice, human resources, and community relations.

The National Agenda was thus wide-ranging in its aims and objectives, and far-reaching in principles. The document re-asserted the multicultural nature of Australian society and its integrative aspects, noting strong patterns of intermarriage of Australians of different backgrounds, with the result that over 60 per cent of the population had at least two different ethnic origins, and 20 per cent had four or more (OMA 1989a:5). Seven of the eight goals referred to *all Australians*, not only to immigrants, and the eighth goal focused explicitly on *the need for a change in society's institutions* through which the aims and principles of multiculturalism would have to be achieved. The document clearly stated:

> The cultural diversity of Australia is not reflected in the key decision-making institutions of society. This is particularly true of our formal political structures.   (OMA 1989a:9)

It specifically noted the limited representation of women, Aboriginal people and people from non-English-speaking backgrounds 'at all levels of the Australian political system'. The public service was also 'unrepresentative of the community at large', and this meant that policy advice and program management was 'based on the unrepresentative personal experience and values of those who staff the public sector'. Other institutions which were mentioned in the same vein were trade unions and various community clubs and associations (OMA 1989a: 9–12).

There was a clear acknowledgement in the National Agenda document that Australian social institutions had not provided equitable access to resources for *all* Australians, and many immigrants of non-English-speaking background and Australian Aborigines experienced problems and injustices. The National Agenda was 'an attempt to redress historic failings and ... to facilitate the processes of continuing adjustment in the future'. This, it was stated, was 'the basic reason' why the National Agenda was needed. The document asserted:

> In the past Australia failed to anticipate and plan for the changes and challenges presented by a rapidly diversifying population. The attitudinal environment was unprepared and the institutional structures unresponsive. This resulted in inequities and inefficiencies – individuals were denied their rights and potential resources were wasted.   (OMA 1989a:7)

A review of the Agenda a year later (OMA 1990) recorded a wealth of activities in many areas: law reform, education, administrative decision-making, communication, health services, and access and equity, among many others. The review document presented the program of the National Agenda as an outstanding success, both in the achievements reached in the previous twelve months and in the extent and diversity of programs in progress. In the foreword to the document the Prime Minister described the Agenda as a 'landmark in the development of our multicultural society', which also

> marked the emergence of a broad consensus on both sides of the political spectrum about the multicultural character of our society and the general policies and programs that governments need to implement in response.
>
> (OMA 1990:3)

There is no doubt that the aims of the National Agenda were not simply to utter rhetorical statements. Much work was being done to implement the program at the federal level, and state governments also developed their own charters on multiculturalism, in education, health and welfare, and in employment policies (Ethnic Affairs Commission of NSW 1987, Department for Community Welfare, SA 1987). However, the Prime Minister's assertion of a 'broad consensus on both sides of the political spectrum' was not reflected in the political realities of the 1980s. There might have been a broad acknowledgement by members of the conservative Coalition of the multicultural nature of Australian society, but the meaning of multiculturalism and the nature of multicultural policy remained a topic with widely differing interpretations, with their added concern about the potential 'dangers' of venturing into such policies.

If there ever had been a bi-partisan approach to immigration and multiculturalism, it certainly evaporated in the 1980s. While the government was engaged in actively promoting the policy of multiculturalism through its National Agenda, the Leader of the Opposition, John Howard, spoke about 'One Australia' and the need to consider 'at what rate immigration from Asia should continue' (1989:122–9). His successor, John Hewson, expressed his views on multiculturalism more directly and in stronger terms: in his widely distributed publication, *Australians Speak: Australia 2000*, he argued that in reply to his invitation to the Australian population to let him know 'what kind of Australia do you want?', over 40 per cent of written responses voiced serious concern about the policies of multiculturalism. He reported that there was 'a feeling that multiculturalism may be promoting a sense of division within Australian society', that multiculturalism 'has got out of hand', that it should be discouraged and assimilation encouraged instead, so as 'to make Australia a united country again'. The document gave an unmistakable impression that Hewson received no replies in favour of multiculturalism when he invited opinions about the future of Australia. He concluded:

The underlying theme of most comments on the multicultural/migration question was that Australia is now running the risk of encouraging cultural 'ghettoism', and that Australia should exercise its right to determine its own cultural direction.   (1990:59)

The views on multiculturalism were thus divided on political party lines and, as it was later acknowledged even by some members of the Coalition (see Chapter 10), those views became a factor in the outcome of the 1993 Federal elections.

It needs to be noted that views against multiculturalism were not confined to the conservative Coalition. Within the Labor Party itself there were opinions that would at best be described as 'lukewarm' towards the notion of multiculturalism, and some were openly antagonistic to it. For example, an ex-minister expressed his view, *inter alia*, as follows:

Eulogising multiculturalism may be a handy device for some politicians to inflate their self-importance and a handy diversion for others who are either unwilling or unable to deal with the country's real problems. But frankly, I don't know what it means in the Australian political context and the verbal garbage put out by the multicultural industry is no help.   (Walsh 1991)

Undoubtedly, the concept of multiculturalism was susceptible to such or similar comments. While the policy was defined in the National Agenda, it was a 'concept in the making', and the term itself was being interpreted in a variety of meanings. The CAAIP report commented at length that Australians were 'confused' about the meaning of the concept and that some people found it threatening. It was on the ground of such reported concerns that the CAAIP report implied, if it did not openly state in precise terms, that maintenance of the social/ cultural cohesion of Australian society should be an important factor in the selection of immigrants in the future. The CAAIP report and its effect on the debate on immigration and multiculturalism is discussed fully in Chapter 9.

The Meanings of Multiculturalism

The concept of multiculturalism was borrowed from Canada where it was put forward in the 1960s as an ideology to unify three ethnic and cultural communities: English, French and others, including the indigenous population. What, then, has been the meaning of multi-culturalism in the Australian context? In common perceptions, in scholarly papers, articles and books, and in the official definitions of government policies, multiculturalism has been the subject of a range of definitions and interpretations. Like most concepts, especially new ones, multiculturalism still means 'all things to all men and women'. One of the 'founding fathers' of multiculturalism, Al Grassby, spoke of multi-cultures in Australia as 'the family of the nation'. The Australian Ethnic Affairs Council (AEAC) identified three principles on which a multicultural society should be built: social cohesion, equality and cultural identity. It defined social cohesion as 'accepted institutional arrangements for allocating social resources and for dealing with conflict over what resources and over what the basis for such allocation should be'. Equality was interpreted 'as equal access to social resources'; and cultural identity meant the 'sense of belonging and attachment to a particular way of living associated with a historical experience of a particular group of people' (AEAC 1977:5). To translate these principles into practice, the AEAC stated its belief in the following words:

> ... our goal in Australia should be to create a society in which people of non-Anglo-Australian origin are given the opportunity, as individuals or groups, to choose to preserve and develop their culture – their language, traditions and arts – so that these can become living elements in the diverse culture of the total society, while at the same time they enjoy effective and respected places within one Australian society, with equal access to the rights and opportunities that society provides and accepting responsibilities towards it.   (1977:16)

The AEAC thus saw multiculturalism as people's legitimate right to preserve their ethnic and cultural identity while accepting the responsibilities of common citizenship. It was simply a claim to the rights of minorities in a democracy. There was an implicit government obligation to ensure and facilitate the exercise of this right, but there was no suggestion, except by inference, of the need for any change in social institutions or in the Anglo-Australian majority.

Following the AEAC statement the meaning of the concept of multi-culturalism and of its application in policy attracted volumes of critique and criticism. In the work of social analysts who became active in that field there have been two distinct approaches, each emphasising a different theoretical concept underpinning the concept of multiculturalism: *cultural* pluralism and *structural* pluralism. For example, Jean Martin, one of the pioneers of studies in immigration and ethnicity in Australia, focusing on cultural rather than structural pluralism, defined the concept in the following words:

> Multi-cultural means something more than cultural diversity ... what I take us to mean by multi-cultural, however, is the existence within the one society of distinct *patterns or systems* of interrelated ideas, values and forms of behaviour, which are identified with particular ways of life that have been developed by separate communities over certain historical periods. These diverse patterns represent *diverse ethnic cultures*.   (1981:180)

The proponents of cultural pluralism argued that the three principles of multiculturalism – social cohesion, equality, and cultural identity – enabled ethnic and cultural diversity to flourish while at the same time developing a common bond of citizenship. As explained by Jerzy Zubrzycki, another pioneer in studies of immigrants in Australia, chairperson of the AEAC in the 1970s and the main author of its report:

> Reduced to its basic ingredients pluralism implies societies in which a number of groups, which differ from each other in ethnicity or religious beliefs, share a common bond. In this sense, Australian society is pluralistic with a wide range of cultural, racial, ethnic, religious and class differences.   (1977:134)

The critics of cultural pluralism have argued that the concept served to conceal structural pluralism, that its acceptance of ethnic diversity served as an ideology to legitimise class inequality because that inequality was then interpreted in terms of cultural attributes of various ethnic groups (Jakubowicz 1981). True multiculturalism, some argued, would have to be concerned not only with life-styles but also with life chances; with 'equality, justice and fairness and not just with tolerance and understanding' (for example, Jayasuriya 1985:23–34).

The proponents of cultural pluralism acknowledged that its acceptance did not eliminate structural pluralism, which meant that the concept of ethnicity could be used to maintain socio-economic stratification. As noted by Zubrzycki, 'ethnic diversity and the promotion of flourishing ethnic communities is likely to interfere with the political goal of equality' (1977:136). Such a development would be clearly undesirable, and for this reason, Zubrzycki argued:

> To avoid the creation of an ethnically stratified society policies have to be devised to assist immigrants and their children in social advancement outside their own communities without at the same time eradicating everything that ethnicity stands for in terms of primordial ties and attachments.   (*ibid.*)

The critics of cultural pluralism had their strongest reservations about the use of that concept by the Coalition government in the late 1970s and early 1980s. They argued that the promotion of cultural pluralism through the multicultural policy aimed to preserve class inequality in the ethnic communities (for example, Jakubowicz 1981, Collins 1988, Castles *et al.* 1988a). By supporting ethnic organisations, the ethnic middle classes which provided the leadership in these organisations were expected also to exercise social control over their communities. The main function of the organisations which were established during that period, such as the Australian Institute of Multicultural Affairs, migrant resource centres, and grant-in-aid workers was to 'set up and institutionalise an "ethnicity model" of disadvantage in which questions of social structure were ignored or mystified' (Castles *et al.* 1988a:70). In other words, these criticisms clearly inferred that the concept of multi-culturalism was used for maintaining capitalist ideology and maximising support for the party which espoused this ideology: in sum, support of cultural pluralism was used to distract attention from the inferior class position of many immigrants, to 'keep them happy' in their ethnicity, and to secure their vote.

Did the policy of cultural pluralism achieve its purpose, whatever that purpose might have been or however it was interpreted? The author of the *Report on Migrant Services and Programs*, Frank Galbally, some years later saw multiculturalism in Australia to be 'both recognised and institutionalised', but also acknowledged at the same time that there was 'little consensus on the concept of multiculturalism' (1985:113). There was certainly no consensus among the analysts, activists, or political parties. As noted earlier, after the Labor Party came to power in 1983, it soon held an inquiry into the Australian Institute of Multicultural Affairs and later commissioned another review of services and programs in that area (ROMAMPAS). The ROMAMPAS committee acknowledged the legitimacy of cultural pluralism, but emphasised that such pluralism should not be used to legitimise inequality and disadvantage. The Committee defined multiculturalism as

> the philosophy that society should accord recognition to ethnic and cultural diversity within a common legal, political and linguistic framework, while ensuring that people are not disadvantaged or discriminated against by virtue of their ethnic, racial or cultural background.   (1986:xvii)

The Advisory Council on Multicultural Affairs (ACMA), in emphasising the need for a multicultural policy, saw such a policy as an instrument for the management of Australian society, the multicultural nature of which was a well established social reality. A multicultural policy had a unifying aim, as it was

> based on the belief that all Australians – Aboriginal Australians, descendants of the First Fleeters, recent arrivals – have the right to develop their cultures and languages. By accepting the rights of Australians to maintain the cultures of their forebears, and to pass them to their children, it allows them more readily to give their loyalty to Australia.   (ACMA 1986:2)

Notwithstanding the number of committees, reports and definitions, multiculturalism has remained a contested area in policy and the concept itself has continued to be interpreted in a variety of ways. Increasingly, too, while the rhetoric continued, the notion of a multicultural society was losing its attraction among the critics, and the conservative Coalition began to challenge the concept itself. Policies of multiculturalism, while still officially maintained by all governments, federal and state, have been criticised from the Left and from the Right, for different reasons. The critics from the Left saw the concept of multiculturalism as a means of diverting attention from the inequalities of a class society, while those from the Right saw it as a 'betrayal of Australia's British heritage, threats to unity of the nation or discrimination against Anglo-Australians' (Sawer 1990:27).

The deteriorating economic situation in the country has also been used as an additional argument against multiculturalism. Arguments have been put forward against high levels of immigration, against immigration from certain countries, especially against immigration from Asian countries, and against immigration as such. Indeed, it has become part of a repeated Australian scenario that when experts and commentators run out of causal explanations of the economic malaise, of unemployment, of foreign debt, immigration is used as an 'explanation of last resort'. However, in some of the arguments against immigration which are advanced on ostensibly economic grounds, there seems to be an implicit desire, or hope, that with a decline in immigration multiculturalism will disappear through the efflux of time, and Australia will return to the snow-white purity of its British-English colonial heritage.

Multiculturalism in Practice

In policy rhetoric and in much of the writings on the subject Australia is presented as a multicultural society. In practice, multiculturalism is perceived and acted upon as an acceptance and tolerance of the multitude of non-English-speaking immigrant communities among the Anglo-Australian majority which certainly does not see itself in any way as 'multicultural'. In common perceptions, in public attitudes and in policy interpretation and application, multiculturalism has become a basic division between the 'multiculturals' or 'ethnics' on one side and the 'true Australians' on the other, with the Aborigines again distinctly somewhere else. At best, 'Australians' are those with the Anglo-Celtic identity and the others are 'hyphenated Australians' – Greek-Australians, Polish-Australians, Chinese-Australians, and so on (Foster and Stockley 1988:6).

Galbally (1985:117) saw evidence of multiculturalism all around in everyday life: in food, in language, in folklore; but people, while experiencing it, seemed to be 'unable to make the leap from the reality to the concept'. Multiculturalism was 'still a word with few associated meanings'; for many, the concept was still baffling.

Certainly, evidence of multicultural influences is easily seen in the urban environment. A walk through areas of Sydney such as Marrickville or Fairfield, or through Carlton and Richmond in Melbourne is a walk through a world far removed from Anglo-Australian conformity. Shop signs display a diversity of non-Anglo names, shop windows display a diversity of non-Anglo goods, and English is only one of many languages heard on the streets. The diversity of restaurants serving food which reflects the diversity of the ethnic communities in the country has also long become part of the scenery, and a similar diversity of foodstuffs can be found on the shelves in all supermarkets. Multiculturalism is evident in the arts: in music, even in some literature. However, there it seems to stop: the closer one comes to the core institutions, the closer to economic, social and political power, the less cultural diversity, the more the traditional Anglo-Australian character comes to the fore. Multiculturalism may be accepted as a 'fact of life' in the visible aspects of social activities, but it has little place in the dominant culture and in the power structure of Australian society. In effect, acceptance of multiculturalism is class-related.

Multiculturalism and the Core Institutions

Multiculturalism in public and policy rhetoric may be reflected in the everyday life of 'average' or working-class Australians, of whatever ethnicity or culture; it is not so well reflected in the prevailing attitudes projected by the media and even less so in the attitudes and practices of what is referred to in this book as the 'core' institutions. The mono-culture of these institutions is overwhelming. After close to half a century of mass immigration of people from non-English-speaking countries, the vast majority of school teachers, university lecturers, public servants and professionals is monolingual, notwithstanding some presence of non-Anglo persons, usually second-generation immigrants, in these occupations. The main newspapers, commercial radio and television, as well as the public radio and television of the Australian Broadcasting Corporation (ABC) project a monolingual, monocultural image of Australia. At times a token 'ethnic' may be thrown into a script, often as a comic or a sad figure, not as a 'normal' person. For example, ABC-TV in its presentation of a 'typical Australian family' in the program *Sylvania Waters*, produced jointly with the British Broadcasting Cor-poration (BBC) in 1992, selected an Anglo-Australian family from the Sutherland Shire, the local council area with the lowest proportion of non-English-speakers of the entire Sydney metropolitan area (Jamrozik and Boland 1993). Was this selection made with the aim of presenting what the ABC considered to be a 'typical Australian family', or was it what the BBC wanted to show to its viewers? Indeed, in the content of its radio and television programs the ABC seems to act like a branch of the BBC and continues to be 'reductively British in its orientation' (Knight 1990:37). The only medium which dilutes the Anglo-Australian norm and acknowledges other cultures in Australia is the Special Broadcasting Service (SBS), commonly referred to as the 'ethnic' television channel.

The culture projected and disseminated by the education system has remained largely unaffected by the multicultural nature of the population (National Advisory and Co-ordinating Committee on Multicultural Education 1987). True, a multitude of remedial courses has been provided for immigrants to learn English, and the value of these services cannot be ignored. However, these are remedial measures which do not affect the core curriculum; on the contrary, the aim is to facilitate the assimilation process and at the same time ensure that the institutions do not have to change. The problem is particularly severe at the tertiary level, especially in the value-laden social sciences and professional education where linguistic difficulties facing the immigrant are exacerbated by the monocultural normative elements embedded in the subject matter itself. Courses in social work and clinical psychology are excellent examples of this issue.

One repeatedly recorded observation from the early years of the post-war immigration program to the National Agenda in 1989, has been concerned with the inadequate, often discriminatory services provided to non-English-speaking immigrants by the public administration bureaucracy and community organisations. This has continued to be the case, despite programs of 'sensitisation' of personnel and 'access and equity' strategies. Clearly, the problem is deep-seated in the institutional cultures. This was noted in the ROMAMPAS report, in relation to the 'access and equity' concept:

> The effective reorientation of general community services requires concurrent changes at three levels: in the manner that services are provided; in decision-making structures and processes; and in the 'culture' of the administering bodies. The goal of such changes must be effective coverage of all users at the same standard of service. (1986:323–4)

Similarly, in considering options for social welfare policies in a multicultural society, and applying the ROMAMPAS argument to that area of concern, Jamrozik and Boland have argued:

> Recognition of equal rights is a necessary prerequisite for recognition of and an effective response to 'special need'. Unless this view is fully accepted and translated into practice, access and equity programs are likely to lead to

attitudes of 'welfarism', the non-English speaking cultural minorities being perceived as 'dependent' population groups, thus eliciting a *remedial* response from the social welfare system rather than a *facilitative* response.   (1988:35)

The conservatism and deeply-ingrained Anglo-British orientation of the core institutions means that issues of multiculturalism have remained peripheral. In public services and administration the perception of non-English-speaking persons as people with 'special needs' is correspondingly translated into *remedial* services. The 'special need' may be a difficulty with the English language, especially with the *bureaucratic* English which presents difficulties for most people who come in contact with such services, be they Anglo-Australians, Greek-Australians, or any 'multicultural' Australians. It may also be, and often is, a problem with the attitudes of the administrators and service providers. As noted in the National Agenda document (OMA 1989a), the public service is 'unrepresentative of the community at large'; consequently, the experience and values of its staff are also different from the everyday experience and values of 'average' or 'ordinary' people, be they 'Anglo' or 'ethnic' Australians.

Multiculturalism: Assimilation in Slow Motion?

Does multiculturalism mean a radical departure from the concept of a socially cohesive and culturally homogeneous society? Or, does it mean acceptance of some diversity in those aspects of social life which are visible, like food, dress, or even the arts, but leaving unaffected those aspects which really matter, namely, the power structures of society? Also, even if policies of multiculturalism work effectively in providing equitable services through 'access and equity' programs, do they not at the same time have an assimilationist effect? Furthermore, as immigrants age and in due course depart to other worlds, and their children have been socialised by the Anglo-Australian education system and by the popular culture of television, recreation and the workplace, does this mean that the issue of multiculturalism is 'time-limited'?

Allan Ashbolt argues that the concepts of assimilation, integration and multiculturalism are not entirely distinct from one another, and they overlap to a large degree. He says:

> ... no one concept has ever been completely discarded in favour of another. There are elements of assimilation and integration in multiculturalism. Indeed, it could be argued that Australia's fundamental policy is still assimilationist (purportedly in the interest of furthering national unity), with both integration and multiculturalism merely methodological by-products of this aim. Or, to put it bluntly, integration and multiculturalism have become ways of assimilation.   (1985:110)

Multiculturalism as assimilation in slow motion is well illustrated by the view that the cultural differences of immigrants may have to be accepted but the second generation will integrate with and assimilate to the Anglo-Australian mainstream of society. Jerzy Smolicz argues that such a view means acceptance of *residual* multiculturalism: it means that assimilation is facilitated by children's speaking mainly English and losing the language of their community (1985:76–87). With the loss of language comes the loss of core values which are embedded in language. A 'milder version' of residual multiculturalism is *transitional* multi-culturalism, or 'assimilation in disguise': an attitude supporting the maintenance of the group's language until such time as the group members have learned the language of the host country. To develop and maintain *stable* multiculturalism, Smolicz says, it is necessary to develop an umbrella of *overarching core values* under which the core values of various ethnic groups can be accommodated. Basing his comments on extensive studies of education in schools and universities, Smolicz maintains:

> The retention and development of ethnic cultures may be perfectly com-patible with the evolution and acceptance of overarching values for the whole society. This holds even though not all cultures interact or overlap equally or readily ... The modification of national cultures and their fitting into the general framework of shared values is not equivalent to their reduction to residues.   (1985: 82-3)

Smolicz thus argues that a multicultural society is feasible and the way to develop such a society is to identify in various cultures in society the core values of each culture and then from these core values develop an umbrella of *common core values*. Multiculturalism would no longer be built on the basis of Anglo-Australian 'mainstream' core values with a periphery of multicultural values which may be tolerated without affecting the mainstream core values, whatever these mainstream core values might be perceived to be. Instead, the mainstream would represent a core of values held by all cultural groups.

What is at stake in the concerns about multiculturalism is the perceived threat of cultural transformation to the hegemony of the Anglo-inheritance. This perceived threat has kept shifting throughout Australian history from one population group to another, with each intake of another group of 'racial' or 'ethnic' immigrants. The antag-onism towards the Irish in the earlier years later extended towards the small number of Italian immigrants of the 1920s and 1930s. From the time the immigration program began in the late 1940s, the antagonism shifted towards immigrants from eastern Europe, then to Italians and Greeks, then to the Lebanese and other persons from the Middle East, and then towards immigrants from South-East Asia. Each new wave of immigrants was perceived to be a threat to 'national cohesion', to the 'Australian way of life', to the 'standard of living'. Chinese people have always been, of course, regarded with suspicion and antagonism; however small the numbers entering the country, they have always been perceived as the harbingers of the multitudinous hordes that would follow. During the years of the Cold War there was the threat of the Soviet Union and China, bringing up to date the perceived threat from Russia in the nineteenth century, the memories of which remain in the remnants of fortifications and artillery emplacements at the entry to each large harbour right around Australia, from Brisbane to Fremantle and down south to Hobart. The Russians never came. In the 1990s people's fears are raised by comments that Asia 'has become the leading source of migrants', and by projections such as that if the trend continues there is a distinct possibility that by the year 2021 over 12 per cent of the population in Australia would be 'Asian' (Wood 1990a). Estimates have been made that, if the 17 000 Chinese students who have been given a temporary permit to stay in Australia after the Tiananmen Square massacre were allowed to remain permanently, this 'may result in a migrant explosion of 300 000 by the turn of the century' through chain migration under the family reunion program (Millett 1992a). Now the estimates of the 'Asianisation' of Australia by the 2020s have been 'revised' to 26 per cent of the population (Jenkins 1993). Clearly, in the field of racism, xenophobia and fear merchandising not much has changed in the last hundred years.

Will Multiculturalism Succeed?

The concept of multiculturalism in Australia evolved from the processes of social change which have been taking place since the late 1940s when the immigration program began. These processes included the increasing ethnic diversity of the population, changes in the structure of industry and occupations, growing affluence and a changing class structure. Cultural integration began in the working-class suburbs where most non-English-speaking immigrants had settled, before the concept of multiculturalism entered the vocabulary of social scientists, media commentators and politicians. It was indeed a *cultural transformation from below*. Government policies were thus a response to the changing social reality (see Figure 5.1).

The future of multiculturalism in Australia is uncertain. The more public assertion there is of the reality of a multicultural society, the more debate and polemical writings about the nature of multiculturalism, the more the policies shift in practice towards Anglo-Australian cultural

Figure 5.1: *Chronology of Social Change and Cultural Transformation, Australia, 1947–1993*

1947–1964: Assimilation

Post-war reconstruction; building up of economic infrastructure and manufacturing industries: full employment and growing affluence.

Immigration program begins, first from Britain, northern and eastern Europe, then from southern Europe; Strict assimilationist policies and attitudes.

1964–1972: Integration

Slowing-down of growth in manufacturing industries; shift of employment to service industries and community services; growth of professional/white collar employment; married women enter the labour force.

Immigration continues from southern Europe, extending to Middle-Eastern countries; English lessons for NESB children; ethnic community organisations become public and more active.

1972–1975: Ethnic Pluralism

Election of Labor (Whitlam) government; focus on social development and political participation; growth of the new middle class; oil crisis; rise of unemployment; free tertiary education and health insurance.

Immigration slow-down; focus on settlement process; concept of 'the family of the nation'; first notions of multiculturalism; 'ethnic' radio introduced.

1975–1983: Multiculturalism Stage 1

Conservative Liberal–NCP Coalition (Fraser) government; economic slow-down; decline of manufacturing industries; changes in social policy towards privatisation; reduction of public sector activities; further rise of unemployment.

Galbally report on migrant programs and services; cultural pluralism accepted as policy; 'ethnic' television; immigration from South-East Asia begins (including boat people).

1983–1988: Multiculturalism Stage 2

Labor (Hawke) government; economic recovery; market deregulation; growth of employment, mainly for women; further growth of service and community industries.

Reappraisal of multiculturalism; movement to 'access and equity'; ROMAMPAS report, criticism of policy of multiculturalism by the Right.

1988–1993: Post-multiculturalism?

Recession 1989, deepening in 1990; industry restructuring; unemployment accelerates; economic rationalism comes into question; Keating replaces Hawke as Prime Minister 1991; policy focus on Asia; pressure for republican Australia; signs of economic recovery.

CAAIP report; National Agenda for a Multicultural Australia; conservative/economic rationalist attack on immigration and multiculturalism; immigration reduced; uncertain future but some signs of a more open society; multiculturalism again under discussion.

homogeneity. Castles *et al.* see the usefulness of policies based on the concept of multiculturalism but express doubts about the future of such policies. They see multiculturalism as based 'on a construction of community through a celebration and fossilisation of differences, which are then subsumed into an imagined community of national cohesion' (1988a:145–6). Acceptance of the concept thus prevents a return to a racist definition of the nation. However, they see the concept as too contradictory and ideologically limited to gain and retain broad and enduring support. They identify four aspects of the concept which make its future uncertain. First, multiculturalism does not reflect power relations in Australia with accuracy, as there are still clear links between ethnicity and socio-economic life chances. Second, at best, in a society with increasing inequality and decline of welfare, multiculturalism presents an equal chance to be unequal; it does not come to grips with inequalities of ethnicity, class, and gender. Third, acceptance of cultural pluralism also runs the danger of creating separate and inferior educational and social systems for different groups. Fourth, irrespective of its manifest acceptance in principle, multiculturalism does not hold much attraction for the Anglo-Australian majority.

Castles *et al.* do not advocate abandonment of the policy of multi-culturalism but emphasise the need to concentrate efforts on dealing with the structural factors which maintain inequality in Australian society. Cultural autonomy of various communities has to be based on equal social, political and economic rights, irrespective of people's race, ethnicity, gender or class.

Other analysts see the issue somewhat differently. For example, Foster and Stockley (1988) argue that multiculturalism, as originally perceived by Galbally in the 1970s and later in the policies of the Labor government in the 1980s, is now dead. They see that the most significant change was in the attitude and recommendations expressed in the CAAIP report, where concerns about multiculturalism were clearly voiced and recommendations made that all immigrants and all Australians should have a commitment to specified values in Australian society. The wide acceptance of the report's views and recommendations by the business community and some public commentators, and implied acceptance by the government, are clear indications of that change. Foster and Stockley suggest that Australia might have reached a stage of 'post-multiculturalism': such a perspective, while perhaps somewhat premature, might enable a more realistic examination of the issues of pluralism in Australian society (1988: 9).

Irrespective of other factors which may intervene, the future of multiculturalism in Australia will depend largely on two related factors:

government policy and the attitudes found in the core institutions. These two factors are closely interrelated because it is the dominant culture and attitudes in the core institutions that influence government policy. In the 1990s the National Agenda for a Multicultural Australia, which figured so prominently in government policy of the late 1980s, has taken a back seat: it may still be there 'on the books' and it may have a place in the rhetoric on public occasions, but it has certainly not been actively pursued for some time.

In the earlier debates on multiculturalism Donald Horne (1983) expressed the view that some years previously he had thought that 'if Australians were to get some more appropriate ideas of who they were, they would have to discard the strongly remaining celebrations of "Britishness"'. However, later he came to the conclusion that such an attitude would not be enough. He then argued:

> I would now say that in the sense that they should seek Australian, not British, definitions of Australia, all multiculturalists in Australia should be as it were 'anti-British'. Failing this, there is a danger that multiculturalism becomes a way of keeping 'the ethnics' quiet while the 'anglos' can go on running things, as destiny demanded they should.   (1983:3)

If there were no signs of such change in 1983, there are even fewer signs in the 1990s that any change in that direction is likely to occur. On the contrary, there is considerable evidence of what may be called a backlash against the concept and policies of multiculturalism. As the policies of both major political parties become increasingly conservative, and economic conditions show only a gradual improvement, multiculturalism is presented as a national threat. Opposition to multiculturalism is not always expressed so bluntly in public, but is clearly a common factor behind the arguments for the reduction of immigration intake and for relating it mainly to the immediate needs of the labour market, for the prerequisite of English language, for the retention of the 'Australian heritage' and the 'Australian way of life', for 'national cohesion'.

Complete multiculturalism would mean the abandonment of the myth of a 'typical Australian', however vague that ideal type of an Australian might be. It would also have to mean a significant 'dilution' of the Anglo core of the society, so deply embedded in the core institutions: education system, professional bodies, politics and government.

The strength of the forces which aim to preserve the white Anglo-Saxon purity of Australian society cannot be ignored, but there are also some signs that these forces might be waning and are now confined to a diminishing although rather vocal minority. The social analysts and media commentators who so authoritatively claim to reflect the views and attitudes of the community might do well to ask themselves whether they indeed do so, or whether the social reality they claim to reflect is a projection onto the community of their own attitudes, prejudices and self-interests. We examine these issues further in later chapters.

CHAPTER 6

Cultural Diversity and Class Inequality

Multiculturalism is an expression of ethnic diversity, with a corresponding diversity of meanings. In the literature on the ethnic composition of Australian society a distinction is drawn between cultural diversity (cultural pluralism) and structural diversity (structural pluralism). This issue raises a number of questions, such as: how far has cultural diversity become part of the economic, social and political life in Australia? Has cultural diversity affected equally all classes and socio-economic strata of the population, or are there distinct differences in the multicultural influences within various classes and strata of the social structure? Or, is cultural diversity gradually absorbed into the class structure of Australian society?

As discussed in Chapter 3, the class structure of Australian society has changed considerably from the time the post-war immigration program began in 1947. The ongoing process of change since then has meant that each successive wave of immigrants has arrived and settled in a somewhat different society. The immigrant waves, too, have been not only ethnically and culturally different from one another, but each brought with them their own social structures, usually different from that of the previous wave. The social structure of the Australia of the 1990s is therefore the outcome of a compound effect of internal changes and the inflow of changing external cultures and social structures, a process that has been going on for nearly half a century.

This chapter examines demographic and socio-economic data from a range of sources and shows that cultural diversity in Australia is not uniformly evident throughout the social structure, but is differentially located in the socio-economic stratification and the class structure. The differences are clearly evident not only in the structure of the labour

117

market but also in the spatial distribution of the population in most Australian cities, especially in the larger State capitals (Burnley 1974, Knight 1990, Jamrozik and Boland 1993). The analysis shows that while the concept of multiculturalism has been accepted in policy rhetoric and in many aspects of social life, in the vital area of 'command over resources through time' the influence of cultural diversity differs widely throughout the social structure.

The Australian Myth of Equality

The myth of Australia as an egalitarian, classless society has been one of the strongest myths, maintained effectively since the nineteenth century (White 1981). In 1930 the historian Hancock maintained the myth by writing: 'Australians show the desire for equality, bordering on the monotonous ... the striking standardisation of material circumstances is emphasised by an equally striking standardisation of habits' (1945:64). It is not quite clear from this observation whether Hancock saw equality as existing or whether he saw only the *desire* for equality, which the popula-tion did not actually experience. Whatever the meaning Hancock intended to convey, in comparison with England at that time Australia would have at least *appeared* rather egalitarian. The myth of equality was doing its work.

The truth was always and continues to be vastly different (Encel 1970, White 1981, Castles *et al.* 1988a). From the early colonial days Australia was a class society; the division between middle class and working class was established early by the affluent settlers who emulated English class divisions, adapted to local conditions. The early middle-class critics of the working class saw its characteristics 'as being distinctively Australian when in fact they were equally a part of the English social order'(White 1981:23). So was the conduct of the early 'aristocracy' of pastoralists, financiers and colonial administrators who modelled themselves on the English upper class. Indeed, when the First Fleet entered Port Jackson it brought with it the body and mind of the English class structure and its spirit of inequality which Australian society has never lost since. As Castles *et al.* note, inequality was a feature of the colony from its earliest days. 'A landed oligarchy developed rapidly, and later merged with trading and manufacturing interests' (1988a:8).

The myth of egalitarianism was created at the break of the twentieth century when the economic wealth of the country was high and Australia was seen to have the highest standard of living in the world. Whether the distribution of that wealth and income warranted the label 'egalitarian society' was another matter: the 'per capita' income did not mean then, no more than it does now, that everyone's income was close to the average. Nevertheless, some steps were taken in the early days of Federation, if not to reduce inequality, at least to lessen the likelihood of extreme poverty. Social legislation on age and invalid pensions passed by the federal parliament in the first decade of the new Commonwealth, and the decision of the Industrial Court in 1907 which established a minimum basic wage for all male workers, created social conditions which Castles (1985) has defined as a 'workers' welfare state'. Legal provisions for a minimum income meant a certain minimum standard of living, and because many people were living at that level, an impression of equality was created. Having obtained the relative security of a minimum income, people seemed to pay little attention to incomes closer to the maximum or to the maximum itself. In this atmosphere a myth of an egalitarian society – even of a classless society – was relatively easy to maintain, and it was maintained by politicians and the print media through jingoism and xenophobia, impressing upon the population the need to keep away the 'yellow and brown hordes' who wanted to invade this 'workingman's paradise'.

The myth was put severely to the test during the Great Depression, but in the affluent years of the post-war period it was brought back to life and was easily demonstrated in the sprawling new suburbs, with their new houses and a car or two in the carport. The myth was again questioned by the re-discovery of poverty in the late 1960s (Stubbs 1966, Henderson *et al.* 1970) but was maintained by removing the poor from people's consciousness through a device called 'the poverty line'. The volumes of 'research' focusing on people 'below the poverty line' provided grounds for a belief that in an egalitarian society people living 'below the line' must be somewhat 'different' from the 'normal' population, not quite a part of the society itself. It was thus only a matter of time for the concept of an 'underclass' to enter the vocabulary of political commentators, economic rationalists, and some so-called concerned citizens.

The myth of equality again became difficult to sustain in the 1980s when the excesses of financial 'entrepreneurs' were flaunted with much publicity as heroic ventures that were going to bring the country to new levels of prosperity. At the same time, people were gradually socialised into accepting the belief that good affluent living was possible but only with a proviso that a certain proportion of 'less useful' people would have to be excluded from access to the resources available to the majority. The mythical equality can thus be maintained for most, but with the exclusion of some others. Places at the table are limited.

As the economic recession deepened and unemployment queues grew longer, the notion of an underclass acquired more popular currency. There was some acknowledgement that the underclass included 'socially disadvantaged' people who were the victims of governments' neglect, such as 'single mothers isolated in inaccessible, sterile public housing suburbs or high rise flats, and the migrants who cannot speak English or find a permanent job' (Crisp 1990:48). However, the people of the underclass were also seen to have personality characteristics which were different from those of the rest of the population. Moreover, those characteristics were 'passed on' from one generation to another. People experience hardships, yes ...

> But for many, the hardships they endure are passed from one generation to the next. It is not just a matter of being poor: their values and behaviour can be askew. Alcoholism is not uncommon, health is neglected and truancy runs unchecked. Too often, the abused becomes the abuser, the dole cheque is familiar to both father and son, the single mother watches her single teenage daughter playing with her new baby ... What is intriguing, even more worrying, is the gradual emergence of a new sub-stratum: a breed of young people who expect society to provide them with the life-style of their choice without their giving anything back. They feel no obligation to work and thumb their noses at most traditional social structures: they are a problem for society but not for themselves.   (Crisp 1990:48)

It is perceptions of this kind, however sympathetic they might be, that evoke public concern but also unwittingly serve to legitimise the conditions of class inequality because they focus on the 'deviant character' of the underclass described. Exclusion of such 'human residue' from the market economy and the mainstream of the class society can then be justified without too much guilt or moral trauma for the comfortable majority.

Culture, Ethnicity and Class Inequality

As discussed in the previous chapter, some analysts of immigration, ethnicity and multiculturalism in Australia have argued that the concepts of ethnicity and cultural pluralism have served to maintain and legitimise structural pluralism, that is, the inferior class position of many immigrants. These critics have perceived multiculturalism as an ideology and have argued that the 'relationship between ethnicity and social class in both theoretical and empirical analyses requires careful explication' (Jakubowicz 1981:4). According to these views, the concept of multiculturalism was introduced because 'the assimilationist doctrine failed to achieve the goals it was intended to implement, those of cultural, normative and economic integration of immigrants into a unitary Australian society' (ibid.: 7). In a similar perspective Marie de Lepervanche has questioned the concept of ethnicity, arguing that while acceptance of ethnic diversity by governments and social analysts may reduce racial prejudice, 'this promotion of ethnicity, particularly when it is elevated to sociological theory, masks conflicting class interests and the nature of class relations' (1980:34).

Grant McCall *et al.* (1985) express the view that to understand better the notion of ethnicity the concept of ethnicity needs to be considered as an ideology. However, they argue, although the concept might be difficult to define, it is not invalid and, like the concept of class, it can be useful in social analysis. The concept of ethnicity, they say:

> can be used as an instrument for exposing inequality, independent of class but related to it at particular points. Sometimes, in fact, the analysis of class divisions is only possible if it is combined with the recognition of ethnic divisions, as indicated by the studies of labour markets segmented along ethnic lines.   (1985:10)

It seems, therefore, that in certain situations ethnicity may be an indicator of the position of a person or a group in the class structure and ethnicity and class may become almost synonymous. In such structural pluralism class structure becomes the dominant social force. On this same issue Fazal Rizvi points out that immigrants who came to Australia 'have not only been seen as different because of their distinctive culture but have also been allocated a particular place within the class structure of society' (1986:19). He argues that focus on ethnic diversity tends to obscure the class relations which are an essential part of immigrants' experience. Furthermore, there are class divisions within culturally distinct ethnic groups, and not all members of a group find themselves in the same class position in Australian society. Whatever cultural bonds might exist in an ethnic group, economic circumstances always have a potential to disrupt such bonds (1986:30–1).

Acceptance of the inequality inherent in the concept of ethnic and cultural diversity also leads to forcing people to assimilate. Rizvi argues:

> For as long as ethnicity is associated with class disadvantage – with higher unemployment rates, a lower standard of living and jobs at the bottom end of the occupational structure – then powerful incentives exist for migrants to assimilate into the mainstream culture since, in economic terms at least, this will improve their chances for a better life.   (1986:36)

Is class position, then, the most important determinant of culturally distinct immigrants, so that it overrides, as it were, the significance of ethnicity and culture? While the analysts discussed here would probably say 'yes' to this question, others (for example, Nicolaou 1991) contend that both class and ethnicity have to be taken into account because each concept represents a different dimension. Loucas Nicolaou also adds gender as a third related dimension. These dimensions are not mutually exclusive; the position of immigrants in Australian society is affected by all three, as all three tend to reinforce one another, creating the effect of a cumulative advantage, or disadvantage. Nicolaou arrived at his conclusions from an extensive in-depth study of immigrant workers in Australian industries and he focused particularly on their place in the trade unions. Immigrants, Nicolaou emphasises, are not a homogeneous group, and understanding and appreciation of the diversity within immigrant communities is essential to the understanding of their position in the Australian class structure. However, within any given class, the characteristic they share is that they are all immigrants and this characteristic makes them distinct from non-immigrants within the same class. For this reason, he argues:

> ... any conceptual framework seeking to analyse immigrants' position in the workforce, in unions and in society in general must incorporate class as an essential dimension. It is this dimension that can provide insights into inequalities resulting from the class structure of Australian society (as is the case with other industrialised societies) ... However, although it is imperative to include class, ... a class model alone is not adequate. This is because people's position within the class structure of a society is also determined by various other historically constructed relationships that interact with each other. Ethnicity and gender are two such relationships.   (1991:260)

The well-documented findings of Nicolaou confirm the findings of the studies mentioned later in this chapter (for example, Campbell *et al.* 1991, Jamrozik *et al.* 1991) on the over-representation of NESB immigrants in the lowest ranks of unskilled and 'dirty' jobs. His study identifies also an additional factor influencing that situation, namely, the power structure in the trade unions and the attitudes of Australian-born and English-speaking immigrant union officials. The vast majority of these officials, Nicolaou found, was either Australian-born or born in another English-speaking country, and this was the case even in unions in which membership included large proportions of immigrants from non-English-speaking countries (Nicolaou 1991:62–72).

Clearly, immigrants in Australia, as in any industrialised society in the capitalist system, will find their place somewhere in the class structure and class relations of that society. An immigrant investor who brings financial capital will be in a different class from the class of a tradesperson or unskilled worker who brings only human skill, or human capital. However, an immigrant, and especially an immigrant from a culture different from the dominant culture of the host society, faces a struggle in being accepted as a fully-fledged member of his or her class. The struggle is about recognition and acceptance as a member of that class, about *a place within the class* to which the immigrant lays claims on some recognised criteria, not a claim for upward mobility, that is, *not a struggle between classes*. This is an important distinction, as emphasised by Przeworski (1977) in his study of class formation. It is a struggle in some ways similar to the struggle of women for gender equality, which is often presented as a struggle for equality between classes but is really a struggle for gender equality *within the existing class structure*. Women in professional middle-class occupations seek equality with their male counterparts of that class, not with women who perform manual and menial tasks in manufacturing jobs or in the services industries.

The position of immigrants of non-English-speaking background in the class structure of Australian society is complex. Classes in contemporary industrialised societies are not homogeneous entities, and each class has its own hierarchical structure of status and power. When the post-war immigration program began, local workers and their unions were assured by the government that the immigrants of non-English-speaking background would not threaten, or compete for, their jobs (Castles *et al.* 1988a, Collins 1988, Kunz 1988,). It was clearly understood that those immigrants would be working 'at the bottom' of the ladder, as labourers or domestics, doing jobs which the locals were unwilling to do, and, furthermore, this arrangement would create unprecedented opportunities of occupational promotion for the local workers. The policies and attitudes of those years became a 'tradition', still applied in practice nearly 50 years later, evident in the position of NESB workers in the occupational structure of the labour market and in the continuing problems that NESB immigrants experience in the acceptance of their educational and occupational qualifications. Whatever explanations or justifications of this situation might be advanced, the overall effect is that cultural diversity is being incorporated into and subjugated to the structure of class inequality of the host society.

The policy of multiculturalism introduced by the conservative Coalition government in the mid-1970s brought the concepts of culture and ethnicity together into one dimension and attempted to incorporate both into the existing class structure. Jakubowicz has argued that it was an attempt to prevent political disengagement of a large part of the working class and the developing middle class from the established power structure (1984:28–48). The policy was not about the acceptance of a class-free cultural diversity but rather a means of preventing eruption of a potential class conflict.

Other analysts who looked at some of the outcomes of social and economic policies introduced in the 1980s have pointed out that these policies increased cultural and ethnic differences in access to resources and thereby reinforced class inequality. For example, Flora Gill notes that while the micro-economic reform of the kind undertaken by Australian government in the 1980s promised a potential flow of economic benefits for the whole community, 'the brunt of change falls on specific economic sectors, geographical areas and occupational and demographic groups. Prime among the losers are middle-aged blue collar workers in the manufacturing industries who possess few transferable skills' (1992:30).

Prominent among the losers are usually the first generation immigrants from a non-English-speaking background. Not only have these immigrants been always prominent in manufacturing industries and in manual occupations generally, but employment data clearly show that in times of economic slowdown or downturn it is these immigrants who tend to be the first to lose jobs (Jamrozik 1991c: Ch. 4).

The labour market is only one of many fields in which inequality in access to resources has increased in the 1980s. In social services generally inequality became a feature of the outcome of policy decisions, especially in access to health, education and child care services (Jamrozik, 1991a). As these services are fundamental prerequisites for adequate social functioning in the market economy, inequality in these areas leads to inequality in other areas of social and economic life. As Gill observes, 'inequality tends to feed upon itself' (1992:45). This means class inequality is a multi-dimensional phenomenon – the cumulative and compound effect of a number of related factors.

A significant factor in the growth of inequality has been the trend towards applying market criteria to certain public services. As market criteria became more and more influential, particular trends, too, became dominant. For example, Simon Marginson points out:

> In teaching, learning and research there is now a tendency to greater utilitarianism. There is a greater emphasis on short-term returns and pre-defined, pre-determined outcomes (commodities). In research, the development of markets means that more research inquiry becomes answer-driven. The client requires a certain answer, the researcher fashions the questions and the methods of inquiry accordingly. The growth of commercial intellectual property is leading to a tussle between individual researchers on one hand, and companies and universities on the other. A growing proportion of intellectual property is falling into corporate hands, where it is much less accessible.   (1992:127)

It is not, however, necessarily a 'tussle' between the researcher and the sponsor. When lavish research funds are available, albeit with certain conditions attached concerning the direction of the desired research, there are always willing researchers to undertake the task. Whether research is government-sponsored or privately-sponsored, the sponsor wants to be assured of obtaining not only value for money but also research which will not put the government or the firm in an unfavourable light. It would be difficult in the later part of the 1980s, for example, to find research emanating from government-sponsored research institutes that was critical of government policies. Gentle criticism, titillating the public, perhaps, yes; but solid intellectually critical analysis, definitely not. Appointment of 'right' persons to directorships and management committees of research institutes and various assessment devices ensure that 'the one who pays the piper definitely calls the tune'.

One outcome of this development has been not only the perpetuation of certain myths about Australian society but the creation of new ones. During the 1980s income inequality increased considerably, the main beneficiaries being earners in the top decile (see Chapter 3). As the egalitarian myth is no longer tenable, growing inequality has been acknowledged in some analyses, albeit retrospectively some years after the trend towards increasing inequality was plain to see for anyone who wanted to see it (for example, Saunders 1993).

Immigration and Class Structure

The post-war immigration program began and continued for some years with the dominant purpose of procuring the labour force for manual, low-skill, low-pay, often unhealthy jobs. For men, the assembly line, the steel industry, heavy construction work and rail and road maintenance became the places where little English was spoken; the equivalent jobs for women were in food processing, textile and footwear assembly lines, and in a variety of domestic work. As a result, immigration policies of the early post-war era were a significant factor in the upward social and class mobility of the native Anglo-Australian population. As Castles *et al.* observe:

> Labour migration helped to increase the size of the working class and to restructure it. Bringing in new workers at the bottom of the labour market gave Australian-born workers the opportunity of upward mobility. Immigrant workers appeared, in the early stages, to be separate from the Australian working class. Widespread racism against 'dagos', 'reffos' and 'wogs' deepened the split.   (1988a:24)

The upward mobility of Australian-born workers was further facilitated by structural changes in the labour market, which accelerated from the mid-1960s onwards (see Chapter 3). As occupational opportunities arose in the expanding non-manual occupations, Anglo-Australians moved up in the occupational hierarchy and the bottom echelons were filled by NESB immigrants. This replacement pattern was established early in the immigration program and for the ensuing decades the NESB immigrants became a distinct lowest-level class of workers in the Australian labour market. From the analysis of relevant data in the 1970s, Storer observed

> [that NESB immigrants] have been disproportionately recruited into low status jobs that Australian-born workers increasingly refuse to do. Because of this migrants have limited opportunities to increase occupation and social mobility – they become 'locked into' the least desirable occupations with minimal incomes.   (1978:75)

The 'least desirable occupations' often meant unpleasant and unhealthy 'dirty work' in the textile, clothing and motor industries, per-formed by men and women, most of whom came from Mediterranean and Middle-Eastern countries. This situation became known as the 'dirty-worker syndrome', of which O'Malley wrote:

> There is little room for doubt that in Australia there exists a 'sub-proletariat' of socially and economically disadvantaged migrant workers and their families. These workers, particularly from Mediterranean countries of origin, occupy a range of roles in the workforce which have largely been abandoned by the Australian-born and migrants from English-speaking countries. In this sense, these non-English-speaking migrants are performing 'dirty-work', i.e. work which is low paid, has poor job security and which involves poor work conditions – work which the relatively advantaged members of the workforce avoid.   (1978:47)

The process of 'replacement' of the Australian-born workers in low-grade manual jobs with the NESB immigrants has now continued for close to 50 years so that to this day the NESB immigrants are found in above-average numbers at the bottom of organisational hierarchies, in process work, in cleaning and general maintenance. For example, a 1988 Melbourne study of a random sample of 272 immigrant workers (178 men and 94 women) born in Greece, Yugoslavia and Vietnam and with at least one year of employment in manufacturing industry, found that upward occupational mobility among them was extremely low. Although the people in the sample came from diverse occupational backgrounds and the time of their arrival in Australia ranged from 1952 to 1987, 127 having arrived before 1970, 95 per cent of them had found their first job in manufacturing industry. Of the 155 men who started work as plant operators or labourers only 24 had found jobs as trades-men or other higher-grade occupations; of the 93 women who started in similar jobs only 15 found higher-grade employment (Campbell *et al.* 1991:172–94). In another study, of support services in the New South Wales public hospitals conducted in the late 1980s, the researchers found that the proportion of NESB workers in those services (cleaning, gardening, laundry, cooking) in the hospitals located in the metropolitan area of Sydney ranged from 50 to 90 per cent (Jamrozik *et al.* 1991). Similar proportions were found in the cleaning services in the State Rail Authority. A sample of 34 workers of both sexes (16 men; 18 women) selected for personal interviews represented 20 ethnic groups or nationalities. A majority of them had lived in Australia for over 10 years (20 per cent over 20 years) and for many this was the first job they held in this country. Some of the work these people were doing was quite unpleasant and dirty. For example, at the State Rail, the methods used to clean railway carriages were rather primitive and had not changed for many years. Carriages were cleaned at night by torch light, the main equipment being a mop and bucket, and water had to be carried some distance. The workers' views of the jobs they held were 'philosophically realistic'; the job was unpleasant but it was a job, and there was not much choice. Some of the younger ones hoped to get a better job in the future; others were resigned to the fact that this was the best they could do. Many of these workers had a limited command of English because after many years there they still worked in an almost exclusively non-English-speaking environment. As one of the women, a cleaner with the State Rail, said when interviewed:

> When we are together at work or at home with the family we always speak our own language. When I first worked here 50 per cent of the cleaners only spoke Greek because they were Greek and that's all we needed.
> (Jamrozik *et al.* 1991:74)

Workers like these may be called a distinct class of 'invisible people in public places'. They are in hospitals, in schools, in hotels, and in public and private offices in the central business districts in all large cities. In a taken-for-granted fashion they provide clean rooms, clean railway carriages, clean offices and hospitals, clean desks and clean beds. They remain invisible because they come in late in the evening or come in and disappear early in the morning – a silent, invisible, multicultural service of the management industries.

There is now also a silent, invisible, multicultural service in the household economy. With the increasing frequency of two income earners in professional families, domestic servants have become part of middle-class households (Jamrozik 1989, Smith 1993). The servant is usually an immigrant woman of non-English-speaking background, doing the cleaning, washing and often cooking as well. Some work as private child carers or live-in nannies. The ABS estimates domestic service in private households to be around 13 000 persons, mainly women, with another

134 000 persons engaged in 'personal services' in a variety of commercial establishments (ABS 1992, Cat. No. 6203.0), but these numbers
represent a considerable underestimate. Much of domestic service is
'black labour' and the people who do it are therefore subject to
exploitation. Being 'black labour', the numbers do not enter the ABS
data, but they are common knowledge in the community. Smith reports
that those most vulnerable to exploitation are immigrant women who
have difficulties finding other jobs; some of them do domestic work for
as little as $3 an hour. Thus, the cultural class division of the formal
labour market now extends into private households as well. In this aspect
Australia follows the trend of other affluent countries such as the United
States, the countries of western Europe, the oil-rich states, Japan and
Hong Kong. Another field of exploitation of immigrant women's labour
has been 'outwork' in the garment industry, increasingly extending into
other areas such as the electronics and packaging industries (Alcorso
1991, Castles *et al.* 1991).

Immigrants and Class Mobility

The occupational mobility of immigrants, especially of those who found
their first employment in low-skill manual occupations has been
notoriously low. Labour force data collected by the Australian Bureau of
Statistics and various research reports certainly indicate that this was the
case even in the 1980s and early 1990s when considerable industry
restructuring was taking place. For immigrants in these occupations
more often than not it was movement out of employment into unemployment rather than occupational mobility upwards. With jobs fast
disappearing in the manufacturing areas which for so many years had
operated with high numbers of NESB immigrant labour, it was that same
immigrant labour force that joined the army of the unemployed.

Has the low frequency of occupational mobility been confined to the
first generation of immigrants, or does it carry through to the second
generation? Data on this issue are rather sketchy because the ABS has
been recording mainly the distinction between Australian-born and
overseas-born people in the labour force. Since 1981 the ABS census
data have provided a basis for intergenerational comparisons of occupational mobility, but studies of this issue have been rare.

One such study was conducted by Ian Burnley who investigated the
intergenerational occupational mobility of certain immigrant groups in
Sydney. Using the 1981 census data, Burnley found that children of those
immigrants who started in low-status occupations and labouring jobs, did
show a considerable degree of mobility to higher status occupations.
Burnley notes that the early immigrants from southern Europe in the

1950s and early 1960s not only had low education and occupational skills, but were 'drawn disproportionately from the propertyless in rural environments'. To offset this 'low skill intake' Australia signed assisted immigration agreements with Britain, Ireland, Germany and the Netherlands and actively sought to recruit immigrants from those countries (1986:67). A two-class immigration intake was thus deliberately created, with immigrants from southern Europe filling labouring jobs, while those from northern Europe filled trade, professional, and managerial positions. This meant that the occupational profile of the latter was similar to that of Australian-born workers, while the profile of the former was distinctly different. The situation was worse for women from southern Europe. The data recorded in the 1966 census show that almost 50 per cent of overseas-born persons employed at the time were in trades, process work and labouring jobs (Table 6.1). Of all employed immigrant women, 31.1 per cent were employed in that category, compared to 11.7 per cent of Australian-born employed women (Ford 1970). Unfortunately, no data are available on the country of birth of these women, but it may be safely assumed that most of them were from non-English-speaking countries. The comparative rates for men in labouring jobs were 57.0 per cent for immigrants and 39.7 per cent for the Australian-born.

To discover the extent of occupational mobility between the first and the second generations of immigrants, Burnley also aimed to identify any differences between immigrants from northern and southern Europe. His analysis showed that children of the southern European immigrants moved to higher status occupations than their parents while children of the northern European immigrants remained broadly at the same level of occupational status as their parents or showed some downward mobility. Burnley concluded that as far as European immigrants were concerned the structural pluralism which was evident in the first generation was not necessarily carried through to the second generation. This did not mean, however, that the second generation had lost its ethnic identity; cultural pluralism was sustained while structural integration, or convergence, was taking place (1986:81).

One explanation of the upward occupational mobility of children of southern European immigrants which Burnley suggested was these immigrants' desire to ensure a better future for their children. For many of those who came from rural backgrounds this was the main reason for their emigrating. Indeed, Storer observed that many immigrants worked in unskilled jobs 'not only for the income but also to provide opportunities for their children via the education system' (1978:76).

However, as mentioned in Chapter 4, many early immigrants who had trade, technical or professional qualifications had to accept manual, low-skill jobs because their qualifications were not accepted. For them, any

Table 6.1: *Changes in Occupational Structure of Employment, 1966–1985:*
Australian-born and Overseas-born Workers

Year/Occupation	(1) All employed '000	%	(2) Australian-born '000	%	(3) Overseas-born '000	%	% of (1)
1966							
All employed	*4856.3*	*100.0*	*3628.7*	*100.0*	*1227.6*	*100.0*	*25.3*
Professionals, technical, etc	459.1	9.5	359.2	9.9	99.9	8.1	21.8
Administrative, managerial	308.0	6.3	239.9	6.6	68.1	5.5	22.1
Clerical	729.1	15.0	603.1	16.6	126.0	10.3	17.3
Sales	382.8	7.9	301.3	8.3	81.5	6.6	21.3
Transport and communication	297.0	6.1	241.7	6.7	55.3	4.5	18.6
Trades, process work, labourers	1748.0	36.0	1136.9	31.3	611.1	49.8	35.0
Service, sport, recreation	369.7	7.6	259.8	7.2	109.9	9.0	29.7
Others (farmers miners, etc)	562.6	11.6	486.8	13.4	75.8	6.2	13.5
1985							
All employed	*6646.1*	*100.0*	*4946.8*	*100.0*	*1699.3*	*100.0*	*25.6*
Professionals, technical, etc	1051.6	15.8	788.7	15.9	262.9	15.5	25.0
Administrative, managerial	450.5	6.8	337.6	6.8	112.9	6.6	25.1
Clerical	1209.1	18.2	958.0	19.4	251.0	14.8	20.8
Sales	607.0	9.1	485.5	9.3	148.5	8.7	24.5
Transport and communication	334.0	5.0	257.3	5.2	76.8	4.5	23.0
Trades, process work, labourers	1858.7	28.0	1265.6	25.6	593.1	34.9	31.9
Service, sport, recreation	643.8	9.7	459.1	9.3	184.7	10.9	28.7
Others (farmers miners, etc)	481.4	7.4	422.0	8.5	69.4	4.1	4.1

Sources: CBCS (1966), *1966 Census of Population and Housing*
ABS (1985), *The Labour Force, Australia, August 1985*, Cat. No. 6203.0

upward mobility that their children might have achieved would have
meant a step towards regaining their previous class position, even if only
in the second generation.

Viewed in a longer term perspective, some occupational convergence
appears to have occurred between first generation immigrants and

Australian-born workers. As shown in Table 6.1, the differences between the occupational structures of the two groups had narrowed considerably by 1985. Overrepresentation of immigrants in manual occupations was still there but to a lesser degree than in 1966 (the occupational classifications shown in Table 6.1 were discarded by the ABS in 1986 and replaced by another system of classification – see tables in Chapter 3). It needs to be noted that these data show the aggregate number of immigrants and do not separate those from English-speaking and non-English-speaking backgrounds. This division is important as more recent data clearly show that immigrants from non-English-speaking backgrounds, particularly women, continue to be overrepresented in manual occupations and in corresponding sectors of industry engaged in material production (see Table 4.3).

Cultural differences thus continue to be reflected in the structure of employment, both in the structure of industries and in the occupational hierarchy. It seems that despite the emphasis on skilled immigration, old and new immigrants continue to fill the places at the bottom of the occupational ladder. Continued immigration has thus been a factor in the reproduction of the class structure of Australian society.

Class Structure in Urban Spaces

Class structure in Australia is also clearly visible in the spatial distribution of population characteristics, being especially evident in the large cities. The larger a city the greater the segregation of its population. Each large city has its affluent 'leafy' suburbs and its poor suburbs, which are either in congested inner city areas or in distant and isolated public housing settlements. This spatial division is not simply a socio-economic one but a class division, as the differences between affluent and poor suburbs are multidimensional, creating cumulative and compound power differentials in the 'command over resources through time'. Affluent suburbs do not have streets with overhanging power lines (although the cost of power is the same as in the poorer suburbs) or chemical factories around the corner. Names like Vaucluse, Mosman, St Ives, Toorak, Hawthorn, Kew, Burnside, Unley Park have distinct connotations and everyone knows that they represent a social world vastly different from Marrickville, Fairfield, Sunshine, Footscray, Elizabeth or Enfield. All these suburbs are household names and most people know their significance. As Barry Jones has argued:

> Postcodes determine life-styles and life-chances, far more than technology: identify someone's postcode and a fair estimate can be made of his or her educational background and prospects for satisfying work.   (1983:4)

People in large cities are segregated according to their 'command over resources through time', that is, according to their social class. The affluent can choose where they want to live; the less affluent and the poor live where they can afford to live. In such a segregated environment one class of people rarely comes face to face with another class. As Knight comments, the suburbs in Australian cities are 'very large and just as largely separated. Anyone could work in Sydney through the late seventies and never see an unemployed person; with equal but better grounded relief, you could live in Liverpool [a distant suburb in Sydney] and never see a yuppy' (1990:132).

In his study of urbanisation in Australia, Burnley has noted that Melbourne and Sydney 'had already taken a metropolitan character before the turn of the century, with a real differentiation of suburbs into working class, middle class and high status areas' (1974:131). He identified ethnicity, social status and familism as the three most important factors in the spatial distribution of certain population groupings which can be observed by such indicators as occupation, education, income, housing quality, ethnicity, and school retention rates, and especially the entry to university studies. He emphasised that spatial distribution of these population characteristics did not simply signify 'differentiation' but social and economic inequality (1974:132).

A study of the distribution of human resources in the metropolitan area of Sydney by Jamrozik and Boland (1993) certainly confirmed some of Burnley's earlier observations and identified some new factors which affected the distribution of socio-economic characteristics of the population. Using the data from the 1986 census, the researchers constructed a 'Vulnerability Index' for all 38 local government areas (LGAs) in the Sydney metropolis, based on a conceptualised cumulative effect of 18 socio-economic and demographic variables. The strongest correlations of cumulative effect of comparative advantage, or disadvantage, were obtained for income, education and employment. The study also showed that while the highest proportions of overseas-born persons from non-English-speaking countries were found to be in the most socio-economically 'vulnerable' areas, average and even above-average proportions were also found in some of the affluent, 'least vulnerable' areas, suggesting some occupational and corresponging class mobility among the immigrant population. Another factor in a high concentration of non-English-speaking immigrants was the distance from the city centre: except for one low socio-economic status distant suburb (Fairfield in Table 6.2), the highest concentrations were in the inner suburbs.

Table 6.2 shows data on income, post-school education and overseas-born population for three States and for selected local government areas in their capital cities. The LGAs selected for each city are those for the

Table 6.2: *Income, Educational Qualifications and Overseas-born Persons in Three States and Selected Local Government Areas (LGAs) 1986*

State/LGA	Income $22 001+*		Post-school qualifications*		Overseas-born**	UK/	
	Men %	Women %	Men %	Women %	All %	Ireland %	NESBs %
Total Australia	22.9	5.3	37.4	23.2	22.4	7.2	15.2
Total NSW	23.5	5.7	34.4	21.8	22.4	6.0	16.4
Sydney City	17.8	9.0	31.1	27.6	44.3	7.2	37.1
Kuring-gai	49.1	13.5	54.1	42.4	24.3	7.6	16.7
Nth Sydney	43.8	22.2	49.3	43.5	35.2	10.6	24.6
Fairfield	14.5	2.0	30.2	16.7	47.3	4.2	43.1
Marrickville	13.7	6.2	27.9	22.8	48.9	3.4	45.5
Total Victoria	23.2	5.6	31.8	18.8	24.5	6.2	18.3
Melbourne City	20.4	11.5	33.5	31.0	40.1	5.0	35.1
Kew	34.7	12.5	44.3	36.5	25.9	5.2	20.7
Hawthorn	34.3	15.3	45.3	40.0	25.1	6.4	18.7
Sunshine	13.4	1.7	27.3	12.6	42.3	4.9	37.4
Footscray	10.2	2.6	26.1	13.8	43.0	4.1	38.9
Total SA	19.9	4.5	32.7	17.4	24.5	10.9	13.6
Adelaide City	25.0	13.0	38.7	34.1	31.8	10.6	21.2
Burnside	36.2	11.4	47.4	34.2	21.4	7.2	14.2
Mitcham	32.2	7.8	47.1	30.2	18.2	9.3	8.9
Elizabeth	11.1	1.4	31.0	13.0	36.9	28.8	8.1
Enfield	10.8	2.1	30.6	14.2	27.2	9.0	18.2

Notes: * Persons 15 years and over
** All persons
Source: ABS, *1986 Census of Population and Housing*

inner city itself, for the two most affluent and for the two least affluent areas. As shown, similar characteristics of the distribution of overseas-born persons are found in all three cities. Two other interesting characteristics are also evident. First, immigrants from the United Kingdom and Ireland appear to be uniformly distributed in all areas, except for a high concentration, as in Elizabeth, South Australia, a satellite town built primarily to accommodate immigrants from Britain who were recruited to work in the General Motors assembly plants established nearby and in associated industries. By contrast, immigrants from non-English-speaking countries show wide differences in distribution, with a consistently high frequency in the inner cities and in some low socio-economic status suburbs, but also an above-average frequency in some high status suburbs. The second interesting feature is that in areas where the frequency of NESB immigrants is the highest, the frequency of immigrants from Britain and Ireland is the lowest: Marrickville and Fairfield in Sydney, and Sunshine and Footscray in Melbourne. The distributional pattern in the other large cities (Brisbane and Perth) was found to be less clear, mainly because the population of NESB immigrants in them is much smaller than in the former three State capitals.

It would appear, therefore, that in the urban environment of large cities cultural diversity of immigrants may not be among the most important factors in the location of particular ethnic groups in certain suburbs, but their socio-economic status and social class are. However, the distinct differences between the localities seemingly preferred by immigrants from England and Ireland and 'the others' suggest that influences other than social class may also be at play. Nevertheless, the largest congregations of immigrants from non-English-speaking countries are undoubtedly found in the 'vulnerable' low socio-economic areas. This low status is clearly visible in the levels of incomes; the frequency of incomes over $22 000 per annum for men (1986 values) in the low socio-economic areas being only about one-third of those in the affluent areas. For women the differences in incomes above that level are shown to be far greater, the frequency of that level of income in the low socio-economic areas being as low as one-tenth of those in the affluent areas, indicating the differences in employment opportunities for women, discussed earlier in Chapter 3. The other indication of differences between high and low socio-economic areas is in education, and, again, the differences are greater for women than they are for men. The overall clear indication from this study gives credence to the comment made by Withers that 'the truly distinctive Australia of the late 80s is the Australia of the suburban multicultural society' (1989:18), notably in contrast to the 'Outback legend'.

Cultural Diversity and the New Middle Class

The new middle class, as identified in Chapters 2 and 3, and examined extensively elsewhere (Jamrozik 1991a), plays an important, indeed crucial, role in society's responses to cultural diversity. The influence of this class on society's response to cultural diversity is wide-ranging, but (and this is of direct relevance to the issue of class inequality) this influence is exercised particularly in four areas: in attitudes towards cultural activities in general, in the fields of music, art, literature, etc; in attitudes towards immigration generally and towards specific ethnic groups in particular; in attitudes towards the working class, accentuated in attitudes towards the immigrant working class; and in attitudes towards new middle class immigrants, particularly those from non-English-speaking countries. The comments which follow certainly entail a degree of generalisation, and exceptions may be found in each of the areas discussed; however, the comments apply to prevailing attitudes which can be directly observed or indirectly inferred from various expressions of views, authoritative decisions, or actions.

In the broad area of 'culture' the new middle class may be receptive to visits by 'exotic' dance groups from other, non-English, cultures, and watch with equal interest 'exotic' folklore displays by local 'ethnics', but there the interest stops. Local theatre, film, radio and television productions, especially television, remain not only almost exclusively Anglo-Australian but also project broadly the middle-class image of Australian society. The Special Broadcasting Service (SBS) is certainly an exception, but, being 'special' and 'multicultural', it is regarded as peripheral to the Anglo-Australian mainstream culture: the channel's foreign films might be watched by the educated Anglo-Australian new middle class but they are watched *as foreign films*. In literature, because the vast majority of the new middle class is as monolingual as the rest of the Anglo-Australian population, its members are not able to read literature in languages other than English. As a result, they have little knowledge or understanding of the culture, history and geography of the lands from which the non-English-speaking immigrants have come. Certainly, there is literature translated into English, but no translation can convey the cultural meanings and nuances of the original.

The education system has remained largely monocultural, although in many schools teachers have endeavoured to widen the cultural perspective by introducing studies of community languages. However, schools not only impart knowledge but also act as important socialising agencies. As Milner says, 'Australians are made not born, and they are made as much as anything by the education system and by the culture it seeks to propagate' (1991:38). There might be acknowledgement of the different cultural backgrounds of students but it is important to note that the educational culture of the curriculum is Anglo-Australian and teaching methods themselves are based on monocultural theories. For many years, bilingualism was seen by teachers and psychologists as a significant inhibiting factor in children's school performance; parental authority over children was decried by teachers and social workers as contributing to young people's problems in relationships with their peers; assistance by children at home or in the family corner shop was criticised as child exploitation. To this day, awareness of, and sensitivity to, cultural diversity in people in the helping professions remain limited.

The members of the new middle class are separated from the working class not only by their socio-economic and cultural characteristics such

Table 6.3: *Comparisons of Earned Incomes, Australia, 1990: Full-Time, Full-Year Workers: Selected Categories*

Category of income earner	Persons '000	Mean gross annual income ($)
All income earners	*5261.7*	*28 920*
Occupations:		
Professionals	768.0	39 380
Para-professionals	363.5	31 820
Clerks	832.3	24 820
Salespersons and personal services	508.4	24 780
Tradespersons	970.3	25 560
Plant operators, drivers	477.0	27 300
Labourers and related	609.1	23 160
Educational qualifications:		
With post-school qualifications	2860.2	32 610
With degrees	698.2	42 700
Without post-school qualifications	2401.5	24 520
Place of birth:		
Australia	3880.4	28 810
Overseas	1381.3	29 230
– English-speaking countries	602.9	31 660
– Non-English-speaking countries	778.4	27 350
Selected countries:		
Malaysia	21.2	35 650
India	26.6	33 790
New Zealand	98.3	31 600
UK and Ireland	452.9	31 520
Italy	116.7	25 730
Greece	59.7	23 080
Vietnam	28.1	23 000
Lebanon	20.2	22 900
China	16.5	20 400

Source: ABS (1992), *1990 Survey of Income and Housing Costs and Amenities, Persons with Earned Incomes, Australia*, Cat. No. 6546.0

as education, occupation and income, and separation in the workplace, but also by spatial separation and corresponding social living environment. Professionals' earnings are, on average, at least 70 per cent higher than the earnings of persons in unskilled occupations. Corresponding educational qualifications account for similar differences (see Table 6.3). The real differences are greater, as averages always conceal extremes.

Differences in spatial separation are especially significant. In examining the spatial distribution of population characteristics in the large cities it becomes evident that the new middle class whose members provide human services in education, health and welfare, tend to live away from the working-class suburbs. Their knowledge of life in those suburbs is, therefore, mainly abstract and second-hand. For example, in the study of spatial distribution of human resources in the Sydney metropolitan area mentioned earlier (Jamrozik and Boland 1993), it was found that people employed in the three top occupational groupings (managers and admini-strators, professionals and para-professionals) lived prdominantly in the affluent suburbs. In the top nine socio-economic local government areas (LGAs) 46.1 per cent of all employed persons living in those areas were employed in the three top occupations; in the eleven bottom LGAs the proportion was 18.5 per cent, a ratio of 2.49 times in favour of the former. The 'helping professions' (medical practitioners, nurses, teachers and instructors, and social professions) showed a similar distribution: 12.5 per cent as against 4.8 per cent, a ratio of 2.60 in favour of the top nine LGAs.

Attitudes of the new middle class towards the working class in general tend to be condescending and often overtly antagonistic. In education, for example, beliefs were strongly held for many years that most working-class children were not able to learn beyond certain levels, were unwilling to learn, or both. Such attitudes were frequently encountered in reports provided to children's courts. The system of streaming in schools was widely practised, and children who did not excel in learning were actively discouraged from continuing at school beyond the compulsory age limit. Even now, higher school retention rates are seen by some educationists as being of little value for many children and are portrayed as the government's endeavour to 'conceal youth unemploy-ment'. Children of non-English-speaking immigrants are perceived as either 'having difficulties in coping with the curriculum', or as 'being pushed by their parents beyond their capacities'.

The problems experienced by working-class persons in their encounters with officialdom and with professionals are well known. Encounters with the helping professions are especially problematic, as such aspects of living as health and illness, child rearing, marital relation-ships, attitudes to work and leisure, are differentially perceived and interpreted according to a person's social class. Working-class immigrants face intensified difficulties in these areas, as witnessed by the entrenched myths of 'malingering' and fraudulent workers' compensation claims. As Caroline Alcorso found in her extensive study of this issue:

> ... Migrants have been identified by sections of the legal and medical professions as being more prone than Australian-born workers to malingering and psycho-somatic complications of back and other injuries ... Similar views are often articulated publicly and reported in the media ... to be a migrant on 'compo' is to invite expressions of cynicism and disbelief from friends and workmates.   (1989:47–8)

Such views and beliefs have been held and propagated by professionals, bureaucrats and media commentators, most of whom have never been inside a factory, a mine, a foundry or smelter works. The most extreme action in that area was the infamous police raid on dozens of Greek immigrant households in Sydney one early morning in April 1978. Some 180 people were arrested on suspicion of fraud and charged with conspiracy in claiming social security benefits. After a few years of court proceedings costing millions of dollars no guilty parties were found (Kondos 1992).

Do immigrant professionals fare better? As discussed earlier, in Chapter 4, Australian immigration policy has presented a contradiction, in that manifest policy emphasis has been on a preference for 'skilled' migration, but the higher an immigrant's occupational qualifications the greater the difficulties that person encounters in having these qualifications accepted for practice in Australia. The reason for this apparent contradiction has been twofold. First, there has been a long-established and actively maintained belief that any educational qualifications and occupational knowledge, skill and experience brought in by an immigrant from a non-English-speaking country was likely to be in some way inferior. Second, skilled and professional immigrants have always been perceived as a threat by the established trades and professions; hence the provision of elaborate requirements for the acceptance of occupational qualifications.

There are considerable, perhaps fundamental, differences on this issue between 'trades' and 'professions', especially social professions such as medicine, social work, psychology, pedagogy. Trades have a large objective knowledge and skills component but a relatively minor normative component: for example, the knowledge and skills necessary to repair the engine of a motor car do not differ much between, say, Italy and Japan or Australia. By contrast, professions, especially the social 'helping' professions have a high degree of cultural specificity and normative elements, in both theory and practice. Such professions also enjoy prestige, exclusivity and power by shrouding their knowledge and skills in secrecy and mysticism, which enables them to invoke the protection of the state from 'invasion of inferior quality', so as to safeguard 'the public interest'. To be accepted into this exclusive community, an immigrant must not only meet the test of knowledge and skill but must also demonstrate a willingness to accept the values and attitudes of the profession. The exclusive community says to the newcomer, 'to join us you must become one of us'. To become one of the professional community the applicant must learn and accept not only the 'what', the knowledge base of the profession, but also the 'how', the practice skills, and the 'why', the values and interests of the profession.

Furthermore, as in professional communities there is a close relationship between work and social life, acceptance of professional attitudes and values is expected to extend into the immigrant's life-style. It is not surprising, therefore, that immigrants from non-English-speaking countries with professional qualifications have had such great difficulties in putting their knowledge and skill into practice in their host country.

Attitudes of the new middle class to cultural diversity present yet another paradox of Australian society. The members of that class are educated and politically aware, they participate in cultural activities both as producers and consumers, and are exposed to other cultures through overseas travel. It might be expected, therefore, that the members of this class would be at the forefront of social and cultural change. However, they are also the guardians of the Australian core institutions, the institutions through which the continuity of the white Anglo-British heritage and structure of power has been maintained. Viewed in this perspective, irrespective of the diversity of opinions, attitudes, cultural pursuits and life-styles that might be found among its members, the new middle class, *as a class*, by virtue of its position in the structure of power, has been a significant force in maintaining the culturally diverse immigrant communities in an inferior position in the class structure of Australian society.

Nevertheless, some of the data in Tables 6.2 and 6.3 suggest that immigrants from non-English-speaking countries are now finding their place in the 'old' or the 'new' middle class. Table 6.2 shows an above-average presence of such persons in some high socio-economic status areas, and in Table 6.3 immigrants from Malaysia and India – countries where English is the common language of the educated population – show average earned incomes above those of Australian-born persons and above those of immigrants from New Zealand and from the United Kingdom and Ireland. It may well be that some elements of a common cultural English background through education, professional activity, public administration or business is relevant here, lessening for immigrants from those countries problems with the acceptance of their professional qualifications. Some of them have probably studied in Australian tertiary institutions. Whatever the reason, the data suggest some 'invasion' of cultural diversity into the class structure of Australian society. Is it this development that fuels the concerns about the 'Asianisation' of Australia, which began to appear in the media in the mid–1980s? This issue is further explored in Chapters 9 and 10.

CHAPTER 7

Religious Diversity in a 'Christian' Country

Cultural diversity in Australia is multidimensional. In addition to the dimensions of socio-economic stratification and class structure, ethnicity, and what some people see as race, another significant dimension of diversity is religion. It is yet another area of social life in which increasing diversity has created social tensions which, while rarely erupting into open conflict or physical violence, continue to simmer below the surface and come out into the open from time to time in the guise of terms such as 'threat to national heritage' or 'lack of loyalty to the nation'. The diversity of Christian denominations which accounted for divisions and cleavages in earlier years has now given way to tensions between Christian and other religious groupings, such as Islam. These 'new' religions are seen by many people as a threat to what has been seen and continues to be seen as a Christian country. The Christian character of the country is maintained in the public image and public consciousness, although some of the so-called 'minority' or 'non-Christian' religions, while still accounting only for two per cent of the population, now have thousands or tens of thousands of adherents (Table 7.1). How the growing diversity of religions is going to be accommodated is one of the important issues to be faced by Australians in the near future.

This chapter examines some of the questions arising out of religious diversity in Australia and relates these to the issues of ethnic diversity and policies of multiculturalism. It then draws some comparisons with situations in other countries in which religious diversity exists without giving rise to any great social tensions, and some others where religious diversity has been a source of tensions and open conflict.

Australia: a Christian Country?

Australia has been regarded as a Christian country. Now, more appropriately, it may be regarded as a country of Christian religious diversity, with a small addition of non-Christian religions and a substantial population described as being of 'no religion' or 'unknown' or 'not stated'. The 1986 Australian census recorded 16 Christian denominations, four non-Christian religions and significant numbers of adherents to 'other Christian' and 'other non-Christian' religions (see summary, Table 7.1). The recording of religious affiliation on the census paper is optional and in 1986 over one in ten persons (11.9%) exercised that option by not answering the relevant question. Another 12.7 per cent recorded 'no religion': this was the largest numerical and percentage increase category of religious (or rather non-religious) affiliation recorded since the census of 1966. In effect, the 'no religion' category became in 1986 the third-largest recorded category after Catholic and Anglican church affiliations. Non-Christian religions accounted only for two per cent of the population, the largest in that group – the Muslim or Islamic religion – recording less than one per cent (0.7%) of the population, followed by Buddhism (0.5%) and the Jewish religion (0.4%). Thus almost three-quarters (73%) of the population recorded its allegiance to Christianity; still a large majority but a significant decrease from the 88.4 per cent recorded in 1966. The major shift over that period has been not to non-Christian religions but to secularism.

Within the Christian churches the largest increase in those two decades was in Catholic affiliation, while the Protestant churches recorded a decrease. To a certain extent these shifts have been an outcome of post-war immigration, but not a very significant one. As shown in Table 7.2, except for the inflow of 205 000 persons of non-Christian religions (6.3 per cent of overseas-born persons), the composition of religious affiliations of the overseas-born persons, including the 'no religion' category (Column 5 in Table 7.2), is not much different from the composition recorded by Australian-born persons.

Australia thus remains a 'Christian' country, but with secularism a growing characteristic. Furthermore, recorded religious affiliation by a person on a census document does not necessarily imply active membership of a religious community, and 'active membership' may also have a range of intensity in the strength of belief, support, or participation in religious activities. However, religious affiliation, even if only nominal, is significant in itself, as it gives people an identity and a sense of belonging; like the extended family, it can play a role in the life of an individual at certain events or stages of life.

Table 7.1: *Religious Affiliations, Australia, 1966–1986*

Religion	1966[1] '000	%	1986[2] '000	%	Change 1966–86 '000	%
Total population	*11 550*		*100.0*	*15 602*		*100.0*
4052		*35.1*				
Christian	*10 205*		*88.4*	*11 382*		*73.0*
1177		*11.5*				
Catholic	3 086	26.7	4 064	26.0	978	31.7
Orthodox	255	2.2	427	2.7	172	67.4
Protestant	6 717	58.2	6 575	42.1	−142	−2.1
– Anglican	3 877	33.6	3 723	23.9	−154	−4.0
– Uniting	2 244*	19.4	1 757*	11.3	−485	−21.6
– Lutheran	177	1.5	208	1.3	31	17.5
– Other	419	3.6	885	5.7	466	111.2
Other Christian	147	1.3	346	2.2	199	135.4
Non-Christian	*76*		*0.7*	*316*		*2.0*
240		*315.8*				
Jewish	63	0.5	69	0.4	6	1.0
Muslim			110	0.7		
Buddhist	13	1.0	80	0.5	234	1800.0
Hindu			21	0.1		
Other non-Christian			36	0.2		
Other	*1269*		*11.0*	*3 904*		*25.0*
2635		*207.6*				
No religion	94	0.8	1 978	12.7	1884	2.004.3
Indefinite	36	0.3	62	0.4	26	72.2
Not stated	1139	9.9	1 864	11.9	725	63.7

The notion of Australia as a Christian country extends beyond recorded affiliations, whether these be active or nominal. It pervades everyday life, language, the law, politics, education, and perceptions of the outside world and its religions. Christianity has been an integral part of the country's history since the arrival of the First Fleet. Later, when the Australian colonies 'agreed to unite in one indissoluble Federal Commonwealth under the Crown of the United Kingdom of Great Britain and Ireland', they were 'humbly relying on the blessing of Almighty God' (*Constitution Act* 1901). That god was certainly a Christian god. The act itself, which described the Australian Commonwealth as 'a self-governing colony' and which is still the basic law of Australia, was an act of the British Parliament, 'enacted by the Queen's Most Excellent Majesty, by and with the advice and consent of the Lords Spiritual and Temporal, and Commons'. The 'humble relying on the blessing of the Almighty [Christian] God' is still repeated at the start of each daily session of Parliament when the Lord's Prayer is recited before the verbal

Table 7.2: *Religious Affiliation, Birthplace and Birthplace of Parents, Australia, 1986*

Religious affiliation	Total population* '000	%	Australian-born persons — Both parents Australian-born '000	%	One-parent Australian-born '000	%	Both parents overseas-born '000	%	Overseas-born persons '000	%
Total population *100.0*	*15 602* *3247*		*100.0* *100.0* *9071*		*100.0*		*1550*	*100.0*	*1221*	*100.0*
Christian	10 205	73.0	6667	73.5	1124	72.5	923	75.6	2292	70.6
• Catholic	4064	26.0	2132	23.5	377	24.3	460	37.7	981	30.2
• Orthodox	427	2.7	18	0.2	20	1.3	145	11.9	250	7.7
• Protestant	6575	42.1	4218	46.5	659	42.5	267	21.9	903	27.8
• Other Christian	346	2.2	308	3.4	68	4.4	49	4.0	162	5.0
Non-Christian	316	2.0	36	0.4	16	1.0	55	4.5	205	6.3
No religion	1978	12.7	1106	12.2	231	14.9	131	10.7	448	13.8
Not stated/indefinite	1926	12.3	1252	13.8	178	11.5	112	9.2	302	9.3

Note: Small differences in addition are due to rounding
*   Includes 513 000 persons birthplace not stated

battle, with the use of more colourful words, begins between government and opposition.

In everyday life, Christian religious instruction is still provided in schools, and most marriages and burials are conducted as religious ceremonies. Every country town, however small, will have its church or two, or more, and large cities will have several, although they may be more difficult to see now that their stone or brick towers are being dwarfed by the concrete-marble-and-glass towers erected to the glory of the gods of finance, business, and economic rationality or – if the experience of the 1980s is to be taken as an example – of economic irrationality.

Christian religions, or rather the Christian church, or churches, came to Australia with the Christian invaders in 1788, and from the outset played an important role in shaping the new society by exerting a powerful influence in politics, education, social policy and social welfare. One of the most significant roles performed by the churches, with lasting influence and effect, was in subjugating local Aboriginal populations to colonial power, destroying their beliefs, culture and social systems. In this Australia was no exception, as Christian churches had performed that role in all invasions by European powers, whether Spanish, Portuguese, French, Dutch or British. The sword and the cross always worked in a close alliance during the centuries of European colonisation of other continents.

Religion continues to be a significant force in Australian society, influencing many aspects of social, political, economic and cultural life. That influence is now more diverse, as the established Christian churches find themselves surrounded by a variety of 'new' forms of Christian religions or cults as well as the growing non-Christian religions such as Islam and Buddhism. The growth of diversity does not mean that more people are now involved in religious activity: on the contrary, the increase in religious diversity has been paralleled by a growing secularism. In some Christian churches the character of the ritual and religious observance has also become secular, as 'holy days' are observed not only for worship but also as 'holidays', for enjoyment (Inglis 1970:471).

The established Christian churches – Anglican, Catholic, Uniting – have been on the defensive. Having become part of the established power structure of a class society and of the monocultural Anglo-Saxon and Anglo-Celtic colonial inheritance, they had much to gain from the preservation of the *status quo*. Over time, they came to be among the largest property-owning corporations, much of the property acquired with government assistance: by engaging in such important social services as health, education and welfare the churches have benefited, and continue to benefit, from financial subsidies for operating expenses as well as transfers of capital. Today, their power hierarchies see their interests threatened, not only by the inroads made into their following by the non-Christian religions and various fundamentalist Christian cults, but also by the apathy of some of their own congregations and demands for change by others. Seeking as they might to adapt their public image to the changing society around them, the established churches tend to act in ways similar to those adopted by other core social institutions: they frequently express concern about unfairness, poverty, disadvantage and discrimination and they engage in activities ostensibly aimed at alleviating these conditions, but at the same time they largely preserve their power structure and political influence intact, as well as their material wealth.

Religion and Politics

Organised religions have never been very far from politics. In the ancient world of the theocratic powers of Egypt, Mesopotamia or Israel, state law was, by definition, also god's law. In Europe, the Greeks and the Romans established civil governments but their gods were never far away from the seats of power. The Romans were accommodating to the influences of other religions, and, as their empire grew, they built a temple, the Pantheon, to accommodate the growing multitude of gods and demi-gods. Their persecution of the early Christians was not because they did not like the new faith but because the early Christians represented a challenge to the divine power of the Emperors and a potential social and political transformation from below. When the transformation could no longer be prevented, the Emperors became Christian and the Roman Empire became the *Holy* Roman Empire. From then on, all political power was deemed to flow from the Christian god and was embodied in the 'divine right of kings': without the authority and blessing of the Emperor and the Pope no power in Europe was considered legitimate. The legitimacy of Rome in allocating power according to god's will was later seriously questioned by such people as Luther and Calvin, but the 'divine right' itself maintained its legitimacy in principle and practice until Thomas Jefferson and his colleagues declared it illegal in their Declaration of Independence in 1776, arguing with logic and eloquence that all people were created equal and power came from and rested with them. The people of France followed suit with their Declaration of The Rights of Man and Citizen, disposing not only of the concept of 'divine right' but also in a most convincing fashion disposing of the incumbent of that 'right'.

In England, after the quarrel with Rome, the 'divine right' was retained: the church and the state remained united as the monarch became also the head of the state religion – the Anglican Catholic Church. Other Protestant churches were later allowed to practise their faith, but not without conflict; some, like the Pilgrim Fathers, found the persecution too oppressive and left the country for another continent. Roman Catholics were less fortunate; after a great deal of bloodshed, disappropriation and discrimination they were eventually 'emancipated' in 1829 and allowed to hold public office (McCallum 1988:941).

It was to be expected, therefore, that in Australia too the power of the British Crown would be accompanied by the power of the Anglican church, and so it was. Other Protestant denominations found their place, although they were often met with antagonism and open hostility. However, the main feature of the history of religion in Australia has been the division between the Protestant and Roman Catholic churches. In the colonial years that division was also a political and 'ethnic' division, as most Catholics were Irish convicts and Irish free settlers, neither being of a particularly friendly disposition towards the British Crown or its representative ruler – the Governor of the colony. It was a social and economic division as well, the propertied class being mainly Anglican or identified with that church. Nevertheless, the Catholic church was recognised and after the passage of the *Church Act* in 1836 the Roman Catholic church was entitled to receive support from government for its charitable activities. In education a dual system of schools was developed: denominational schools, including Catholic, which were subsidised by the state, and public, non-denominational schools operated by general boards of education. However, in 1869 the Colony of New South Wales withdrew state aid to church schools and established a universal secular system of education. Church schools continued their work without government assistance and the Catholic bishops then began to establish more Catholic schools and improve their own system of education. Catholic parents who continued sending their children to non-Catholic schools were warned by bishops that they 'had committed a serious moral offence' (Mol 1970:476).

At the time of Federation (1901) about a quarter of the population of Australia was Catholic and predominantly of Irish working-class descent. White notes that some division appeared among the Catholics at the time: those of Irish descent who had been taught in their church schools saw their loyalty to be to Australia and their (Irish) Church, while other Catholics held their loyalty to be to Australia and the British Empire, seeing no inconsistency with their membership of the Catholic Church and its Irish heritage (1981:112). The theme of the twin identity – of being Australian and British – was the popular rhetoric at the time and the majority of the population 'identified with the government school tradition of Protestant God, British King and Anglo-Australian country' (*ibid.*).

The division between Protestants and Catholics remained for a long time one of the persistent and profound divisions in Australian society: it has been reflected in politics, in attitudes to social and moral issues, in culture and in the class structure. In the writings on religion in Australia, Australian Irish-Catholics have been perceived as fundamentally different from the majority of the, largely Protestant, population. Social analysts such as Mol (1970), Inglis (1970), Encel (1970) and Hickman (1977) have focused their attention almost exclusively on the Protestant/Catholic division, giving relatively little or no attention to differences within the Protestant denominations themselves or to non-Christian religions. Catholics have been perceived to differ from the Protestant majority in their attitudes to marriage, divorce, contraception, politics, even death (Inglis 1970). The reported findings suggest that differences between Catholics and Protestants in some of these aspects have existed and continue to exist but that they tend to be exaggerated. For example, the often expressed belief that Catholic families tend to have many more children than Protestant families is scarcely supported by evidence: the data recorded in the 1986 census (ABS 1992, Cat. No. 2514.0) show that the mean number of children borne by all women in Australia was 1.889 per woman and for Catholic women it was only slightly higher at 1.971; even when the data were standardised for age the mean rose to 2.032, hardly a huge difference.

In politics Catholics have been identified with their allegiance to the Australian Labor Party (ALP), and studies of voting intentions carried out in the 1960s certainly indicate that Catholics, more than persons with any other religious affiliations, were inclined to vote for the ALP (Encel 1970:166). However, while this might have been the case, Catholicism was never the sole factor in Catholics' support for the Labor Party. The ALP emerged late in the nineteenth century from the trade union movement as a working-class party and Irish Catholics were prominent in the working class. Thus early ALP politics were grounded not so much in Catholicism *per se* but rather in the working class; they were also grounded in Irish ethnicity and culture, competing for power against the Anglo-Australian establishment – an establishment that was solidly Protestant, mainly Anglican. The Catholic church did play an important role in Labor Party politics at certain times, as, for example, during the conscription debate in World War I, and in the 1950s when fear of a 'communist takeover' of trade unions and the Labor Party reached its peak; this resulted in a split in the ALP which took many years to heal and kept the party out of office until 1972.

In more recent decades, the focus on the significance of religion in politics has shifted to immigrant communities, and political parties became active in courting the 'ethnic vote'. However, with the exception of some immigrant communities where the issue of religion was perceived in the context of the Cold War and communist power in their home countries, religion as a factor in immigrants' allegiance to a political party does not seem to have been significant. Like the Australian-born population, the main, if not the sole, factor in the voting preferences of immigrants is social class. If immigrants tend to vote for the Labor Party it is because the majority of them are, and see themselves to be, working class. The exception may be those immigrants who have found their place in the 'old' or the 'new' middle class, and are likely to vote for the conservative Coalition parties, or become 'swinging' voters, who behave politically in the same way as their Australian-born counterparts.

The religion of immigrants re-emerged as a political issue of wider significance during the conflict in the Persian Gulf in 1990–91, when the Islamic communities were suspected of 'disloyalty' by certain sections of the population and the mass media. However, although Islam evokes strong and strange attitudes and emotions among many Australians, the issue of religion during the Gulf War was part of the wider issue of ethnicity, race, and the question of 'what does it mean to be an Australian?', revived at the time by media commentators. The suspicion of disloyalty among non-English-speaking immigrants, of whatever religious affiliation they might be, even after they had become Australian citizens, seems to linger in the minds of some Anglo-Australians and comes to the surface on certain interesting occasions, usually through the action of an 'authoritative commentator' in the mass media. At times, loyalty to Australia has been equated with loyalty to England: for example, during the Falklands/Malvinas conflict the newspapers and television media were searching out immigrants from Argentina and questioned them as to whose side they were on. The colonial inheritance, it seems, is still very much alive in certain sections of the Australian population and is 'cultivated' by certain sections of the media whenever the occasion promises the desired effects.

The colonial inheritance is well embedded also in some Christian churches, especially in the Anglican church. The links with the British Crown are also religious links, as the Queen is the head of the Anglican Church and Defender of the Faith. On these grounds the change in the Oath of Allegiance which is taken at naturalisation ceremonies has caused grave concern among some church dignitaries, for two reasons: invoking god is now optional and what was a pledge to the British Crown has become a pledge to Australia (Murray 1993). It would seem that the belief that Australia had no state religion might be one of the Australian myths.

Religion and Ethnic Pluralism

Most religions aim to present a universalist orientation, appealing to values which transcend national, ethnic and racial boundaries. Many have succeeded in achieving this aim and have established a presence in all parts of the globe. At the same time, some religions, including those with universalist aims, have acquired national or ethnic characteristics in many countries or regions, through certain historical events and developments such as threats of invasion by powerful neighbouring nations, or political and religious oppression by foreign occupation. It was in such situations that people would gather around their religion and church to seek protection and preserve their national or ethnic identity. Historically also, priests, monks, pastors, nuns, rabbis and imams have been people's educators, conducting schools and universities, disseminating not only their faith but also secular knowledge. Through such activities organised religions became vehicles of history for nations and ethnic communities, and people's ethnic or national identity became also their religious identity. Universities were originally religious organisations and to this day the main Christian denominations have their colleges at Australian universities. Formal academic dress is modelled on the habits of monks and church dignitaries and in western countries, including Australia, all official university (and many school) mottos on coats of arms are in Latin.

In commenting on the significance of the relationship between religion and ethnicity or nationhood, McCallum observes that religion can be a powerful force in uniting or dividing people and nations. He says:

> This power is inherent in religion because it is the cumulative tradition of the faith of a people in history ... As part of the tradition of a people, it is one dimension of ethnicity, perhaps its primary feature. Religions create relatively stable, formal social structures which bind groups of people together, giving them common purpose.   (1988:938)

McCallum further observes that 'religion is clearly one of the key factors determining the social culture of a nation. Religions carry the important signs and moral codes that define cultures'.

In Australia, from the early colonial days the Anglican and other Protestant churches were 'English' or 'British' and the Catholic church was 'Irish'. Later in the nineteenth century there were also the Chinese with their own religions which they kept to themselves, but mostly they were forced to disappear from the scene when Australia 'turned white'. Other ethnic groups remained small in numbers and their religions were not an issue on a national scale, although adherents might have met with unfriendliness at times or in some localities. Larger groups of immigrants, such as the Germans who settled in South Australia in the mid-nineteenth century, established their own local communities and 'erected churches and schools as soon as they had obtained the basic necessities for living' (Seitz and Foster 1985: 420), thus maintaining the unity of their religion, ethnicity and language.

With post-war immigration came other ethnic groups and their religions. Those of the Catholic or Protestant faiths found their churches already well established in the host country but the reception of the newcomers was not always without some tensions and strains. Catholic immigrants, particularly, found the attitudes of the local church hierarchy to be assimilative and thus something of a threat to their own ways of religious expression and their ethnic identity (Lewins 1976: 126–35). Other national or ethnic communities, such as those of the Orthodox religions – Serbs, Greeks and Russians – established their own church buildings, and by following their traditional religious practices they aimed to preserve their ethnic identity.

As Burnley notes in his study of ethnic communities in Sydney:

> Historically religion has been a crucial factor in the preservation of ethnic identity in some home countries, especially those which experienced long periods of foreign domination: the Serbian Orthodox Church under Austrian and Turkish occupation; the Greek Orthodox Church under Turkish suzerainty ...   (1985:185)

As a means of expression of ethnic, cultural or national identity, religion is important because it facilitates that expression's being made collectively, that is as a community and in public. For this reason, a member of an ethnic community may not be necessarily religious but will attend religious services in his or her church to maintain the tradition and ensure that such action will 'be at least a surface manifestation of identity' (Burnley 1985:187).

It is in the forms of religious expression that significant differences between some immigrants and their host churches in Australia became evident. For example, as Pittarello points out, while for Anglo-Australians religion is rather a private affair, 'for Italians religion is primarily a social experience and only secondarily a private one' (1990:6–10). Among Italian Catholics anti-clericalism is also prominent, something which Anglo-Australian Catholics find difficult to understand. Yet, anti-clericalism has been a feature of Catholic church followers in many European countries, where people see their priests and bishops as guardians of the faith as well as guardians of church power and they differentiate between the two, accepting the first but keeping a critical and watchful eye on the second. Mindful of history, European Catholics know that power is power, whether it be symbolised by a crown or a mitre.

Notwithstanding the problems experienced by some immigrant communities in establishing their own church organisations as a means of preserving their own faith and cultural and ethnic identity, the diversity of religions has not been a source of great conflict in Australian society. With growing secularism, there has also been a degree of tolerance of religious diversity, and any divisions and antagonisms that might have occurred have not approached the degree of hostility which was present in the earlier years between Protestants and Catholics. The trend towards secularism has been paralleled by a growth in various Christian fundamentalist groups and a multitude of semi-religious or 'new age' cults in which people, mostly members of the new middle class, seek to find fulfilment and spirituality, or re-discover their sexuality, intellectual or emotional potential, or the proverbial 'meaning of life'. The frequency and diversity of these trends does not seem to unduly disrupt the social order: in an affluent society the search for the meaning of life takes various forms, and for some people who have money to spare the more exclusive the form in which that search is offered, the more attractive it becomes.

As noted earlier, the religion which has caused anxiety in some sections of the population is Islam. In addition to being a non-Christian religion, Islam is a 'visible' religion and has been in the forefront of international issues for some years. In Australia, Islam has been perceived by some people as an 'Arabic outpost', a rather hostile element, representing a 'foreign' power and a repressive culture. Such perceptions are often fuelled by the media: the picture of an Islamic mosque with a minaret evokes emotions different from those connected with the sight of a Christian church with a spire; and repeated images of assemblies of men bowing to the ground, *en masse*, suggest the power of a regimented multitude and stir viewers' or readers' emotions even further. It somehow does not seem to occur to the people in the media that congregations in Christian churches also stand, sit, kneel, bow their heads, raise their hands and sing rather strange chants.

In contrast to the perceptions of Islam, other religions such as Buddhism and Hinduism, although also foreign and non-Christian, tend to be perceived in a different light: saffron robes, incense, and multitudes of lighted candles present images of peace. These Eastern traditions also attract interest from the Anglo-Australian population, especially from the new middle class, because they are seen to offer a kind of refuge from the pressures of an industrialised society, but not as a direct challenge to that society, as Islam may be seen to be.

On a nation-wide scale, the growth of non-Christian religions has not led to open hostility and violent conflicts, but the situation tends to be different in some local communities. Non-Christian religious communities, whether perceived as 'threatening' or 'peaceful', do not find a warm welcome in Australian towns and suburbs. The negative and at times overtly antagonistic attitudes of 'Christian' Australians towards non-Christian communities rise to the surface in certain circumstances, especially when such communities want to build their own meeting places, schools, or places of worship. On such occcasions racist elements come to the fore, whipping up emotions and fears. Difficulties experienced by Islamic and Buddhist communities in Sydney in obtaining approval from local councils for building their places of workshop are well known. In some cases delays with such applications have persisted for years and petitions opposing approval from local lobby groups have raised thousand of signatures (Allison 1991). In a number of places:

> local residents' reactions to proposals for new mosques, temples or religious schools ranged from simple concerns like increased traffic or parking problems to outright fears of Muslim or Asian invasions of their suburbs.
> (*Ethnos* 1990:74)

The perception of the Muslim community as one large and homogeneous ethnic, racial or national group 'invading' Australian suburbs is completely erroneous. They may perhaps not cover quite the same extent of ethnic diversity as do 'Christian' groups in Australia, but Muslim communities have come to Australia from a number of areas, ranging from north Africa to Malaysia and Indonesia (Clyne 1991:131–7). Indeed, while some Muslims are Arabs, most Muslims in Australia are not Arabs, and most Arabs are not Muslim, but rather Christian, mainly from Lebanon and Syria (Henderson 1991). Furthermore, while a common religion is undoubtedly a unifying factor in ethnic or national groupings, different national identities may be more important in dividing various ethnic groups than the power of the common religion is in unifying them. The more universal a particular religion, the more likely it is that its members want to maintain their ethnic or national identity. This is as true of Christian as it is of non-Christian religions, not only Islam but also Buddhism and Taoism (Bennoun *et al.* 1984:102–24). Within each of these religions, too, as European history of religious conflicts among the various branches of Christianity vividly attests, differences arise which at times turn into violent upheavals and wars.

Religion, Multiculturalism and Social Class

Inasmuch as the concept of multiculturalism in Australia is difficult to reconcile with the concept of an undisturbed Anglo-British heritage, religious diversity does not fit easily into the concept of a Christian country. The concept of a Christian country implies that non-Christian religions may be tolerated and some of their activities, such as schools or welfare services, may even be supported by the state, but in the public mind and institutional power structures they remain secondary to the Christian mainstream. The very division of 'Christian' and 'non-Christian' indicates that this remains the basic division in the diversity of religions and their institutions. It is a division which pervades many aspects of social life. In the rooms of almost every hotel one finds a copy of the Bible; in the courts swearing on the Bible is automatically assumed unless the Koran is requested, or taking an affirmation rather than an oath is insisted upon.

Religious expression is a cultural expression in more than one way. Organised religions do not confine their interests and activities to spiritual aims such as 'saving souls'; they are in the forefront of such important social areas as education, health services, child and family welfare and care of the aged. They also act as teachers and guardians of social values and social morality, expressing views on, and aiming to influence, laws, politics, family life. It follows then that in a Christian country the dominant role in these areas of social life would be performed by the Christian churches.

In the early colonial days in Australia the Anglican Church was dominant in these roles. As Anderson comments:

> The First Fleet brought not only British civil and military authority, but also spiritual authority in the form of representatives of the Church of England. The latter regarded itself as the custodian of morals and manners as well as the religious welfare of the first white residents and, among other things, soon took initiatives in providing schooling for the young.   (1988:215)

Other churches, especially the Catholic Church, took up the challenge and thus gave birth to what became a dual education system. As mentioned earlier, church schools were initially supported by public funds but this support was withdrawn in 1869, and for the next hundred years church schools operated without state support, although they enjoyed a variety of tax concessions as 'charitable organisations'. Responsibility for school education has remained with the States, and State governments have supported church schools in a variety of ways: special grants, tax concessions, teacher training. Direct financial support by the Federal government was resumed in the 1960s by the conservative Coalition (Menzies) government and was later formalised in the early 1970s by the Labor (Whitlam) government. Financial support for church and other private schools by both federal and state governments is now a well established policy.

Private schools now account for approximately a quarter of Australia's student population: this is one of the highest proportions of students in private education among all OECD countries, second only to Spain where the proportion is 35 per cent (Anderson 1991:147). At the latest count, in 1991, 72.1 per cent of children and young people attending school were in government, or public, schools; of the remainder, 19.5 per cent were enrolled in Catholic schools, and 8.4 per cent in other non-government, or private, schools (Table 7.3). At the primary school level, the numbers in public schools were higher (74.9 per cent), but in secondary schools the numbers in public schools were considerably lower (68.2 per cent). The greatest difference between the numbers in primary and secondary schools was in Anglican schools: at primary level these schools accounted for 1.5 per cent of all school enrolments, but at secondary level Anglican schools accounted for 4.5 per cent (ABS 1992, Cat. No. 4221.0). At secondary level Anglican schools have been and remain the elite schools.

Private schools are distinguished by significantly higher retention rates to the final year of secondary education (usually Year 12) and considerably higher rates of their students' entering into tertiary education (Table 7.3). Differences exist also between the Catholic and other Christian schools, the latter recording higher retention rates and higher rates of entry into universities. As the tuition fees in these schools are beyond the resources of most families, 'Anglican and non-conformist church schools ... are now noted more for their social distinctiveness than their Christian ethos' (Anderson 1988:216). Indeed, the 1986 census 'revealed a strong relationship between the level of annual family income and the likelihood of a child in that family attending a non-government school' (ABS 1989, Cat. No. 4119.0). For example, nearly 40 per cent of children in primary schools whose family annual income was over $50 000 were attending private schools, compared to less than 20 per cent of children whose family income was $18 000 or less. In secondary schools, more than half of the children whose families' annual income was over $50 000 were attending private schools.

Like the private schools in England on which they were modelled, private schools in Australia have been important institutions in the reproduction of class structure (Encel 1970: 152–64). Certainly, there are differences within the private school system. Catholic schools divide into the parish schools which cater for children of families in particular localities and focus mainly on primary education, and the elite schools, which take both primary and secondary students, but concentrate more on the latter. Protestant schools, with their high fees, tend to be elite schools, drawing their student population from affluent families (Anderson 1991:148–9) and focusing clearly on educating 'future leaders'. A private Protestant school background is undoubtedly a prominent

Table 7.3: *Schools in Australia, 1991: Student Numbers, Retention Rates and Transitions to Higher Education* (N = '000)

Schools/retention rates/transitions		All schools	All public	Schools All private	Anglican	Catholic	Other
Schools							
All schools	N	3075.1	2217.2	857.9	84.1	598.2	175.6
	%	100.0	72.1	27.9	2.7	19.5	5.7
Primary schools	N	1786.5	1338.6	447.9	26.2	342.9	78.8
	%	100.0	74.9	25.1	1.5	19.2	4.4
Secondary schools	N	1288.6	878.6	410.0	57.8	255.3	96.8
	%	100.0	68.2	31.8	4.5	19.8	7.5
Retention rates							
To Year 10	%	98.7	98.7	99.0	105.5	96.0	103.9
To Year 11	%	86.0	84.1	90.3	109.3	82.3	103.5
To Year 12	%	71.3	66.9	81.6	104.7	71.9	98.4
Transition to higher education							
Left school in 1991	N	275.6	202.8	65.5	n/a	n/a	n/a
In May 1992:							
At university	N	75.6	42.6	30.3	n/a	n/a	n/a
	%	27.4	21.0	46.2	n/a	n/a	n/a
At TAFE	N	64.3	49.1	14.3	n/a	n/a	n/a
	%	23.3	24.2	21.8	n/a	n/a	n/a
Other tertiary	N	11.3	8.1	3.2	n/a	n/a	n/a
	%	4.1	4.0	4.9	n/a	n/a	n/a
Not attending	N	124.4	103.0	17.7	n/a	n/a	n/a
	%	45.1	50.8	27.0	n/a	n/a	n/a

Sources: ABS (1992), *Schools, Australia*, 1991, Cat. No. 4221.0
ABS (1992), *Transition from Education to Work, Australia 1992*,
Cat. No. 6227.0

characteristic of persons occupying high positions in business, in the professions and in the higher echelons of the public service (Pusey 1991:50–6). In the past most politicians and leaders of the conservative parties came from private Protestant schools (Encel 1970: 238) and the situation is not much different now. Moreover, more Labor Party politicians now come with a private school background, both Protestant and Catholic.

Not all private schools are directly related to an organised religion, but most of them are. Some ethnic communities have now established their own schools, usually operated under the auspices of their church or in association with such a church. The most prominent among these are

Jewish, Greek and Italian schools, which provide a complete primary and secondary curriculum. The Islamic communities are now establishing their own school system, as are other non-Christian communities and various small fundamentalist Christian religions. Most ethnic communities have established at least 'Saturday' or 'Sunday' schools, providing religious and language instructions for their children, thus aiming to maintain the community's religion as well as its culture and ethnic or national identity.

The influence of organised religion in education is not confined to the operation of the private religion-related school system. Religion as a subject is taught in most public schools, although the subject is usually non-compulsory; parents may choose for their child to attend lessons of a particular religion (or denomination) or not to attend any such lessons. In some schools, however, a lack of clear communication to parents regarding their rights gives the impression that religious lessons are compulsory. Difficulties are also experienced in providing religious classes for Muslim or Buddhist children (Connell 1993). The introduction of comparative religion as a school subject in some states has met with strong objections from some parents and community groups, expressing fears that such courses would 'undermine Christianity' by exposing young children to religions such as Islam or Buddhism. There was a danger, some argued, 'of breeding a generation that knows virtually nothing of Christianity, which underpins the ethical structure of the country' (Eccleston 1991).

The social activities of churches are not confined to education: another important field of their activity has been in charitable work. As far back as 1801 the Reverend Samuel Marsden preached in Sydney on the 'community responsibility for destitute children, and urged the importance of securing their moral character' (Dickey 1987:9). In the same year the Orphan Schools were established in Sydney, one for boys and one for girls. At first these were the responsibility of the Anglican Archdeacon, but some years later (in 1840) they were further divided into two for Protestants and two for Catholics. The Benevolent Society of New South Wales, established in 1813, had the full name of 'The New Society for Promoting Christian Knowledge and Benevolence in these Territories and the Neighbouring Islands' (ibid.: 12–13).

With the passage of time the charitable work of the Christian churches extended into diverse areas of social service activity. Organisations such as the Brotherhood of St Laurence, the Catholic Welfare Bureau, Anglican Community Services, Uniting Church Central Missions, the Salvation Army, the Society of St Vincent de Paul are now household names in Australia. Some churches have also been active in work with refugees and immigrant groups. While this involvement signifies the churches' interest in immigrants' needs, it is not possible to ascertain here whether they have overcome their earlier assimilationist tendencies and have now accepted a multicultural orientation. Some progress in that direction appears to have been achieved by the Catholic church.

In immigrant communities men and women are very much involved through their religious organisations in education and social welfare work. The larger communities, for example the Greek, Jewish, Polish, Italian, Lebanese and Vietnamese, have established their own social welfare agencies, either under the auspices of their religious organisations or in association with them. Indeed, there are very few, if any, immigrant groups in Australia in which a religious organisation does not play a role in the maintenance of the language, culture and ethnic or national identity of the community. Religious organisations in many immigrant communities have also played an integrative role between these communities and the wider society, as some of their activities in education and social welfare involve personal and organisational contacts with other immigrant communities and with the Anglo-Australian mainstream.

Religion and Multiculturalism in the 1990s

Australia is not unique in having a wide diversity of religions. Many countries in the world today are multi-religious or multicultural or both, with different degrees of accommodation to this diversity. Those people in Australia who decry the growing cultural and religious diversity of society and speak of the necessity to preserve the 'British heritage', do not seem to notice that much of the United Kingdom has also become multicultural and multi-religious. Many of the English sportsmen and sportswomen (whom one often sees on Australian television) or their ancestors came to England from former colonies, and population movements in Europe in more recent decades have meant that British society has not been immune to further diversity. Indeed, Britain and England itself has always had to a certain extent a multicultural periphery around its monocultural institutional core and class structure. In looking at this aspect of British history, Waldinger *et al.* observe:

> In London's Brick Lane, the Bengali community is served by a mosque that served as a synagogue from 1898 to 1975, and was built in 1744 as a church for French Huguenots. In Bradford, Yorkshire, the first centre of migration from Pakistan, Howard Street, is within a hundred yards of the late nineteenth-century German Evangelical Church and the church of Our Lady of Czestochowa, serving the post-1945 Polish community.   (1990:107)

In today's England ethnic diversity may not be very welcome in some places and animosity to immigrants from Britain's former colonies may manifest itself also in religious antagonism; but religious diversity *per se* does not present serious problems, in our view.

What is eminently clear is that in societies where religious diversity appears to lead to tensions or open, even violent, conflicts, there is always an underlying non-religious factor. In Northern Ireland, an example *par excellence*, the underlying factor in the religious division is class inequality and what one of the antagonists sees as a common bond through history with another country, while the other side sees it as the continuity of an oppressive foreign occupation. In Canada, religious division is also a division of culture, language, social order, and an outcome of certain events in history, but the division, while threatening to convert into complete separation, has not led to open conflict and violence. In the United States of America religious divisions are interrelated with divisions of culture, language, ethnicity and race and, above all, social class. The Netherlands has been a multi-religious and multi-ethnic society for a very long time, functioning effectively without any serious tensions. In any such society, religious divisions lead to conflict when they serve as, or are related to, social and economic inequality. Mostly issues of religion and politics are also closely interrelated, so that assertions of religious identity and political demands go hand in hand.

Alford has argued that the 'connection between religion and politics arises as a problem only in nations which are not religiously homogeneous' (1969:321). This proposition may hold true in some cases but it does not hold true in all situations. For example, in a religiously homogeneous country like Poland religion was used for many years as a political force opposing the power of a one-party state. In some South American countries which are also religiously homogeneous, liberation theology has been used as a countervailing power to the political, economic and cultural oppression of the lower classes. However, when a religion, as an organised church, is united with state power or is closely related to it, it presents a problem of a different kind, namely, it becomes itself a power of oppression and social control. Historically, the latter has been true more often than the former.

In Australia, although there has never been a legally established state religion, the Anglican church has acted as such for many years, and to this day continues to be influential in maintaining the Anglo-British character and class structure of Australian society. The Catholic church originally played a role in opposing this, but with increased numerical and material strength it also became a significant force in the maintenance of the social order and class structure. With the inflow of Catholics from non-English-speaking countries, local Catholic churches welcomed new members but the church's assimilative tendencies, such as insistence on obedience to the established church hierarchy, were resented by the newcomers. Other Christian churches, while maintaining their identity, and some even developing a degree of separateness and exclusivity, have certainly not disturbed but rather have served to reinforce the social order and class structure.

Although Australia has become an increasingly secular society, organised religions have maintained their power and influence through a range of activities, such as education, social welfare and health services. Most of these activities are supported by the state through subsidies and capital transfers, increasing the material wealth of religious bodies with gifts of public funds.

For the established churches, the inflow of immigrants has meant the potential of increased membership, and immigrants were sought and assisted by some of them for that reason. Acceptance of new members, however, also entailed acculturation and assimilation of the newcomers to the existing hierarchy of power, methods of control over the flock of believers, and often the acquisition of immigrants' communal property. In the Catholic church, this attitude of the local church hierarchy created a division and antagonism between the Anglo-Irish Catholic establishment and Italian, Ukrainian and Polish Catholics. Ukrainian Catholics have experienced an additional problem because of their different religious ritual which the local Catholic church hierarchy found difficult to understand and accept.

On a broad scale, tensions remain between the Christian and the non-Christian religions, especially between the Anglo-Christian community and Islamic communities. Islam is a 'visible' religion and, as Gellner observes, it is 'more perhaps than other religions, a blueprint of a social order' (1969:127). In a 'Christian' society, the people of the Islamic communities encounter problems with the laws of marriage and divorce, relationships between the sexes, parental authority, even their manner of dress, especially for women. A different day of worship (Friday) and the obligation for devout Muslims to pray five times a day bring serious problems in the work environment.

Religious diversity may be accepted in Australia, but very little, if any, modification of customs, laws, and practices has taken place to accept this diversity on equal terms. For example, most public holidays are based on Christian holy days such as Christmas or Easter, and no allowance has been made for the holy days of Orthodox Christians, Muslims or Buddhists, for instance. Like Catholics in the earlier years, the adherents of these religious traditions undoubtedly see this neglect as somewhat discriminating.

As we have shown, religions, even those which claim universality, are historically interrelated and interwoven with the politics, ethnicity, culture and social structures of various places and nations. From the earliest colonial days Australia experienced problems in religious affairs, the Protestant/Catholic divide having been a political as much as a cultural divide: this division related not only to internal political, cultural and class interests, but also to the relations with the British Crown and Anglo-British dominance. To come to terms with the religious and cultural diversity which now exists in Australia, the notion of a 'Christian' country will need to be reconsidered so that minority religions, including the non-Christian ones, can contribute to the development of multiculturalism on fair and equitable terms.

CHAPTER 8

Cultural Transformation and its Effects

Australia in the 1990s is certainly a different country from what it was in the 1940s. A visitor returning to the country after a few decades of absence would find, in addition to a much larger population, brighter and more colourful cities, a previously unheard of diversity of languages, a previously unseen diversity of eating places and previously unseen foodstuffs with strange names on the shelves of supermarkets. The old decaying inner-city suburbs have become attractive places, with terrace houses spruced up and surrounded by greenery.

At the same time, if the visitor opened a newspaper or magazine, or entered a government office, she or he would find that not much had changed. The newspapers would have coloured photographs but the content would present an Anglo-Australian view of internal and external events and issues. The stories in men's magazines would be about Anglo-Australian sporting heroes, as they always were; those in women's magazines would be about the sex lives of the members of the British royal family rather than, as they used to be, about their sporting prowess in polo or about their latest clothes. The overall content would be almost as Anglo-Australian as it ever was: monolingual and monocultural. Certainly, there might be some newspapers on the stand in languages other than English (there are in fact more newspapers in Australia published in languages other than English than in English), but none of those would rank as a major newspaper. Switching on radio or television, the impression of a monocultural Anglo-Australia is the same. 'The proverbial visitor from outer space would have difficulty identifying Australia's cultural, linguistic or racial diversity if he or she relied solely on images from the mainstream media' (Ingram, in Trevitt and Rish 1989). The exception would be the television station operated by the Special Broadcasting

161

Service, but as the service now relies increasingly on income from commercial advertising, the earlier messages on community matters presented from time to time in various languages have been largely replaced by messages from Kelloggs Cornflakes, Coca-Cola and McDonald's McFoods of every kind.

In public offices the impression would be similar. The surroundings would be more spacious, more luxurious, with greenery in the reception area and the ubiquitous computer screen on every desk; but the language, methods of working and attitudes towards the client would have the familiarity of the past. In some offices the visitor may find information pamphlets in non-English languages but, with rare exceptions, the personnel will be monolingual.

Thus, in effect, the returning visitor would find that much has changed and not much has changed. The first impression, the surface one, would be one of an ethnic and cultural diversity which was not visible earlier, but beneath the surface little change from the years past would be noticeable.

What then, if anything, has changed in Australia in the cultural sphere over the past near-half century? Has there been any significant cultural transformation in any aspect of social life, and, if so, what has been the nature of this transformation and with what effects? This chapter considers these questions by examining some of the changes which have taken place in Australian society over recent decades, focusing on those areas in which the cultural influence of various ethnic groups is most evident. It looks particularly at two areas of social life and economic activity which bear a distinct imprint of that influence: food production and corresponding eating habits, the hospitality industry and tourism; and urban renewal and change in the life styles of the urban population. It then evaluates the effects of these changes on the society's wider social and cultural life and the concomitant outcomes in the economic sphere. In doing this, the chapter raises the question: what has been the value of immigration to Australian society?

Cultural Transformation from Below

As discussed in the earlier chapters, Australian policy and public attitudes towards the post-war immigrants were for a long time assimilationist. Immigrants from non-English-speaking countries and cultures were actively discouraged from maintaining their language and customs, and were pressed to think and act like the local Anglo-Australian population. Later, the policy changed towards acceptance of some diversity through integration, to be replaced later again by a policy of multiculturalism. In practice, however, assimilationist tendencies remained strong, and, if the claims of some authoritative analysts and public commentators are to be believed (see Chapters 9 and 10), the policy of multiculturalism has not received universal acceptance by the Anglo-Australian population. Whether such claims can be substantiated is an open question; it is however clear that acceptance of the concept and policy of multiculturalism is not evident in the attitudes and operation of what we term the core social institutions. The multicultural society is visible and audible in the streets, markets and shopping arcades, in eating places and workplaces, in the architecture of some buildings and in art galleries, but not in the Anglo-Australian power structure embedded in these core institutions.

Whatever cultural transformation of Australian society has taken place it has been 'transformation from below'. Transformations of this kind normally occur for two reasons and in two corresponding ways. First, if some aspects of an imported culture are strong or attractive, they become irresistible to the host population; these attributes then influence and transform local customs, attitudes to work and leisure, lifestyle, eating habits and so on. Second, if the host society is exclusivist, isolating immigrants from the social and economic mainstream, it tends to facilitate, as it were by default, the maintenance and further development of the imported culture among the immigrant population, some aspects of which in due course breach the walls of resistance and affect the local culture.

In Australia both these phenomena have occurred. Some aspects of the imported cultures became irresistible and in time some sections of the host population adopted them, notwithstanding resistance from conservative quarters: changes in diet and eating habits, and recreational activities on Sundays are two clearly visible examples. On the other hand, the exclusivist attitudes, evident especially in the non-acceptance of immigrants' educational and occupational qualifications, have influenced – and at times forced – immigrants to engage in activities in areas in which the barriers were low or non-existent: the milkbar, the corner shop and a variety of small family businesses which became the mark of immigrant enterprises.

Immigration policy and public attitudes towards immigrants from non-English-speaking countries thus produced two different effects: on the one hand, the negative effect has been a waste of human resources with corresponding negative effects on the economic development and cultural life of the country; on the other hand, immigrant entrepreneurship has developed new or previously neglected areas of economic activity, with a corresponding positive effect on the economy and on the culture of everyday life in Australia. The examples discussed below illustrate two areas of social life in Australia where such cultural transformation from below has occurred and produced effects of considerable cultural and economic significance.

Food Production, Culinary Art and the Hospitality Industry

The change in diet and eating habits has been one of the most visible cultural, social and economic changes in Australia in the second half of the twentieth century. This change has pervaded food production and processing, the hospitality industry and tourism, as well as home cuisine. The influence of immigrants from non-English-speaking backgrounds and the economic and social effects of their contributions to these fields of activity are unmistakable. These effects are now taken for granted because this influence has been integrated into the local Anglo-Australian culture and economy. Within the context of the conceptual framework presented earlier (Figure 4.2), the skills in food production and the culinary arts which immigrants brought to their host society have been transferred to others, incorporated into the production of goods and services and, to a large extent, integrated into the broader culture of Australian society.

As Richard Beckett recalls in his book, *Convicted Tastes*:

> In 1982, when the Australian Broadcasting Commission ran a series of programs about migrant hostels in the great post-World War Two years, the horror that remained engraved in the minds of most Europeans was the food. Insults from officials, refusal to accept qualifications, terrible accommodation, and an English language that was incomprehensible to anyone but a native-born Australian; all these paled into insignificance in comparison with the food.   (1984:145)

Food on Australian tables in those years was certainly simple, monotonous and rather tasteless, and food in the transit camps where immigrants first encountered Australian cuisine was notoriously bad. Viewed in a historical perspective, the narrow utilitarian attitude to food in Australia was rather interesting, as the country was well endowed with resources conducive to growing a variety of food, especially fruit and vegetables. The situation was also interesting because horticulture in Australia, especially vegetable growing, as well as food processing, had been well developed since the mid-nineteenth century, but it was mainly in the hands of non-English-speaking immigrants. German settlers in South Australia had produced and processed their own kind of food since the mid-1800s, and Chinese immigrants supplied the market with vegetables, as Italian, Greek and Bulgarian immigrants did after them and still do today. These early immigrants also retained the diet and food culture which they brought with them, but their culinary art did not reach in to the Anglo-Australian community where an imitation of English diet and eating habits persisted without much change. The culinary transformation occurred only in the second half of this century. In this process the Anglo-Australian population became less averse to extending their tastes to new kinds of food and also discovered new ways of preparing the food which had always been available but used only in a limited and unchanging fashion.

Nowadays, a visit to the fruit and vegetable markets in all state capitals provides clear and impressive evidence that the supply of these goods comes, more than ever before, almost entirely from the non-English-speaking multicultural world of Australian society.

The impact of post-war immigration from non-English speaking countries was first noticeable in the new food products in corner shops, delicatessen outlets, milkbars and restaurants. Over time, these products aroused curiosity in Anglo-Australian consumers and found their way into their family cuisines. Many of these products were at first imported but were later grown and processed locally. The skills which immigrants brought to this area of economic activity have been of considerable significance to the developing tourist trade which is now one of the most important and expanding industries in the Australian economy. Of no lesser importance has been the influence of immigrants on Australian attitudes towards nutrition and health, and with this influence has come a growing appreciation of certain cultural values related to food.

The contribution of immigrants to improved nutrition and to the development of the hospitality industry can be better understood and appreciated if viewed in retrospect, for example, by reading Charles Price's colourful description of the Australian hospitality industry before the post-war immigrants became active in this field.

> Food, except for that served by a few enterprising French or Chinese restaurants, or by hotels located in the old German or Italian areas, was cooked in English style, often in degenerate form. Hence the weary traveller, arriving late one hot summer's night in a remote country town, might find a small Greek-owned restaurant still open and then be served, not with Greek or Italian dishes, not with refreshing salads and cheese, but with tired slabs of bacon or steak hidden beneath greasy fried eggs. In the larger cities he might be even less fortunate: few restaurants stayed open after 9 o'clock in the evening and the traveller felt himself lucky if able to buy a stale sandwich at the railway refreshment bar.   (1968:96)

One may add at this point that if there was a 'small Greek-owned restaurant' in a country town, the owner would be providing the kind of meals the local people would eat. Extending the menu beyond the traditional 'steak 'n' eggs' would have been commercially risky, and introducing 'ethnic' food might have produced a boycott of the enterprise. Now, the young and not-so-young people who delight in the diversity of ethnic cuisines in the city restaurants of the 1990s would not know (or would not want to remember) that a few decades earlier any such innovation in the culinary arts was regarded by Anglo-Australians with the same antagonism as was the sound of any non-English tongue in a public place.

The growth of the hospitality industry and its ethnic and cultural diversity 'just happened'. In a review of developments in this field, based on many years of experience, Lothar Bringmann (1988) points out that a considerable period of time had elapsed since post-war immigration began and the appearance of these enterprises on the Australian landscape. Until the late 1950s there was no organised hospitality industry, either as private enterprise or as a trade organisation. Since then, hospitality establishments have appeared in ever-increasing numbers, ranging from top-class restaurants to fast-food and take-away outlets. There are now thousands of such establishments, employing thousands of people and generating many hundreds of millions of dollars in turnover (ABS 1989, Cat. No. 8655.0).

The influence of various ethnic groups resulted in an increasing diversification in the diet of Anglo-Australians, each new ethnic community introducing a new kind of food. Ethnic cafes and restaurants grew in numbers mainly in the large cities, but gradually they have extended also into small country towns. For example, Anthony Dennis reports that Chinese restaurants had appeared in country towns already in the 1950s where they 'offered a respite from culinary philistinism, a world where the rissole was a taste sensation' (1991:24). Now, in the 1990s, a country town without an ethnic (usually Chinese or Vietnamese) cafe or restaurant would be an exception.

Eating habits in Australia have certainly changed also. Increasingly meals are being taken outside the home, either in a restaurant, in a fast-food outlet, or bought from a take-away establishment. Ethnic outlets, providing Chinese, other South-East Asian, or Middle Eastern and southern European dishes, compete with the universal transnational American McDonald's and Pizza Huts. The diversity in food on offer is great, and hospitality establishments range from low-price restaurants to expensive *haute cuisine* places, and from 'cuisine-specific' to those offering choices between European (Greek, Italian, French, etc.) and Asian (Chinese, Thai, Vietnamese, etc.) dishes. This diversity in culinary fare is not confined to meals taken outside the home. Under the influence of an expanding range of food served in commercial outlets home cuisine has also changed. The earlier prejudice against 'ethnic' food has disappeared from significant sections of the population, and experimenting with various cuisines has become especially prevalent among the new middle class. In that class, people might not have accepted multiculturalism in their hearts and minds, but they have certainly accepted it in their taste buds and stomachs. As Webb and Manderson observe:

> The diet of the mainstream culture has been influenced by increased mobility and international travel as well as by increasing immigration. Each wave of migration has made a contribution to the cuisine(s) of Australia, which today include cooking styles using ingredients from a variety of European, Middle Eastern and Asian cuisines.   (1990:156)

Some of these foodstuffs are imported but much is now also produced in Australia. The range of fruit and vegetables, even grain, now grown in the country, is impressive, and processed food is produced by new as well as old-established firms, including some multinationals. Processed food has also increasingly become an important source of export revenue, and immigrants' initiatives in this area have been of considerable significance.

With the increasing diversity of food available people have become more aware of the relationship between food and health. Ethnic influence on diet and eating habits has attracted the interest of researchers, and numerous research monographs have been published on the nutritional value of a variety of 'new' food now grown and consumed in Australia (for example, Greenfield *et al.* 1980, 1984). In addition, epidemiological research is being conducted at various Australian universities with the aim of ascertaining the relationship between diet and health in various ethnic communities. Research findings indicate a close relationship between culturally-related diet, eating habits and social environment, and the prevalence or absence of certain illnesses. For example, immigrants in certain ethnic communities who record a lower frequency of particular ailments in the early years after arrival, later tend to acquire patterns of ailments similar to those of the Australian-born population (Reid and Trompf 1990). These findings suggest that either people's health is affected by changes in diet or by changes in their social and physical environment and life-style, or by both.

Parallel with the growth of the hospitality industry has been the growth of tourism, both internal and external. The tourist industry in Australia began to take shape only in the late 1960s. Bringmann (1988) records that there was no international hotel system in the country before then; in the mid-1950s there were only 350 air-conditioned hotel rooms in Sydney and the situation was similar or worse in other large cities. From 1951 to 1955 the yearly average of short-term visitors from

other countries was 48 000, and in the next five years the yearly average
rose to 68 000 persons. In comparison, in 1990 the number of short-term
overseas visitors was 2 214 900 persons (ABS 1991, Cat. No. 3101.0).

The growth and diversification of the hospitality industry and associated activities since the late 1940s has been directly related to the
inflow and changing ethnic composition of immigrant intakes. Each
successive wave brought in new foods, new skills and new enterprises,
and through this chain of events a culinary cultural transformation has
taken place in Australia. As shown in Figure 8.1, this cultural transformation did not come through any deliberate government policy or as an
initiative of established Anglo-Australian enterprises: it was in every sense
a *transformation from below*.

The growth of the hospitality and tourism industry has created a need
for the education and training of chefs, waiters and hotel managers.
These skills are taught mainly in schools and colleges conducted under
the auspices of Technical and Further Education (TAFE), and such
schools are now operating in all States. For example, the Ryde Food
School (TAFE) in New South Wales was established in 1978 and now has
a teaching staff of around 100 persons, most of them (85 per cent)
immigrants from non-English-speaking countries (Jamrozik *et al.* 1990).
In the earlier years of the school's operation the proportion of NESB
teachers was even higher but this was gradually diluted by the first generation of the school's Australian-born graduates (many of them children
of overseas-born parents) who had gained international experience and
on return took up teaching positions. As the head of the commercial
cooking section of the Ryde School, himself an immigrant, put it:

> Looking at the hospitality industry in general, you can see that immigrants
> have had a huge impact in every shape and form; roughly 60 to 70 per cent of
> staff in big hotels are overseas-trained, and as high as 80 per cent would have
> migrant backgrounds. I always tell my students, you may find me hard to
> understand at times, but you better get used to my accent, because in this
> industry you're always working with 'foreigners'.
>
> (quoted in Jamrozik *et al.* 1990:73)

Evidence of immigrants' contribution to the food industry, hospitality
industry, tourism and eating habits in Australia are plain to see. Behind
the visible effects – restaurants, diversity of food on supermarket shelves
and so on – is an extensive food production and food processing
industry in which immigrants from non-English-speaking countries
continue to provide the stimulus for expansion, through their initiative,
knowledge and skills, and participation in the labour force. This
contribution has been multi-dimensional, and for this reason it cannot
be calculated in simple economic terms, solely as an input into the Gross

Figure 8.1: *Immigrants and Food Production/Consumption: Transfer of Knowledge Skills, Attitudes and Values*

Period	Activity
Late 1940s to early 1950s (European influence)	Skills of individual immigrants used at first in the kitchens of migrant hostels and work camps. First 'ethnic' cafes and small restaurants begin to appear.
Later 1950s to 1960s (Southern European influence)	More 'ethnic' eating outlets opened. New food production expands: vegetable growing, small goods manufacture, pasta, etc.
1970s (Asian influence)	Asian influence on culinary art begins to expand. Changing attitudes towards eating out. Fast foods/take-away industry expands. Awakening of tourism interest and its economic potential.
1980s (Cultural integration)	Expansion of hospitality industry. Government interest in tourism. Food processing expands to meet domestic demand and (some) export. Studies in nutrition and epidemiological studies of dietary habits and their effects. Extending cultural acceptance of new foods.

Source: Based on L. P. Bringmann (1988), *The Hospitality Industry in Australia* (unpublished)

Domestic Product. In spite of the resistance from the Anglo-Australian population to 'ethnic' food during the early post-war years, this culinary diversity is now taken for granted. For example, an informative publication, *Towards Better Nutrition for Australians*, issued by the Commonwealth Department of Health and Community Services (1987) elaborates at length on the health value of various food products and the economic importance of the food processing industry, but the term 'immigrant' does not appear once in all of its 112 pages.

The Building Industry and Urban Renewal

The building industry is part of the broader construction industry which includes the construction of factories, offices, bridges, houses, etc. Employment in this industry accounts for about 7 per cent of total employment (559.3 thousand or 7.2 per cent in August 1993) but the numbers fluctuate with the state of the economy. The industry employs an above-average proportion of immigrant labour: in August 1993 it was 25.2 per cent, second only to manufacturing at 33.4 per cent, and compared to the average of 24.2 per cent in the total employed labour force. Most immigrants employed in construction are from non-English-speaking countries.

Immigrants' contribution to the building of an industrial infrastructure during the post-war reconstruction period is well known, especially their legendary performance in building the Snowy Mountains hydroelectric scheme and similar large-scale work in Tasmania. Another area of construction where immigrants have made a contribution of particular economic and cultural significance has been in the house-building industry. In this field immigrants have provided labour and specialised skills, and of particular value has been their contribution by way of knowledge and skills to the restoration of heritage buildings and the renovation of old dwellings in the inner suburbs of Australia's cities.

The retention and restoration of heritage buildings became an issue of public debate and government action only in the early 1970s, during the brief period of the progressive Labor Party government under the prime ministership of Gough Whitlam. Since then many beautiful buildings of historical value, which would have been pulled down – had earlier attitudes prevailed – have been restored. However, the renovation of old dwellings began almost two decades earlier. It is a matter of history that in the late 1940s and early 1950s some of the inner suburbs of Sydney and Melbourne (and to a lesser extent of other state capitals) were regarded, with justification, as city slums, but have since become fashionable gentrified urban areas. In this transformation, which began in the 1950s, immigrants from non-English-speaking countries played an important role.

In this urban renewal a number of factors were at play. The availability of relatively cheap housing was one factor and the desire for a more communal urban way of living rather than isolation in distant suburbs was another. Added to these was the immigrants' attitude towards 'old' dwellings: people who had lived in towns and villages where buildings were hundreds of years old could not understand why anyone would want to pull down buildings that were still relatively new. Living in old houses and high density neighbourhoods meant for them a certain continuity of their culture and communality in social life. By their attitudes and actions immigrants preserved their communities and also humanised the sterile, alienating urban environment which was so typical of Australian cities. Marrickville, Cabramatta or Carlton may not be the leafy suburbs high in real estate values but they are alive with people visible on the streets and in shops, cafes and restaurants, not hiding behind high walls and alarm systems like Sydney's 'leafy North Shore' or Melbourne's Toorak. One is a community, the others just 'a good address'.

Renovation and restoration of old buildings calls for specialised knowledge and skills which were rather rare in Australia before the start of post-war immigration. Most of the skills needed came with the immigrants, especially those from southern Europe. The economic value of their contribution has been not only in urban renewal but also in the subsequent growth of enterprises and products engaged and utilised in renovation work generally. The extent of these activities, their economic value, and the extent to which the knowledge and skills have been incorporated into education and training programs has been one of the significant but now taken-for-granted benefits of post-war immigration. As with food and the hospitality industry, the value of immigrants' contribution in the area of building renovation and construction has not been solely economic but also social and cultural: in ideas and in the less-tangible contribution to the quality of life.

Immigrants from non-English-speaking countries have been (and continue to be) well represented in the building industry, as employers, self-employed and employees. For example, Burnley noted in his analysis of data from the 1966 census that Italians predominated in plaster, concrete and terrazzo work and in bricklaying occupations, to the extent that '68 per cent of all concrete workers in Melbourne were Italians' (1975:15). The majority of building enterprises consisted of small-scale employers or self-employed persons, and many of these were immigrants. This is still the case now. Among the large-scale entrepreneurs with non-English-speaking backgrounds the names of Tristan Antico (Pioneer Concrete), G. J. Dusseldorp (Lend Lease) and Franco Belgiorno-Nettis (Transfield) are well known (Glezer 1988). There are also outstanding immigrant architects who have contributed significantly to the character of Australian cities. The most notable among them is Harry Seidler, whose work includes such well-known buildings as Sydney's Australia Square, MLC Building and Grosvenor Place, as well as the Australian Embassy in Paris. His work 'spawned imitations and opened up Australia to new ideas and influences' (Sheaves 1988). The new Parliament House in Canberra is also a creation of an immigrant architect, Romaldo Giugola; and the most famous building of all in Australia, Sydney Opera House, was conceived and designed by Jørn Utzon from Denmark who, regrettably, unable to complete his work because of the bureaucratic heavy-handedness of state government authorities, left Australia swearing never to return (Ellis 1992).

The most significant contribution that immigrants have made to urban renewal has been in the restoration and renovation of old buildings in the decaying suburbs of the large cities, as previously noted. In the 1950s and 1960s, when the push to the open spaces of the ever more distant suburbs was creating the urban sprawl, immigrants from non-English-speaking countries were transforming the inner slum-like suburbs into attractive urban areas. Documentation of this process of transformation is rather scarce, and the 'trendy' gentrified inner suburbs are now taken for granted. As McCall *et al.* note:

> Indeed, it was the immigrants from Southern Europe that began the residential revitalisation process in the inner suburbs of Sydney, Melbourne, Adelaide and Perth, later taken over by middle class and/or alternative lifestyle groups. (1985:19)

Brief accounts of the immigrants' role in that process can be found in Burnley (1974:131–46) and Jupp (1984a:110–28), and a more extensive account in Kendig's *New Life for Old Suburbs* (1979), which records the history of post-war urban renewal in Sydney, Melbourne and Adelaide. Kendig records that in the immediate post-war years the inner-city suburbs of the three cities were in an advanced state of decay. In Sydney, a special Council (Cumberland County) was established in 1945 to plan the city's future development. The Council found some inner suburbs to be in such a state of decay that any preservation of old housing in these areas was to be regarded as only a 'temporary expedient' measure until the housing shortage was relieved and redevelopment had started. In 1947 the Council estimated that '40 000 inner-suburban dwellings, a third of the stock, were so bad that they required immediate replacement'. Another 49 000 dwellings would have to be replaced in the following 25 years and yet another 29 000 in 50 years' time, a total of 118 000 dwellings. The inner suburbs had 95 per cent of the Sydney's total housing designated as substandard (Kendig 1979:106).

People living in those suburbs were reluctant to meet the high costs of renovation, especially as they expected that a large-scale planned redevelopment was going to take place at some time in the near future. Many dwellings were occupied by tenants, not owners, and neither the owners nor the tenants were inclined to do much maintenance work; the former because of cost, the latter because they expected to move out to new public housing estates as soon as houses became available. At the same time, the inner suburbs attracted the attention of the recently arrived immigrants from non-English-speaking countries who were used to living in cities or in small towns with high-density dwellings. A transition thus occurred in the 1950s, with the Anglo-Australians moving out to new suburbs further away from the city centre and immigrants moving in, buying the old dwellings at low prices and beginning to renovate them. As Kendig records:

> Part of the increased value of the properties resulted from improvements by the new owner-occupants. During the late 1950s, the number of houses that were renovated increased further. Even poor owners, who could not afford the

major alterations and additions ... did a considerable amount of cleaning, and repairing roofs and plumbing.   (1979:115)

In the early 1960s immigrants were still the major buyers of the inner-suburb terrace houses, but by the late 1960s the gentrification process had begun. In less than two decades an area such as Paddington in Sydney, which was declared a slum by post-war planners, became an elegant suburb of beautifully restored terrace houses and an example of the gentrification phenomenon to be followed throughout Australia. Similar processes took place in the inner suburbs of Melbourne and Adelaide.

In his study of urban politics of the 1960s, Jakubowicz notes that it was the southern European immigrants who 'did most to invalidate the planning projections for urban renewal that were developed for the major cities' (1974:329–43). The 'spontaneous rehabilitation by owner-occupants' in the 1950s prevented the large-scale demolition plans of the authorities and preserved the character of the inner suburbs. Although excluded from any actual decision-making, these immigrants had effectively redefined the nature of the urban environment. The new middle class took over the renovation and preservation process only after the immigrants had shown what could be done with old decaying buildings and slum areas. This transformation process, as shown in Figure 8.2, is still continuing.

How significant was the immigrants' contribution in this cultural transformation, and how can it be evaluated? The attitudes towards urban living which the immigrants brought with them, the appreciation of 'old' buildings, the willingness (partly motivated by the necessity of acquiring relatively cheap housing) to restore old buildings, and the skills to do it – all played an important role in changing the environment in Australia's cities. The demonstrable effects of these efforts also led to the awakening awareness in Australians of the value of preservation and conserving of the country's heritage.

By and large, this contribution is not only unacknowledged, but some critics have perceived immigrants' attraction to city living in a negative light. For example, Colin Hay expressed the view that the impact of immigration on the environment of the cities was 'almost entirely unfavourable' (1978:103–14). Hay argued that no provisions were made at the time for the scale of population increase in city planning, land-use regulation, housing development, or for the provision of sewerage and storm water disposal; as well as there was the question of air pollution. He did not blame the immigrants directly for these problems but the inference of the need to keep immigrants away from large cities, or stop immigration, is clearly there. He considered the feasibility of directing immigrants to new growth areas, but he saw inevitable 'serious

Figure 8.2: *Immigrants and Urban Renewal: Transfer of Knowledge, Skills, Attitudes and Values*

Period	Activity
Late 1940s	Inner suburbs of large cities in a decayed state, many areas in slum condition. Authorities consider large-scale demolition of buildings and re-development, some of it in the form of high-rise residential buildings.
1950s to early 1960s	Immigrants from non-English-speaking countries move into the inner suburbs and become owner-occupiers of old dwellings. Renovation, alteration and addition to dwellings begins to take place.
Late 1960s to early 1970s	As the previously decaying and slum areas change character they become attractive to young new middle-class Anglo-Australians. Immigrants sell their dwellings and move out to the adjacent suburbs. Attitudes to urban living change.
Late 1970s to 1990s	Gentrification process almost completed in the inner suburbs and extending to adjacent suburbs. Revitalised inner areas now sought after by the affluent new middle class. Attitudes towards conservation generally also changing, higher density housing (not high-rise) encouraged by local councils and state governments. Renovation skills now incorporated into trades and used also by do-it-yourself people.

Source: Based on H. Kendig (1979), *New Life for Old Suburbs: Post-war Land Use and Housing in the Australian Inner City*, Sydney

integration problems' in such a solution, 'given the fact that future migrants are likely to be heavily Asian in background' (1978:111). More recently, similar voices have also been raised (for example, Barnett 1990), expressing concern at the negative effects of immigrants' tendency to settle in large cities rather than in smaller country centres. It seems from these expressions of concern that immigrants settling in the large cities pollute the environment, unlike the locally-born Anglo-Australians who also live there in large numbers. Such views are rather strange, especially as there are also concerns expressed from time to time at the depopulation of inner-city suburbs, a trend which the immigrants have at least slowed down because of their interest in inner-city living (Sheridan 1990).

Cultural Transformation in a Wider Perspective

The two areas of economic activity presented in this chapter as examples of the influence of non-English-speaking immigrants on the cultural life of Australia are certainly not the only areas where their influence is now evident. Many immigrants recruited as manual labour in manufacturing and other industries engaged in material production remained in such jobs and experienced little occupational mobility. Others wanted to be independent, established their own enterprises, usually small family businesses, and became quite successful in their ventures. Such business ventures were usually of the kind that Anglo-Australians did not find attractive and which did not require enormous amounts of capital but a great amount of physical work and long hours. The fish-and-chip shop and the milkbar, which are open long hours, have been part of the Australian urban scene for decades. Small business became the trade mark of immigrant entrepreneurs, and in some immigrant groups the proportion of self-employed persons is above the average for Australian-born persons.

Small business enterprises are a feature of immigrant communities in most countries of western Europe, the United States and Canada. As Waldinger *et al.* record (1990), coffee shops, restaurants, corner shops, and service industries generally, have been established by immigrants in all these countries. Often such enterprises are established to meet, in the first instance, the special needs of an ethnic community itself, but later their activities are extended to serve a wider community.

Self-employment in the small-business field among immigrants in Australia has followed a similar pattern. In an extensive longitudinal study of small business enterprises covering the whole country, Strahan and Williams (1988) examined a sample of 4113 immigrant entrepreneurs conducting a total of 2130 enterprises. Most entrepreneurs (73 per cent) were born in Europe, 20 per cent were born in Asia, and the remainder in Africa, the Americas and Oceania. The largest group of enterprises was in retailing (37 per cent), followed by various kinds of enterprises in the service industries (34 per cent), manufacturing (16 per cent), and wholesale trade and primary industries (13 per cent). Most of the businesses (70 per cent) were conducted by the people who established them. The majority were successful, but in the period of study, 1973 to 1984, 47 per cent of them had failed. The researchers concluded that immigrant entrepreneurs in small business were comparatively better performers than people operating small businesess generally, but small business is a risky area and failure rates are always high.

In another study of small business ventures in the Sydney metro-politan area, Castles *et al.* (1991) recorded results similar to those of

Strahan and Williams. The reported reasons for the above-average frequency of self-employment among certain immigrant groups were the desire for independence and autonomy, previous difficulties in obtaining recognition and acceptance of educational and occupational qualifications, and unemployment. Castles *et al.* found that the price paid by the entrepreneurs for the freedom to conduct their own business was high and involved 'long working hours, few holidays, the need for unpaid work by the whole family'. They also concluded from their study that the 'high presence of migrants in the small business sector in Australia highlights a hitherto unrecognised economic contribution of immigrants, especially by those from NES [non-English-speaking] countries' (1991:13).

Immigrants' contribution to the development of business enterprises was acknowledged by the then Minister for Immigration, in a report on small business ventures initiated and successfully operated by non-English-speaking immigrants. The Minister wrote:

> ... no sector of the Australian economy has been more influenced by the vigour and resourcefulness of our immigrant entrepreneurs – men and women who adopted Australia as their new home, who brought with them great skills and talents, and who are now playing a critical role in the reconstruction of Australia's economic foundations.
>
> (G. Hand, in Pascoe 1990)

Once again, the value of the contribution of immigrants to the development of industry in Australia cannot be adequately measured in narrow economic terms alone, and has to be seen also in its social and cultural dimensions. The two case studies discussed earlier are particularly important in this regard because they illustrate how cultural transformation of considerable significance has occurred through the influence of 'ordinary' working-class people who on arrival in their new country saw certain opportunities for economic advancement, which the local Anglo-Australian population either did not see or did not want to exploit. The immigrants also saw the need for change in certain areas of social life in their host society, which they found strange and in some ways somewhat primitive.

The examples in this chapter illustrate the significance of what could be seen by some people as the strength of a 'folk culture', but the examples also illustrate the significance of the strength of a social class. In Europe, as well as in other parts of the world, the continuity of cultural identity has been maintained by farming and industrial working-class communities. It is such communities that have always been the carriers of culture and vehicles of history. Profound political changes, wars, oppression and shifting national boundaries have not destroyed the language, cultural traditions and ethnic identity even of small communities. Immigrants in Australia, beginning with the early involuntary Irish immigrants, have demonstrated that the continuity of cultural identity can be transferred to another country and maintained, despite social and religious discrimination and economic disadvantage. The post-war immigrants from non-English-speaking countries resisted deliberate and often overtly assimilationist pressures from the dominant culture and power structure, and have retained their cultural identity. Moreover, as the examples in this chapter show, some important aspects of their cultures became irresistible to the host society, either for economic reasons or for reasons of taste.

It is the contemporary new middle class 'trend setters' who live in the charming terrace houses of Paddington or Richmond, or in the 'maisonettes' of Norwood. They sip their cappucinos and chew Danish, French, Italian or Lebanese pastries, sitting under colourful parasols in the outdoor cafes of Lygon, Oxford or William Streets, discussing their latest or forthcoming travels to Thailand, Fiji, Italy or England. They buy a variety of 'ethnic' foodstuffs in gourmet shops and entertain friends in their homes by demonstrating their knowledge and skills in preparing and serving exotic ethnic dishes. When they feel off-colour they probably take some 'natural' medication which, they have heard or read, is effectively used in India, China or Thailand. Their working life, however, is spent in government or private business offices, or in professional chambers, where only English is spoken, where most people are Anglo-Australians or immigrants from England or perhaps from the United States. If there is an immigrant from a non-English-speaking background employed in such a workplace, he or she will be well educated and thoroughly assimilated to the Anglo-Australian atmosphere, even to the point of a changed name to ease difficulties in pronunciation and spelling.

Cultural transformation for most Anglo-Australian middle-class people is thus limited to the acceptance of pleasures in new food, drink, entertainment, style of living and travel, and an occasional 'ethnic' film on SBS television. This is how far cultural pluralism in this class goes; but beyond this, in the seats of power Anglo-Australian exclusivity remains virtually untouched.

Has cultural transformation therefore been an illusion? To answer this question one needs to keep in mind that although the cultural influences illustrated by the examples in this chapter have been ethnically-specific, they have produced somewhat different outcomes in each case. In the first example, the ethnic origins of the influence are visible, but in the second example the change has acquired a universal character to the extent that interest in building renovation has become widespread and preservation of heritage buildings is now of national interest. Another area of cultural influence has been in the arts, that is music, painting and sculpture, theatre, and literature. In all these fields individual immigrants, and now their children, have made and continue to make significant contributions to the cultural transformation of Australian society (Australia Council 1986). However, the arts in Australia, a multi-cultural mosaic with distinctive influences from many cultures, is an area we cannot explore further here.

The one area of society which has remained relatively immune to non-Anglo cultural influences has been the power structure, as already noted. This does not mean only the political parties which form governments but also the whole system of core institutions which constitute that structure and the interests, ideologies, values and attitudes which are part of it. In effect, the dominant social class has resisted cultural transformation, resulting in a dichotomy of cultural transformation 'below' and mono-cultural continuity 'above'. This dichotomous outcome may appear strange at first sight but is not unusual. Indeed, there have been notable examples in history of cultural diversity and cultural transformation in certain aspects of social life co-existing with, and being deliberately used to maintain, an overarching monocultural or mono-ideological power structure: the Roman Empire, the British Empire, and the Soviet Union have been outstanding examples. In Australia, Jakubowicz (1981), de Lepervanche (1984), Collins (1988) and others have argued that the policy of multiculturalism promoted by the conservative Coalition government in the late 1970s and early 1980s was used to maintain that government in power and to preserve the class interests which that government represented and wanted to protect. Since then the rhetoric of change has not been reflected in the operation of the core institutions; on the contrary, voices against the acceptance of ethnic diversity have grown louder in some quarters. It is a sobering thought, however, to note that throughout history all such attempts, attempts to maintain a certain power structure and resist cultural transformation, have resulted in due course in the demise of those structures. There seems to be a lesson for Australia in this, somewhere.

The Effects of Cultural Transformation

The arguments against immigration and multiculturalism are examined in greater detail in the next chapter. The aim of this chapter has been to demonstrate that the cultural transformation which has occurred in certain aspects of social life in Australia through the stimulus provided by NESB immigrants has had, and continues to have, economic value of considerable magnitude. The fact that the role of immigrants in the areas of economic activity where such transformation has occurred is now taken for granted is an indication that the knowledge and skills they brought into the country have been transferred to other persons, incorporated into the production process and integrated with the host culture (cell 4(iv) in Figure 4.2).

In the reductionist arguments advanced against continued immigration intake, which became so prevalent in the late 1980s and early 1990s, the potential value of the transfer and integration of knowledge and skills referred to above is ignored and the value of immigration is perceived solely as a necessary supplementary labour force in times of labour scarcity (cell 1(i) in Figure 4.2). The analysts and commentators who present such views fail to see the very important economic contribution immigrants have made and continue to make precisely through their own culturally different approach to economic matters. It has been exactly this kind of different perceptions of resources and opportunities that has enabled those immigrants to become instrumental in transforming Anglo-Australians' perceptions and awareness of certain resources and thus become prime movers in the cultural transformation of Australian society. Further, we may ask if such anti-immigration arguments are arrived at through sound economic analysis, or are spurious economic reasons advanced with the aim of keeping old prejudices and fears alive in order to safeguard certain vested interests? Are the arguments motivated by fear that continuous immigration of people from non-English speaking countries, particularly if such immigrants are well educated and skilled in trades or professions, will mean greater pressure for social change and cultural transformation, not only in food, eating habits, or urban surroundings, but also in education, professional attitudes, public administration, and perhaps political structures as well?

Assessments of Australia's imported human resources purely as commodities akin to goods that can be purchased in a supermarket, conducted in a conceptually-confined perspective of economic reductionism, ignore the social and cultural as well as economic values immigrants do or potentially can contribute to the development of skills and to the production process. Because human production, be it material or mental, is a cultural product, the full value of that production cannot be realised without cultural acceptance by, and cultural transformation of, the social environment in which the production takes place. That social environment has to include the environment of the social institutions through which the 'command over resources through time' is exercised. In other words, for society to achieve the full potential of the human resources imported through immigration, conditions need to be created for cultural transformation to encompass the entire social structure.

CHAPTER 9

The Monocultural Resistance to Change

Although Australia has undertaken a high level of importation of human resources for some decades, the country's economic and social development has lagged behind other industrialised and industrialising countries. Why has this been so? It is argued in this chapter that one important reason for this decline has been the cultural conservatism embedded in Australia's social institutions and class structure. The cultural diversity which has grown through the impact of the immigration program and is now present in many aspects of social life is not very evident in the core social institutions, such as the tertiary education sector, the public service (especially in its higher echelons), the political parties and the government, and the established Christian churches. Resistance to cultural transformation is particularly evident in the professions, such as medicine, teaching, social work and the law.

This chapter analyses the role of these core institutions in the resistance to cultural change. It looks more closely at some of the processes which are not readily visible in organisational operations except by inference, but which are highly significant in the resistance to change. It also examines some of the arguments advanced by so-called expert analysts, public commentators and politicians who present ostensibly logical arguments against immigration and multiculturalism, but whose actions in fact serve to revive old prejudices and fears in the Anglo-Australian population. It is a curious situation which raises the Roman question, *cui bono?* This is because the arguments and issues put forward do not seem to be substantiated by empirical evidence or reflected in the everyday life of Australian society.

The Culture of Resistance to Cultural Change

Resistance to change may be individual or institutional, and in this chapter the focus is mainly on the latter. It is appropriate to consider institutional resistance to change because institutions are the vehicles of continuity and, as such, they function on principles of stability and predictability, not change. Institutions tend to exert pressure on individuals to conform to established values, attitudes and practices, and it is through such pressure that individual attitudes and values, including resistance to change, become institutionalised and become part of a society's culture. These characteristics are common to all social institutions: the family, the school, the church, the professional association, or the bureaucracy of public administration. These institutions also interact with their environment; they project, and in certain situations impose, the institutionalised culture on the community. This may be done by the law which they administer and also by a variety of socialising methods aimed at achieving people's acquiescence to the values and interests of the institution.

The history of institutional attitudes to immigration in Australia is a history of a *culture of resistance to cultural change*. This resistance became institutionalised last century, expressed at first through the antagonism towards Chinese immigrants, later extended to other ethnic or national groups and then culminated in the White Australia policy. Although this policy was eventually abandoned in the 1960s, each successive national or ethnic group arriving in the country during the post-war immigration program evoked fear of a threat to British or Anglo-Australian traditions and cultural homogeneity. Fears expressed in the early post-war years about eastern Europeans, Italians and Greeks were later replaced by fears of Chinese, Vietnamese and Khmer people, commonly referred to as 'Asians', and fear of people practising Islam, commonly referred to as 'Arabs'. Yet, it is also an established fact that Australian society has accommodated itself to successive influxes of newcomers without undue strain or conflict. Why, then, does this attitude of fear and antagonism persist, and why has this attitude intensified in the late 1980s and early 1990s? Who have been, and continue to be, the actors in the formation and maintenance of these attitudes? In which social institutions is resistance to cultural change particularly evident?

What follows is an attempt to examine these questions and provide some explanations. Beginning with some comments on the policies of successive governments, the chapter then examines some empirical evidence and looks at the role of the media and some of the commentators and analysts who have used the media to propound their views.

Finally, the question is posed as to what extent the resistance to cultural transformation is in fact a defence of class interests.

Government Policies and Policy Reviews

Looking back over the years, it is not difficult to see that the immigration program has brought great economic and cultural benefits to Australia. At the same time, as we have already discussed, there has also been a waste of imported human resources and their potential: an irretrievable loss which Australia has incurred through policies based on rather primitive, narrow, sometimes crude views of immigrants. The attitudes of governments, public administrators, professional bodies and trade unions have hindered rather than facilitated the process of utilising imported talents and skills and integrating them into a developing new cultural environment. This pattern of inhibition and hindrance was set up from the outset by recruiting immigrants with a wide range of knowledge and skills but then reducing all occupations for non-English-speaking immigrants to two categories: 'labourers' for men, and 'domestics' for women. To this day, any occupational qualifications above that of labourer or 'unskilled worker' which might be claimed by an immigrant from a non-English-speaking background have to be examined, tested and approved by government officialdom as well as a professional body or trade union. After nearly half a century of conducting an immigration program, the progress the country has achieved in this area has been minimal.

In addition to these inhibiting factors, a feature of government actions relating to settlement and integration has been one of 'slow learning'. This is clearly evident in the chronology of government initiatives aimed at assisting immigrants in the settlement process. The immmigration program began in 1947 but government responses of the facilitative kind came much later, for example:

- The Translation Unit in the Department of Immigration was not established until 1960.
- A Language Training Program for Migration Officers in, or selected for, overseas service with the Department of Immigration was introduced in 1965.
- The Committee on Overseas Professional Qualifications (COPQ) was formed in 1969.
- The Telephone Interpreter Service (TIS) was introduced in 1973.

The situation changed in the 1970s and continued to improve in the 1980s, but towards the end of that decade a distinct reversal in this trend began and continued strongly. This shift occurred despite the government's avowed commitment to the continuation of the immigration program and explicit actions taken towards further development of the policy of multiculturalism. Some indication of how the shift occurred and what forces were at play in that shift can be gleaned from a brief examination of certain events which took place at the time.

In the later 1980s three government-sponsored bodies each published a document on immigration and multiculturalism. Viewed together, the three documents give a distinct indication that behind the government's manifest policy of sustained immigration and promotion of a multicultural society an increasingly powerful reaction was building up in certain sections of society and in some parts of government administration, exerting pressure for a change in policy. The voices of that reaction advocated a reduction of immigrant intake or even a complete cessation of immigration, on economic grounds, arguing that in times of high rates of unemployment immigration exacerbated the problem. Other ostensibly economic arguments such as high foreign debt, capital outflow, pressure on resources and so on were usually added for good measure. However, with these 'economic' arguments were interwoven arguments about dangers to social cohesion, threats to 'the Australian way of life', national disunity, disloyalty to Australia, and a host of other similar arguments.

The three documents were: *Don't Settle for Less*, Report of the Committee for Stage 1 of the Review of Migrant and Multicultural Programs and Services (ROMAMPAS), published in August 1986; a Discussion Paper, *Towards a National Agenda for a Multicultural Australia*, by the Advisory Council on Multicultural Affairs (ACMA), published in September 1988; and *Immigration: a Commitment to Australia*, by the Committee to Advise on Australia's Immigration Policies (CAAIP), submitted to the government in May 1988, but released to the public later that year. All three reports have been mentioned here in earlier chapters, but they need to be considered together so that their significance as instruments of attitude formation and policy validation may be appreciated.

The ROMAMPAS Committee (Professor James Jupp, Chairman) was established in December 1985 and its brief was to 'advise on the Federal Government's role in assisting overseas-born residents to achieve their equitable participation in Australian society'. The committee was given fairly simple terms of reference:

(a) propose appropriate principles to guide the development of the Federal Government's role and policies; and

(b) advise on essential elements of, and priorities within, a strategy to implement the Government's role and policies over the next decade. (ROMAMPAS 1986: v)

To achieve these objectives the committee was to examine the needs of immigrants in the settlement stage, identify the existing arrangements and services in that area, suggest and recommend appropriate policy and administrative remedies, and identify likely constraints on resources if the suggestions and recommendations were to be adopted. The committee was also to take into account the roles and activities of state governments and non-government sectors such as unions, employers, community organisations and ethnic communities; and the need for wide consultations with these organisations and other relevant bodies.

The committee undertook a wide range of consultations and received a large number of submissions. In its report it traced the history of immigration in Australia and then focused on the situation in the 1980s. It concluded that immigration had had demonstrable positive economic, social and cultural effects for Australia, but to enhance the value of the imported human resources the settlement process of immigrants needed to be facilitated by certain provisions based on democratic principles of equity, participation and acceptance of cultural diversity under the concept of multiculturalism. To fulfil these objectives, the committee argued, there would have to be a significant institutional change. The report stated, *inter alia*:

> There is considerable evidence of inequities arising from the failure of many institutions to take appropriate account of the linguistic and cultural differences in the community, and to involve clients and consumers of services in determining the nature of those services. To effectively address these shortcomings requires significant institutional change: in the manner in which services are provided; ... in organisational decision-making structures and processes; ... in awareness and knowledge ...   (1986: 93)

Indeed, the need for *institutional change* was the main theme in the committee's recommendations. The committee argued that to facilitate immigrants' settlement and enhance their equitable participation in Australian society, government policy 'must address not only the changes that the individual must make to function effectively in Australia but also the changes required of the institutions of society and society itself to adjust to diversity' (*ibid*.: 323).

Negative attitudes and resistance to multiculturalism in public institutions were issues which the committee viewed as problems of considerable magnitude. Recalling the committee's inquiries in a conference address, the Chairman of the ROMAMPAS commented that despite national and state programs designed to assist the non-English-speaking communities, the committee had found in public institutions 'general indifference or even hostility' to actually doing something positive in that area. He observed:

> Few, if any public agencies expressed open hostility towards catering for those who were not of British or Irish origin. But many regard this whole area of public policy as marginal and unimportant – unworthy of allocating financial and human resources beyond what was already available.   (Jupp 1988a:65)

The establishment of the Advisory Council on Multicultural Affairs (Sir James Gobbo, Chairman) was one outcome of the ROMAMPAS report (the other was the establishment of the Office of Multicultural Affairs in the Department of the Prime Minister and Cabinet). The ACMA Discussion Paper (1988) followed broadly the direction outlined in the ROMAMPAS report. As requested by the, then, Prime Minister, R. J. L. Hawke, ACMA was to assist in the preparation of a 'National Agenda for a Multicultural Australia', and its Discussion Paper was written for that purpose. Its commitment to the concept and policy of multiculturalism was explicit, and, like the ROMAMPAS report, this paper asserted:

> Multiculturalism is above all else about institutional change. It is not basically about introducing special measures to aid immigrants or NESB Australians, although at times such measures are necessary to ensure equity. Far more fundamentally multiculturalism involves making sure that the institutions and processes of society are genuinely responsive to the needs and aspirations of *all* members of the community. (ACMA 1988:160)

The change advocated by ACMA was comprehensive, one could say holistic. Substantiated by the arguments for equal access to resources, its report focused on access to services, employment, political participation, recognition of overseas qualifications, language resources and other related areas. The report emphasised the significance of cultural factors, pointing out that cultural and linguistic barriers in government programs created unfairness and waste, and the reason for this was the inherited British monoculture. It explained the issue as follows:

> At the core of this situation is the fact that most of Australia's structures and mechanisms are derived from a particular cultural tradition, that of Britain. For much of the last 200 years it has implicitly been assumed that Australia was a British society transplanted to the other side of the world. (1988:161)

The report pointed out that this orientation was no longer appropriate, even for economic reasons such as trade which was increasingly being conducted with the neighbouring South-East Asian countries. Demographic and cultural reasons were equally important, as less than half of the Australian population was solely of Anglo-Celtic descent and almost one in four Australians had no such ancestry. The inequities and inefficiencies persisting in Australian institutions were thus due to the mismatch between the monocultural British tradition and the country's multicultural population. Institutional change was therefore needed to effect a structural responsiveness which would lead to social cohesion rather than cleavages and divisions in the multicultural society. Social institutions had to reflect social reality.

Both the ROMAMPAS and the ACMA reports advocated the necessity for maintaining public awareness of the multicultural nature of Australian society, and emphasised the responsibility of the government for that function. The ROMAMPAS report recommended, among other things, the establishment of a parliamentary Standing Committee on Ethnic Affairs and Multiculturalism, 'to examine the participation of overseas-born residents and their families in the community and the general development and promotion of multiculturalism in Australia' (1986: 351). The ACMA report noted that in consultations with the community suggestions had been received for consideration to be given to the passing of a multiculturalism act, similar to the then recently introduced Canadian Bill 'for the preservation and enhancement of multiculturalism in Canada' (1988:137–8). The ACMA thought that these suggestions warranted discussion on the advisability of such an act, and on its purpose and content. Both reports thus sought to obtain political accceptance of multiculturalism and possibly give it a permanent nation-wide legal basis through parliamentary endorsement.

The report of the Committee to Advise on Australia's Immigration Policies (Dr Stephen FitzGerald, Chairman) was an entirely different document, and its arguments and recommendations presented a powerful antidote to those of the other two reports. The CAAIP terms of reference stated that the Committee should address all pertinent matters including, in broad terms, the following:

• the relationship between immigration and the economy, including the effects on the labour market and economic development;
• the relationship between immigration and Australia's social and cultural development as a multicultural society;
• the relationship between immigration and key population issues;
• the overall capacity of Australia to receive significant immigration intakes; and
• the relationship between immigration policies including compliance, and the administrative and legislative processes involved.

The committee certainly interpreted its terms of reference 'in broad terms': it did examine the economic aspects of immigration and expressed its support for a continued, even numerically extended immigration program, but at the same time it provided extensive arguments which could be interpreted as arguments against immigration, and certainly against immigration from non-English-speaking countries. Furthermore, it presented these negative arguments not as arguments of the CAAIP itself but as arguments prevalent in the community. The CAAIP report (entitled *Immigration: a Commitment to Australia*) was indeed an interesting document, for the community views it reported were of the '*on dit*' variety: nowhere in the report was it stated from which sections of the community the negative arguments had come, but the impression was given that these views were widely held. Moreover, as some excerpts from the report quoted below indicate, although the reported views were ostensibly against continued immigration, they were really arguments against the changing culture of Australia and against the policies of multiculturalism. For example, the report stated:

> Problems with current immigration policies are not limited to numbers. Widespread mistrust and failing consensus threaten community support of immigration. The program is not identified in the public mind with the public interest, and must be given a convincing rationale ...
>
> Many Australians are not convinced that immigrants are making a commitment to their new country. Inevitable changes to their society, brought by immigration, trouble them. Poor rates for the taking up of citizenship disturb them ...
>
> Confusion and mistrust of multiculturalism, focusing of the suspicion that it drove immigration policy, was broadly articulated. Many people, from a variety of occupational and cultural backgrounds, perceived it as divisive. The majority of these people also expressed concern about immigrants' commitment to Australia and to Australian principles and institutions. (1988:xi–xii)

The difference in the perspectives projected by the ROMAMPAS Committee and the CAAIP is striking. As shown in the two comparative excerpts quoted below, the former acknowledges some resistance and antagonism to ethnic and cultural diversity but overall it presents fairly positive attitudes in the community. The latter emphasises the negatives and gives a clear impression that negative attitudes are widely held in all sections of society, including immigrant communities.

> ROMAMPAS: There is considerable support for the view that community awareness, understanding and acceptance of Australia's social diversity should be promoted. The main reasons advanced for this are that it would assist in reducing what is seen as considerable ignorance of – and prejudice toward – immigrants and Australian born people of non-English speaking background, and their contribution to the development of Australian society. (p. 71)
>
> The Committee is not persuaded there is a level of tension between people of different ethnic and cultural backgrounds which poses a major threat to social cohesion, and which should cause the abandonment of multiculturalism as an appropriate response to the diversity of the Australian community. (pp.81–2)
>
> CAAIP: Multiculturalism, which is associated in the public mind with immigration, is seen by many as social engineering which actually invites injustice, inequality and divisiveness. (p. 5)
>
> The Committee can find little to rejoice at in the suspicion towards immigrants and immigration which is reflected in community suspicion of multiculturalism. But that is also a fact. Of all immigration issues, strong feeling about multiculturalism seems to extend most widely, across politics, from traditional Labor voters to traditional Liberal and National voters, from

trade unionists to business people, from blue collar workers to academics, and from older generation to newly arrived Australians. (pp. 10–11)

The reports of the two committees were produced two years apart and the impressions of each committee were gained from surveys and consultations in the same society. Yet the reported findings of each committee were quite different, and particularly different were the interpretations of findings, conclusions and recommendations. The ROMAMPAS report accepted the social reality of ethnic and cultural diversity in Australia and called for *institutional change* which would reflect that reality. The CAAIP report emphasised certain Australian values – parliamentary democracy, freedom of speech, religion, equality of women, universal education, etc. – and also a high standard of living and open, relaxed life-style, the values to which *immigrants should show commitment*. An impression was created in the report that 'many people' saw these values threatened by immigration and the policy of multiculturalism.

The CAAIP report used the low rate of take-up of Australian citizenship by immigrants as an indicator of the lack of commitment to Australia. It was somewhat ironic that it gave prominence to the concern about cultural cohesion which it saw being threatened by questionable immigration selection procedures and emphasised the importance of English in immigrants' usefulness for Australia; but at the same time it found that the low rate of the take-up of Australian citizenship was particularly prominent among immigrants from Britain. It noted that according to the 1981 census data, 43 per cent of overseas-born residents who were eligible to become Australian citizens had not done so, and about 60 per cent of these were immigrants from the United Kingdom and Ireland (CAAIP 1988:11).

Undoubtedly the authors of the CAAIP report intended to highlight the concerns expressed to them about immigration and multiculturalism, but even a sympathetic reader of the report would not escape the impression of a bias favouring critical and negative views on these issues. By contrast, opposing views received only passing comment, as did submissions from ethnic communities. Furthermore, the report stated that the 'immigrant voice the Committee heard most was an institutionalised voice' (1988:33), thus creating an impression that opinions which questioned immigration and multiculturalism policy had come from 'concerned citizens', while those in favour of the policy had come from organisations which had a vested interest in the policy – the 'ethnic lobby'.

One of the main concerns of the CAAIP was clearly the perceived threat of cultural diversity and the lack of loyalty among immigrants to their new country, Australia, which the committee saw in the views it received from 'concerned citizens'. The committee wanted to overcome this problem by recommending to the government to

> examine ways of restricting public benefits to non-citizens as a means of enhancing the value of citizenship, ... entitlement to sponsor immigrants be limited to Australian citizens, except in instances where those being sponsored are spouses, dependent children, or refugee/humanitarian cases ... [and] citizenship ceremonies be made more meaningful by linking the grant of citizenship with a declaration to respect fundamental institutions and principles in Australian society, and that this declaration be foreshadowed when immigrants are selected.   (1988:121)

Unlike the recommendations of the ROMAMPAS Committee or the views of the ACMA, the CAAIP report certainly did not see any need for institutional change so as to reflect the cultural diversity of Australian population. On the contrary, the report clearly indicated that cultural diversity would have to be compatible with what the committee perceived to be the fundamental institutions and principles of Australian society. The report did not advocate a return to the assimilationist policies of the 1950s and 1960s, but its comments certainly could be interpreted as suggestions for such policies.

Public Attitudes and Authoritative Opinions

Which of the views reported in the three documents reflected the views of the general public? Each committee had to perform its commissioned task with somewhat different although similar terms of reference, but it is also transparently clear that each committee approached its task with clearly different attitudes. Consequently, each report presented findings with a particular emphasis and differential weight given to certain community views, and so reached very different conclusions.

What, then, were community views on immigration and multiculturalism at the time? Some indications of public attitudes to these issues were recorded in a nation-wide survey commissioned by the Office of Multicultural Affairs and conducted in 1988, at about the same time as the CAAIP conducted its inquiries (OMA 1989b). The survey obtained opinions from four samples of the population: a general random sample of 1552 persons; a sample of 823 persons whose parents or one parent were born overseas; a sample of 986 immigrants from non-English-speaking countries; and a sample of 1141 persons who had arrived in Australia since 1981. In the general random sample 1306 persons (84.1 per cent) were Australian-born and 246 persons (15.9 per cent) were naturalised immigrant citizens. Some data extracted from the results of that survey are shown in Tables 9.1 to 9.5.

Recorded attitudes to immigration policy are shown in Table 9.1, indicating that the majority of replies was in favour of higher immigration levels or at least maintaining the existing levels. This majority in favour of sustained immigration held these views in regard to immigration as a whole as well as to each ethnic or regional immigrant group mentioned in the survey. Views in favour of increasing immigration were distinctly higher in the sample of non-English-speaking immigrants and in the sample of recent arrivals. A high percentage of views in favour of British immigrants was recorded almost at the same level by all four samples; attitudes to other ethnic groups varied, being higher in favour of immigration in the samples of non-English-speaking immigrants and the recent arrivals than in the other two samples. A large majority in all four samples was in favour of bringing in immigrants who would do work that no Australian wanted to do, somehow indicating that in their views this might still be one of the aims of the immigration program.

Table 9.2 shows respondents' replies to questions about multiculturalism. There is no indication in these replies of any great antagonism to multiculturalism, and there is a remarkable consistency of replies in all four samples. Only in three questions did the replies in the general sample indicate a fairly high frequency of negative attitudes which were not shown to the same extent in the other three samples: the belief that multiculturalism deprives Australians of jobs (44.0 per cent); that immigrants get too much help from government (51.0 per cent); and that multiculturalism undermines loyalty to Australia (43.0 per cent).

Table 9.3 lists replies to specific questions about attitudes to ethnic diversity. The views of the respondents suggest a somewhat higher level of equivocation on certain issues, with greater differences among the four samples than in the attitudes to immigration intake and multiculturalism. Negative attitudes in the general sample were expressed with regard to public funds being used for immigrants' cultural activities and to ethnic groups' maintaining their own way of life. It is rather interesting to note that the majority of respondents in all four samples did not see the knowledge of English as a necessary prerequisite for 'getting ahead' in Australia, which is in contrast to all authoritative statements from policy makers and public commentators.

Tables 9.4 and 9.5 give data on personal attitudes to certain ethnic groups. In the survey the respondents were asked for their views on 20 different groups, some defined in broad categories such as 'Europeans', or 'Asians', and others defined as specific ethnic or national groups such as 'Italian' or 'Chinese'. Tables 9.4 and 9.5 show the results on what appear to be the 'most acceptable' and the 'least acceptable' immigrant groups in the broad categories. The questions concerning each group are not discrete categories, in that the sum of answers for each group in

Table 9.1: *Attitudes to Immigration Policy, Australia 1988*

Attitudes	General sample N = 1552 %	Second generation N = 823 %	NESBs N = 986 %	Recent arrivals N = 1141 %
All immigrants				
– accept more	23.4	25.1	40.4	65.9
– accept the same	33.0	40.5	34.9	26.1
– accept fewer	42.6	33.9	22.9	6.5
British immigrants				
– accept more	39.3	33.8	34.5	40.8
– accept the same	49.8	52.7	52.3	45.1
– accept fewer	10.2	13.0	11.7	11.9
Southern European immigrants				
– accept more	26.9	31.3	33.4	41.2
– accept the same	55.5	56.3	53.5	47.9
– accept fewer	16.5	11.9	11.3	8.4
Middle-East immigrants				
– accept more	13.2	18.8	17.6	34.7
– accept the same	43.2	47.0	44.3	42.1
– accept fewer	42.8	33.5	35.9	20.9
Asian immigrants				
– accept more	16.8	20.8	21.1	50.2
– accept the same	37.7	39.7	41.2	33.4
– accept fewer	44.7	39.0	36.0	14.8
Who do work no Australian wants to do				
– accept more	29.9	37.0	39.8	55.5
– accept the same	40.9	40.8	35.0	24.7
– accept fewer	27.2	20.9	23.2	17.2

Note: Not stated/'Don't know'/have been omitted.
Source: Office of Multicultural Affairs (1989), *Issues in Multicultural Australia, 1988: Frequency Tables*. Canberra.

each sample comes to 100 per cent (the 'not stated' answers have been omitted in Table 9.4). This means that the answers show a gradient of acceptance, and the higher the positive answer to the first question the lower are the answers to subsequent questions.

As Table 9.4 shows, 'Australian people' and 'British people' were the most acceptable and 'Muslim people' were the least acceptable. Positive answers to the first question, 'welcome as a member of family', vary considerably and the only case where the answer exceeds 50 per cent is in the general sample with regard to the 'Australian' group. The interesting feature is the difference between the pattern of answers to the first question, where positive answers decrease from the general

Table 9.2: *Attitudes to Multiculturalism, Australia, 1988*

Statement/ Attitudes	General sample N = 1552 Agree/Disagree (%)		Second generation N = 823 Agree/Disagree (%)		NESBs N = 986 Agree/Disagree (%)		Recent arrivals N = 1141 Agree/Disagree (%)	
Multiculturalism is the basis of Australia's immigration policy	81.8	14.2	84.4	11.5	80.0	11.8	88.5	6.8
helps tourism and trade with other countries	85.1	12.9	90.7	8.3	88.6	7.9	92.4	4.7
deprives Australians of jobs	44.0	54.4	35.8	33.4	31.1	65.5	30.8	65.2
provides a greater variety of food, music and dance	93.2	6.3	96.3	3.4	95.8	2.6	93.8	4.5
means that immigrants get too much help from government	51.0	45.5	38.5	58.3	35.0	59.1	28.3	66.3
promotes a fair go for all members of the community	62.2	34.5	73.4	24.3	79.1	15.4	84.3	10.6
creates suburbs with high concentration of ethnic groups	87.1	11.0	84.6	14.4	77.0	19.1	75.3	29.5
is necessary if people from different cultures are to live in harmony	77.0	20.6	82.3	16.9	79.2	17.1	87.3	7.6
undermines loyalty to Australia	43.0	54.4	36.4	61.6	36.8	67.1	37.4	59.4
is a fact of life in Australia today	95.0	4.0	96.0	3.5	93.1	4.3	92.3	5.1

Note: Not stated/'Don't know'/have been omitted.
Source: Office of Multicultural Affairs (1989), *Issues in Multicultural Australia 1988: Frequency Tables*, Canberra

Table 9.3: *Attitudes to Issues of Ethnic Diversity, Australia, 1988*

Issues/ attitudes	General sample N = 1552 Agree/Disagree (%)		Second generation N = 823 Agree/Disagree (%)		NESBs N = 986 Agree/Disagree (%)		Recent arrivals N = 1141 Agree/Disagree (%)	
Governments should provide money for cultural activities	41.4	58.4	53.9	45.9	55.0	44.2	70.1	29.3
Australia would be a better place if ethnic groups kept their own ways of life	23.5	75.9	27.7	72.0	35.0	64.0	55.6	43.6
If a person is committed to Australia it doesn't matter what ethnic background they have	88.0	11.6	91.1	9.0	94.9	4.8	92.8	6.6
If ethnic groups want to keep their own culture they should keep it to themselves	53.4	46.3	48.2	51.5	64.5	34.7	67.3	32.0
People who come to Australia should change their behaviour to be more like Australians	66.1	33.7	54.5	45.5	66.6	32.8	63.3	36.3
Having lots of different cultural groups causes lots or problems	69.0	30.5	62.1	37.9	59.2	40.0	44.3	53.8
A person who doesn't speak English has no right to get ahead in Australia	44.7	55.0	30.3	69.5	39.2	60.2	39.4	59.7

Note: Not stated/'Don't know'/have been omitted.
Source: Office of Multicultural Affairs (1989), *Issues in Multicultural Australia 1988: Frequency Tables*, Canberra

Table 9.4: *Expression of Attitudes to Various Immigrant/Ethnic Groups, Australia, 1988*

Q. How close are you prepared to be with ...?	General sample N = 1552 %	Second generation N = 823 %	NESBs N = 986 %	Recent arrivals N = 1141 %
Australian people				
Welcome as member of family	55.6	42.9	36.1	21.3
Welcome as a close friend	28.1	35.2	38.6	41.6
Have as a next-door neighbour	9.1	13.1	15.9	23.0
Welcome as workmates	3.2	3.8	4.6	7.1
Allow as Australian citizen	3.0	4.3	3.5	6.1
Have as visitor only	.3	.2	.3	.3
Keep out of Australia altogether	–	–	.1	.1
British people				
Welcome as member of family	35.8	24.8	21.8	11.7
Welcome as a close friend	28.9	34.3	38.9	33.9
Have as a next-door neighbour	15.1	17.7	17.5	26.6
Welcome as workmates	5.8	6.7	8.3	12.8
Allow as Australian citizen	9.5	10.3	8.5	8.8
Have as visitor only	2.8	3.8	2.2	3.7
Keep out of Australia altogether	1.4	1.9	2.0	1.6
Aboriginal people				
Welcome as member of family	15.8	12.5	11.6	7.9
Welcome as a close friend	23.3	28.3	27.1	25.3
Have as a next-door neighbour	16.5	15.3	18.6	27.4
Welcome as workmates	20.5	20.2	20.0	18.4
Allow as Australian citizen	16.2	14.7	14.8	16.4
Have as visitor only	2.2	2.6	1.9	1.9
Keep out of Australia altogether	3.9	5.5	4.3	.8
Black people				
Welcome as member of family	13.7	12.8	10.6	8.2
Welcome as a close friend	22.9	31.8	26.7	26.4
Have as a next-door neighbour	18.0	18.6	20.4	27.1
Welcome as workmates	13.9	11.9	16.3	16.0
Allow as Australian citizen	14.5	12.5	10.4	12.4
Have as visitor only	9.5	6.8	8.3	5.2
Keep out of Australia altogether	6.4	5.1	5.7	3.2
Asian people				
Welcome as member of family	13.1	10.9	11.8	13.7
Welcome as a close friend	18.6	26.0	26.5	35.2
Have as a next-door neighbour	16.2	14.1	18.5	22.2
Welcome as workmates	10.5	11.3	14.4	11.7
Allow as Australian citizen	14.5	14.5	9.7	8.9
Have as visitor only	13.7	12.8	8.2	4.6
Keep out of Australia altogether	12.4	9.7	9.8	2.7

Table 9.4: *(Cont.)*

Q. How close are you prepared to be with ...?	General N = 1552 %	Second generation N = 823 %	NESBs N = 986 %	Recent arrivals N = 1141 %
Muslim people				
Welcome as member of family	8.8	7.9	9.4	8.9
Welcome as a close friend	14.9	22.5	21.9	21.1
Have as a next-door neighbour	16.0	13.9	16.4	23.0
Welcome as workmates	11.9	13.4	13.5	14.9
Allow as Australian citizen	14.8	15.6	11.3	14.3
Have as visitor only	16.5	12.4	11.3	8.6
Keep out of Australia altogether	15.3	13.9	14.3	7.4

Table 9.5: *Expression of Attitudes to Various Immigrant/Ethnic Groups,*
Australia, 1988: Summary

Q. How close are you prepared to be with ...?	General N = 1552 %	Second generation N = 823 %	NESBs N = 986 %	Recent arrivals N = 1141 %
Per cent sum of: welcome as family member, as close friend, as next-door neighbour				
Australian people	92.8	91.2	90.6	85.9
British people	79.8	76.8	78.2	72.2
Aboriginal people	55.6	56.1	57.3	60.6
Black people	54.6	63.2	57.7	61.7
Asian people	47.9	51.0	56.8	71.1
Muslim people	39.7	44.3	47.7	53.0
Per cent sum of: welcome as family member, as close friend, as next-door neighbour, as workmate				
Australian people	96.0	95.0	95.2	93.0
British people	85.6	83.5	86.5	85.0
Aboriginal people	76.1	76.3	77.3	79.0
Black people	68.5	75.1	74.0	77.7
Asian people	58.4	62.3	71.2	82.8
Muslim people	51.6	57.7	61.2	67.9

Source: Office of Multicultural Affairs (1989), *Issues in Multicultural Australia*
1988: Frequency Tables

sample to the sample of recent arrivals, and the pattern in the remaining questions where positive answers are either fairly even or decrease in the reverse direction. Certainly, the second pattern is to some extent determined by answers to the first question, but the answers seem to indicate that while people might be reluctant to see various immigrant groups as members of their families ('they're alright but I wouldn't want one to marry my daughter'), they would be prepared to accept them as friends, neighbours or workmates.

This 'levelling off' in acceptance is shown in Table 9.5. In the first part of this table, the percentages for the answers to the first three questions have been aggregated. As shown, the result is that only the 'Muslim' group scores below 50 per cent by three of the four samples, and 'Asians' score under 50 per cent only by the general sample. The second part of Table 9.5 shows the sum of percentages for the first four questions, and at that level no immigrant group scores under 50 per cent. Furthermore, except in relation to the first two groups, 'Australian and British people', where the answers by the general sample tend to show a higher level of acceptance, in the remaining groups the level of acceptance almost universally rises from left to right.

Four broad conclusions may be drawn from these replies. First, there seem to be certain differences in the acceptance of various ethnic, national or religious groups: acceptance of Muslims is shown to be comparatively lower than acceptance of other groups. Second, while people might generally be cautious in accepting others from immigrant groups as family members, their dispositon towards friendship, neighbourliness and working with others is quite positive. Third, people with immigrant background and new immigrants have generally more friendly attitudes towards other immigrants than have Australian-born people. Finally, the proportion of people who would not want to admit certain immigrants into the country is extremely low.

The results of the survey appear to be rather at odds with some of the impressions recorded in the CAAIP report. Certainly, there are indications of ambivalence and negativism towards ethnic diversity and some disagreement with the policy of special provisions for immigrants, but there seems to be a relatively high level of acceptance of multiculturalism, if only as a fact of life in Australia. On the whole, the survey recorded a diversity of both positive and negative attitudes to immigration and multiculturalism, rather similar to the views recorded in the ROMAMPAS report two years earlier.

One survey, however extensive and unbiased it might be, and one or two public reports commissioned by government, do not necessarily produce a complete picture of the views held in the community at large. Yet the findings recorded and interpreted by these methods cannot be dismissed as invalid or untrue. For these reasons the different pictures presented by the ROMAMPAS and the CAAIP pose some important questions about value judgements and biases in such reports. These questions need to be raised because the two reports were commissioned for the purpose of informing government policy, but their respective findings and recommendations were hardly similar or complementary. Considering the fact that the two committees were given rather similar terms of reference and used similar methods of enquiry, how, then, did they produce such different outcomes? It needs to be noted that both reports and the survey were produced at a time when the immigration program and the policy of multiculturalism were beginning to be increasingly questioned by some members of academia, press commentators, politicians and lobby groups. Some of these commentators substantiated their claims by their own expertise in certain areas, such as the economy, but others used 'on dit' arguments, claiming to reflect the views of the public. Yet the views of the public, recorded in a nation-wide survey, did not support these authoritative 'expert' opinions.

It may be suggested, therefore, that the ROMAMPAS report was useful to the government as a confirmation of a broad, if not universal acceptance of ethnic diversity in Australian society. The report served as the basis for the abolition of the Australian Institute of Multicultural Affairs and for establishing the Office of Multicultural Affairs, located in the Department of the Prime Minister and Cabinet, thus being placed under direct government control. The report also provided the rationale for establishing the Advisory Council on Multicultural Affairs which was to prepare the ground for the government's proposed National Agenda for a Multicultural Society. At the same time, the government had to respond to the increasingly vocal critics of the policy (and to some critics within its own party) who questioned the high immigration intake on economic grounds and perceived the policy of multiculturalism as a threat to social cohesion and traditional 'Australian' values and way of life. The government responded to these critics by establishing the CAAIP, but the report of that committee brought new arguments into the debate, and revived some old ones which questioned the policy on immigrant selection and even more so the policy of multiculturalism.

The observations and arguments presented in the CAAIP report revived public debate on immigration and multiculturalism and became powerful weapons in the hands of the analysts and commentators who opposed both but especially the concept of multiculturalism. Arguments against multiculturalism became multi-dimensional. As noted by Sawer (1990), multiculturalism was seen to encourage racism, it was 'importing old hatreds from overseas', it presented a danger of a 'fifth column', it represented cultural relativism, it threatened Australian 'core values', and it was used by politicians to attract the 'ethnic vote'. These arguments projected the threat of immigration from Asia, an issue of high sensitivity which never completely disappeared from the debate even if it was not always openly stated.

The argument presented in the CAAIP report, that selection of immigrants needed a 'sharper economic focus, for the public to be convinced that the program is in Australia's interest' (1988: xi), provided a field for economists to argue against immigration. However convincing some of their arguments might have appeared to be, their strength lay more in the rhetoric used than in their substance. The great weakness of the economic case advanced against immigration has been the one-dimensional nature of the analysis, notwithstanding its being presented with wide-ranging inferences. Economic commentators have viewed immigration as a direct causal factor in such things as unemployment, the country's external debt, inflation through increased demand for goods and services, or public expenditure. They have attempted to link immigration to 'problems' of a non-economic nature, thus reviving old fears and prejudices. For example, the economics editor of a national daily newspaper who commented regularly on immigration wrote:

> Many Australians are apprehensive about what they perceive as an excessive, and excessively rapid, change in the population mix – the 'Asianisation' of Australia. Many more are beginning to question the economic benefits of mass migration, worried about the impact on their job security and standard of living, including their urban and national environment and general quality of life ... Like it or not, it is the racial factor that many people focus on in considering immigration and it is information they are entitled to have and, if they wish, base judgments on.   (Wood 1990a)

It is an interesting 'economic' comment, with the threat of 'Asianisation' thrown in for good measure, for the benefit of the people 'out there', who apparently hold racist views. The comments on 'Asianisation' are interesting, especially as the arguments in the article were prefaced with a quotation from the CAAIP report referring to people's views that they were not receiving the facts on immigration. In regard to views on Asian immigration the CAAIP report was quite specific, noting that, considering earlier attitudes to Asian immigration and the White Australia policy, 'the accommodation to immigrants from Asia is remarkable'. Further, the report stated:

> In the Committee's consultations, also, perhaps five out of 587 indiviuals we spoke to were overtly against Asian immigrants on grounds of nothing other than race. And the written submissions from organisations representing hundreds of thousands of Australians and from many individuals did not even take this as an issue.   (1988:6–7)

Antagonism to multiculturalism reached new heights in the opinions and comments expressed in the late 1980s in the media by the well-known and respected historian, Professor Geoffrey Blainey, such as the following:

> Multiculturalism is an appropriate policy for those residents who hold two sets of national loyalties and two passports. For the millions of Australians who have only one home and one loyalty this policy is a national insult.   (1988a)

Or further and more specific comments on the supporters of multi-culturalism:

> Its ardent supporters are the ethnic groups who live in a cultural or physical ghetto. They are essentially monocultural, but they find a useful camouflage in forming a protective alliance with many other ghettos under the spurious banner of multiculturalism. The typical ghetto of new immigrants is a haven of racial preference and discrimination. It rightly enjoys the democratic privilege of speaking its own language, of always employing its own kinsmen when the opportunity arises, of worshipping in its own church, reading its own foreign-language press, patronising its own clubs and cafes, occasionally setting up its own creches and marrying within the ghetto.   (Blainey 1988b)

Such and similar comments have continued into the 1990s, and became more strident as the economic recession deepened and unemployment kept rising. It was an interesting phenomenon to see university faculty members who normally prefer to publish their views in the 'learned journals' joining journalist commentators in addressing their views to the public directly through the mass media. As shown in the examples below, which have been selected from volumes of similar comments, the repeated themes were wide-ranging: the views included the notion of 'powerful ethnic lobbies' exerting strong pressure on government policy, although they did not really represent most immigrants' views; issues of citizenship and loyalty to Australia; concern about the cost and the economy; concern about 'social cohesion'; unfairness to 'Australians'; and concern about current and future overcrowding. An interesting feature of many comments was the use of emotive language and the 'on dit' kind of reporting mentioned earlier.

Powerful, unrepresentative ethnic lobby: 'Key decisions determining the immigration program and population growth have been taken on the narrow political basis of placating particular sections of the ethnic community'. (Wood 1990b)

Citizenship and loyalty to Australia: 'Those who now apply for citizenship do not even have to forswear allegiance to their previous nation … Mr Hawke's citizenship laws have quietly undermined the case for compulsory voting. Why dragoon a new voter who knows little about the land, whose loyalties may lie elsewhere, and whose knowledge of English can be scribbled on a postage stamp?' (Blainey 1989)

Cost to the economy: 'It is beyond any reasonable doubt that the present immigration programme is seriously aggravating our short and medium-term economic problems. Its mostly non-economic focus enhances the damage'. (Walsh 1990)

Social cohesion: 'Immigration risks backlash because in some suburbs of Sydney and Melbourne it is hard to hear an Australian accent. Of course parts of Australia's big cities have been immigrant ghettos for a generation. The change is that today's immigrants look as well as sound different from most Australians ... The issue is the sort of Australia we want our children and grandchildren to inherit. Will it be a relatively cohesive society that studies Shakespeare, follows cricket and honours the Anzacs; or will it be a pastiche of cultures with only a geographic home in common? ... Race matters – but only because it usually signifies different values, attitudes and beliefs. The real problem is not race, but culture'. (Abbott 1990)

Unfairness to 'Australians': 'As new migrants, especially refugees, often receive a high priority for public housing and as such housing is now scarce, some groups must suffer if others are to gain. It is the Australian homeless who too often wait in the queue while the new migrant jumps ahead of them. The present migration policy, in effect, discriminates against the Australian homeless. It is one of the ironies of a government which claims to oppose all ethnic discrimination that it has no hesitation in discriminating against Australian Australians'. (Blainey 1990)

Current and future overcrowding: 'If there is to be a reduction in migration, it had better be soon because Australia is now linked to countries with immense emigration pressures. Management of the selection system is now just about out of control, with migration officers swamped by applications overseas and here. The latter have exploded through change of status applications on spouse, compassionate and refugee grounds. Nearly 40 000 were in the pipeline as of June 1990, with about half the applicants located in Sydney'. (Birrell 1990)

'Sydney 2021. The Harbour City is a sprawling metropolis of nearly 5 million people – close to the present day populations of Melbourne, Brisbane and Adelaide combined ... Racial tensions have increased dramatically as Sydney, with over 40 per cent of its population overseas-born, now rivals New York in terms of its ethnic composition.' (Millett 1990)

There is a certain 'undertone' in all these statements, conveying something that perhaps should not be said aloud in polite company, but something that everyone understands, they share the sentiments expressed. The common element is the projection of fear.

The debate on immigration and multiculturalism, which intensified following the CAAIP report, continued until 1992 and abated only after the government reduced the immigration intake to 70 000 for the year 1992–93 and placed the policy on multiculturalism on the proverbial 'back burner'. Nor was the debate one-sided, consisting entirely of monologues against immigration and cultural diversity, although comments of that kind prevailed. There were other voices which aimed to demonstrate the economic and cultural benefits gained by Australia from immigration and cultural diversity, and argued for the continuation of the immigration intake and for further development of multiculturalism. Some of these contributions have been noted in the earlier chapters and some are examined in the next chapter in the context of the issues, current and future, which affect   Australian attitudes to cultural transformation.

The debate of the late 1980s and early 1990s brought to the surface some of the forces of resistance to change and cultural transformation. In particular, it showed how opponents of immigration projected fears by claiming to reflect concerns and fears of the population at large. The debate did not disappear, but rather its focus changed in the later part of 1991 when the leadership of the Labor Party changed. This change also shifted media attention to the forthcoming elections and to the differences between the policies of the two major parties on immigration and multiculturalism. Some aspects of these differences are discussed in the next chapter.

The Media

The debate discussed in the preceding sections took place mainly in the mass media, especially in the popular widely-read daily press. The authors of many of the arguments claimed to *reflect* public views, but it would be more accurate to interpret their arguments as efforts to *influence* public views. Indeed, some authors claimed that the government was reluctant to have the issues of immigration and multiculturalism discussed at all and that people were therefore not given their rightful opportunity to express their views. To say the least, this sudden concern about democracy by the so-called experts on these matters was rather surprising.

As noted earlier, the mass media in Australia have presented and still present a uniformly monocultural Anglo-Australian image of Australian society. The resistance to change is so deeply embedded in the media that they have remained the bastion of Anglo-orientation, projecting this perspective onto the community. Ethnics may be mentioned on occasions, either when they do a great deed, or, more likely, when they do something like committing an offence against the law. A sporting hero may be an Agostino, a de Castella, a Veletta or Dipierdomenico, but they are all 'Australians'. However, any such name appearing in a court case as an offender will appear in the print media as an 'Italian', a 'Greek', or a 'Vietnamese'.

Television and radio follow the same path. Commercial radio and television 'entertain' but in doing this they promote an Anglo-Australian life-style of a particular kind. They appeal to prejudices and Anglo-Australian chauvinism through an admixture of crudity, especially prominent in advertising. 'Papa Luigi' making pasta sauce and 'Con the greengrocer' selling vegetables in not very salubrious surroundings are caricatures, intended to be funny, but presented in bad taste so that many people find them offensive. The national broadcaster, the Australian Broadcasting Corporation (ABC), does not engage in such crudities and is free of advertising, but as a medium of monocultural entertainment and socialisation it has been the most consistent vehicle for transmitting the British, or more specifically English, cultural inheritance. As one of its critics comments:

> Rather than keeping Australia's flame, the ABC was carrying a torch for Britain. The television service was, in effect, the BBC's third network … the organisation ran what was, in effect, a White Australia Policy. It gave WASP broadcasting. Or, rather, WASA: White Anglo-Saxon Anglican. (Adams 1993)

This critic, Phillip Adams, further comments that 'after 37 years of television, Australia's ethnic minorities are still the invisible people. The main networks, public and commercial, haven't even got around to tokenism'. The comment is quite valid, but it is also apposite to note that Adams himself conducts a program on ABC Radio National ('Late Night Live') in which, while often discussing world events and drawing on contributions of commentators from other countries, usually Britain or the United States, he rarely takes up issues of ethnic minorities in Australia or multiculturalism. One may only assume that the program is directed at a particular audience for whom the issues of multiculturalism are of little interest.

Not only is the ABC oriented towards England and entirely mono-cultural; it also remains solidly committed to promoting middle-class values. In its radio and television programs which deal with social and political issues, such as the family, work, women, social policy (for example, ABC Radio's daily 'Life Matters'), it presents Australian society as consisting almost exclusively of the new (Anglo) middle class. The projected 'average' Australian family is the two-income family of professional people, with the child in the state-subsidised child care centre (and an 'ethnic' domestic help who is carefully concealed from the viewers or listeners, only on rare occasions receiving a mention, almost by accident, it seems); the 'average' woman, is a university-educated professional person; the 'average' worker is a professional in the public service or a consultant. Books which are frequently discussed and recommended in these programs are usually concerned with issues of 'personal fulfilment', 'relationships' and why people ought to use more professional help in anything from conception and child rearing to marital relationships, happiness or grief.

The exception, as noted earlier, is the Special Broadcasting Service (SBS) which came into being because the ABC was not interested in extending its vision, and declined the government offer made in 1976 to establish radio stations in Sydney and Melbourne which would provide programs for non-English-speaking communities (Kramer 1990). It needs to be noted that, except for films and serials produced in all parts of the world presented in the original languages with English sub-titles, and news from a number of countries (in the morning sessions), SBS television presents its programs in English. It is rather unfortunate that SBS now also relies on commercial sponsorsip for its revenue and advertising has been on the increase in its programs. However, it is important to add that advertising on SBS is confined to breaks between programs, unlike the practice of the commercial channels.

Resistance to Change and Social Class

As discussed earlier, especially in Chapter 3, from the first days of colonisation the history of Australia has been a history of immigration, accompanied by a fear of 'foreign' cultures which were supposed to be a threat to the British or Anglo-Saxon or Anglo-Celtic inheritance. It has also been a history of racism, first directed against the native Australians, then against Chinese immigrants, and later enacted in the *Immigration Restriction Act* of 1901 and in the White Australia policy, which did not disappear from the laws and party platforms until the 1960s. The fear of 'foreign' cultures and 'non-white' races might not have disappeared entirely from public perceptions and attitudes, but the empirical evidence suggests that Australian society as a whole has become more open to other cultural influences. Negative attitudes to certain ethnic groups and non-Christian religions persist but in an attenuated form, except for occasional outbursts from some fringe groups or in certain localities. The millions of immigrants who have settled in Australia since the 1940s have met at times with an unfriendly reception or with indifference, but not with physical violence.

Resistance to cultural influences has not been uniform across the socio-economic strata and class structure. The 'average' working-class

Anglo-Australian might have been negatively predisposed towards the newcomers, by tradition and socialisation, but having met them in the workplace and in the neighbourhood, initial fears tended to dissipate. Working-class suburbs in the cities where non-English speaking immigrants have settled in large numbers have not been distinguished by social conflicts or violence. If fears have been maintained, or revived, more often than not such fears have been fuelled by some 'authoritative' opinion propagated through the media.

The question thus arises whether, or to what extent, the negative views on immigration, ethnic diversity and multiculturalism that emanate from social analysts, public commentators and professionals and their organisations, are expressions of concern with public interest, or manifestations of resistance to cultural change with the aim of protecting professional exclusiveness and class interests. As we have said, arguments against immigration and multiculturalism are usually formulated in terms of the public interest, but active discrimination against immigrants from non-English-speaking backgrounds is most systematically applied among the middle classes. Negative attitudes and protective actions of professional unions aimed at preventing or restricting professionally qualified NESB immigrants from practising their professions have persisted with undiminished rigidity. Organisations such as, for example, the Australian Medical Association or the Australian Association of Social Workers, justify their resistance by claiming responsibility for the maintenance of professional standards and the protection of public interest, but their requirements for admission to membership present the newcomers with insurmountable barriers. In some cases, immigrant medical practitioners have been allowed to practise but only in certain 'approved hospitals', usually in country towns or in working-class suburbs (Visontay 1989).

Important positions in public administration and in community services – health, education, social welfare – remain almost exclusively in the hands of Anglo-Australians. The same situation continues in the management and control of professional organisations. There are no objections to an 'ethnic' office cleaner, tea-maker or gardener, or even an interpreter or 'ethnic aide' in schools or child care centres; but an 'ethnic' doctor, social worker, or senior public servant is an entirely different matter.

Bureaucrats and members of the established professions, who have their interests protected by legislation and/or strict prerequisites for admission to membership and practice, have a vested interest in the maintenance of the *status quo*. Furthermore, as Pusey found (1991), the federal government's policy advisers perceive most issues from the perspective of economic rationalism and economic reductionism. In such a one-dimensional perspective there is little room for consideration of social issues, let alone issues of ethnic and cultural diversity.

In the field of community services, the monocultural perspectives of the helping professions create pressures on immigrant families to adopt 'Australian norms' in such functions as child rearing and parental authority. The attitudes towards the different cultures are not much different from those displayed for many decades towards Australian Aboriginal families whose child-rearing practices were condemned, and removal of children from their families was the accepted policy and practice (Read 1982). Furthermore, these attitudes are grounded in the values and norms of the new middle class, which the professions regard as the 'right' norms and values against which other classes can be assessed and judged. These attitudes continue because the education and training of professionals such as medical practitioners, nurses, psychologists, teachers, social workers and the great variety of specialised counsellors is grounded solidly in the socialisation of students in monocultural and class norms which are presented as if they were universal norms of an unquestionable 'scientific' nature (Boland 1989, 1991).

In the business world, class-based resistance to cultural change continues in the form of 'we don't discriminate against migrants but our clients do'. Evidence from personnel recruiting agencies indicates that such excuses are frequently used by firms in the selection of professional or management personnel. Even a foreign-sounding name is often sufficient to disqualify an applicant for a position (Moeller 1991, Williams 1992).

In the public sector, the federal policy of 'access and equity' (A&E) promulgated under the National Agenda for Multicultural Australia in 1989 has achieved limited improvements in service provision. An evaluation of the program conducted in 1992 for the Office of Multicultural Affairs revealed some progress in the implementation of the A&E strategy, but also reported significant barriers to its successful implementation. The evaluators found that cultural barriers 'existed on both sides of the counter' and affected the quality of service, especially to young people and the aged, to women who did not speak English, and to Aborigines and Torres Strait Islanders. The strategy for the implementation of the policy intended it to work 'top down', but it 'has not, however been effective in filtering down to APS [Australian Public Service] staff at the client interface', and departments and agencies 'were not able to demonstrate that they had significantly addressed A&E issues in internal audits'. One of the key findings of the evaluation was that:

> ... managers were not using the tools already available to them as a conse-
> quence of the range of management reforms of the 1980s to fulfil their A&E
> implementation obligations; nor were they adequately assisted to do so. As a

result, A&E was inclined to be considered as an added 'extra' and therefore as an additional resource cost managers often felt too hard pressed to meet.

(OMA 1993a: 11)

Resistance to cultural influences thus appears to be well entrenched through the whole spectrum from public administration to business corporations, to professional bodies. It is maintained by restrictive practices in the professions, by monocultural socialisation of future professionals, and by portraying multiculturalism as a threat to economic well-being, social cohesion and what are called 'Australian values' and 'Australian way of life'. What these actions protect, however, is the inheritance of a class culture from Britain, now adopted and maintained by the new middle class in the institutions in which this class has found its power and economic interests.

CHAPTER 10

Cultural Transformation: The Australian Search for Identity

The impression that the reader undoubtedly has gained so far is one of a profound dilemma experienced by Australian society in its search for identity. While everyone agrees that Australian society has been changing, at least in its visible aspects, the extent and direction of change and its likely outcomes remain unclear.

We have attempted to demonstrate that over the past decades, specifically from the start of the immigration program in 1947, two kinds of change have been taking place simultaneously in Australia: social change and cultural transformation. Social change, causally linked to changes in technology and related changes in the structure of industry as well as the occupational structure of the labour market, has been multidimensional, entailing changes in the relations between sexes and age groups, in the distribution of income and wealth, and in the institution of the family: the overall outcome has been a significant change in the class structure. One of the main features of this change has been the growth of a social stratum which has become known as the new middle class. Another salient feature has been the growth of what may be called the 'human residue' of the market economy, a population stratum excluded from the social mainstream, mainly through unemployment, sickness or family breakdown, and referred to by a variety of names, such as 'the disadvantaged', people 'below the poverty line', or in stronger terms such as 'the underclass'.

Cultural transformation has also been multidimensional, but it has been uneven in its various aspects and with different effects across the class structure. The transformation has been more extensive in those sections of society where Australian-born people have come into direct contact with the immigrant population in the course of their everyday life, in the workplace and in the towns and suburbs in which they live. Indeed, in working-class communities certain signs of transformation are visible in the patterns of everyday life, but in the middle-class suburbs and in the core institutions little, if any, change has taken place.

As a result of the social change which has affected its class structure and the varied extent of cultural transformation in that structure, Australia has become a society of cultural diversity but directed and controlled by a monocultural structure of power which is deeply embedded in the British, or Anglo-Celtic, tradition. From the political and legal system, to educational institutions and the professions, the core institutions carry this monocultural inheritance as 'colonial baggage'. It is these unchanging institutions that serve to maintain the class nature of Australian society and act as what may be termed 'colonial ballast', which makes the Australian search for identity such a laborious process.

The analysis in this chapter focuses on the choices Australian society faces now and in the years ahead. Viewed in a global perspective and bearing in mind the shifting centres of world power and economic development, unless society is willing to change the Australian situation may become increasingly precarious both politically (because of its colonial inheritance) and economically (because of its reliance on commodities for export revenue). Both the internal diversity of its population and its geographical location in a fast-growing and changing region will present Australian society with problems which will not be solved easily within the inherited mode of thought. To solve these problems Australian society will need to jettison the inherited colonial ballast and dispel some of the myths which have prevented it from finding its own identity and independence of thought. Australian society certainly has the human resources to do this, and recent events suggest that it might in fact do so.

Social Change and Politics

In March 1993 Australia held a general election to choose its federal government for the next three years. To all political commentators and analysts (except one) the results of the elections were a foregone conclusion. The Australian Labor Party had been in office for ten years, its longest ever period in office; the country was in the middle of a severe recession, with unemployment exceeding one million persons, or over 11 per cent of the labour force and no improvement in sight. The conservative (Liberal–National Party) Coalition was so confident of winning office that arrangements had been made by them for a meeting with Treasury officials for the day following the election.

Yet, when the results came out people could scarcely believe them. Not only did the Labor Party not lose office, but it increased its majority in Parliament: the percentage vote for Labor actually had increased, the first time since 1966 that a party in government increased its vote at a general election. The effects of this totally unexpected and unprecedented outcome have reverberated throughout the nation ever since. What happened, then, and why?

The voting pattern in the 1993 election echoed the traditional class vote, especially in working-class Labor-held electorates where the margins of Labor candidates increased by some remarkable percentages. Most marginal electorates, however, remained marginal, some shifting to Labor, others to the conservatives. The Labor Party won more of these than the Coalition, in some cases by only a handful of votes.

Has the multicultural nature of Australian society affected the election outcome, thus affecting the class-based pattern of political allegiance? A definitive answer to this question cannot be given here, but the voting patterns indicated strong support for the Labor Party among the non-English-speaking communities. Other sources of data also indicated that such support was well etablished. For example, in the survey conducted for the Office of Multicultural Affairs in 1988 (OMA 1989b, see Chapter 9) over one-half (51.8 per cent) of new arrivals (since 1981) expressed support for the Labor Party and only 15.3 per cent for the Liberals; 27.3 per cent expressed no clear support for any party. Expressed support for the Labor Party among NESB voters was 42.6 per cent, 40.2 per cent among the second generation of immigrants and 37.7 per cent among the general sample. Expressed support for the Liberal Party was lower in all four samples, ranging from 31.7 per cent in the general sample, to 24.3 per cent in the second generation, 20.7 per cent among NESB voters and 15.3 per cent among new arrivals. 'No committed support' for any party ranged from 17.6 per cent in the general sample to 25.2 per cent in the second generation, 29.0 per cent among NESBs and 27.3 per cent among new arrivals.

In the 1993 election campaign immigration and multiculturalism did not appear to figure prominently as an issue, but it was undoubtedly on the minds of immigrant voters. The issue appears to have been a proverbial 'sleeper' which was not identified by media commentators at the time because it was not tested by the pollsters and was not publicly debated by the leaders of the two major parties. As public debates, media comments and analyses concentrated on the major issues of unemployment and Coalition taxation proposals, the potential significance of the ethnic vote was given little attention.

In retrospect, there were many reasons why the ethnic vote was important. The post-CAAIP debate on multiculturalism and immigration which was so vehemently conducted through the print media right up to 1992, must have been fresh in people's minds. The substantial cut in the immigration intake for 1992–93 and tightened conditions of entry were not well received by the ethnic communities. An even less favourable impression was created by the tough stand taken with the 'boat people' who had arrived from Cambodia; they had been confined in detention camps in the desolation of Port Hedland on the north-west coast and in Sydney for years while their applications for admission as refugees were tested by immigration authorities and courts of law. These actions did not endear the government either to the ethnic communities or to wider sections of the population. The detention camp at Port Hedland especially attracted much attention and accusations of inhuman treatment, racism, and abuse of human rights were levelled at the government: the treatment of people in that camp was called a 'national shame' (Bunk 1992:38–45).

If the Labor government adopted a tougher stand on immigration and multiculturalism as a policy was put 'on the back burner', the conservative Coalition went much further. The views expressed by its politicians against multiculturalism and in favour of a monocultural 'One Australia' envisaged policies reducing immigration or stopping it altogether, policies of excluding immigrants from unemployment benefits for two years after arrival, policies of 'no English language, no vote' (Millett 1992b); all these threats must have had an effect on immigrant voters. The policy of 'One Australia' which had been promulgated by the Liberal Party since 1988 was seen as a stance encouraging antagonism towards immigrants, especially those from Asia, and unwittingly inviting the racism latent in some sections of society to come to the surface. Even the commentators in the conservative press were extremely critical of John Howard, then leader of the Coalition, for his comments on the need to restrict immigration from Asian countries. 'Howard's prejudice shames us all' wrote one columnist (Sheridan 1988); 'Mr Howard is a politician who thinks he has found a good issue. He is not a racist; he's about exploiting racism', wrote another (Walsh 1988). The *Financial Review* editorialised, 'Howard takes a dangerous road' and pointed to the evident purpose of such talk:

> If Mr Howard is eyeing, as a last desperate throw, the vote of the 'righteous remnant' who seek to turn the clock back to a homogeneous Australia, he too runs the risk of being marginalised. He has the right, like the Blaineys, the Ruxtons and the Caseys, to say his piece. But once uncorked the racial argument rampages at will, and has a cannibalistic capacity to devour its progenitors.   (5.8.88)

Such warnings went unheeded. As noted in Chapter 5, in his *Australians Speak: Australia 2000* (1990), John Hewson, who became leader of the Coalition after the 1990 elections, wrote that many people thought that multiculturalism 'has got out of hand' and were worried about the risk of 'cultural ghettoism'. Hewson was thus reflecting the views of those commentators who from their own limited perspectives, developed in separation from the social reality of the everyday life of the community, seemed to believe their own illusions, that is to say illusions created by themselves.

It was these illusions that brought on the shock of the election results. It seems the conservative Coalition believed that by raising fears of a threat to the Anglo character of Australia and promising, by inference if not in a direct way, to stop policies of multiculturalism, they would attract voters to their camp. They completely misread the electorate, especially the electorate in the working-class areas. The country has changed and cultural transformation from below had evidently gone further than the experts claimed to know: the projected fear did not work. When working-class people were faced with the choice between a monocultural class society with the vestiges of colonial inheritance on one side, and a multicultural communality of democratic pluralism on the other, they chose the latter. Certainly, there were other reasons as well, but they all had one thing in common, namely, a choice between the collective or 'communal' character of such provisions as universal health insurance and industrial relations based on some regulatory principles; and the promise of an individualistic competitive, atomised society which devalues collective or communal effort and elevates the class power of capitalism to the level of the first principle.

Stephen Knight, in writing about the 'Australian mind' observed the decline during the 1970s and 1980s of the previously present 'ideology of the collective' in Australia; he saw the collective spirit to be 'thoroughly swamped by an individualist craving for material comforts' (1990:5). The election results of 1993 suggest, and *only suggest* because no clear evidence is yet available, that perhaps that 'craving' might have reached its peak and is now in retreat. It is apposite to note at this point that most immigrants from non-English-speaking countries follow a more collectivist ethos than Anglo-Australians, both in working together and in social pursuits, leisure and recreation.

In the results of the 1993 elections differences on immigration and multiculturalism became apparent along class lines. In effect, from the time the bi-partisan approach to immigration and especially to multiculturalism was openly ruptured in 1988, issues of immigration and multiculturalism became class issues.

The outcome of the elections means that many issues on which the conservative Coalition was confident of representing the attitudes of the Australian community at large are in need of a fundamental reassessment. The post-election views expressed in the media by people from a wide cross-section of the community provided a clear indication that the politicians, social and economic analysts and other commentators in the media did not reflect the views of the majority of the population as they so arrogantly claimed. A one-dimensional future of economic reductionism and economic rationalism was not acceptable to the voters, and nor were the fears that were implicitly and explicitly projected about a republican future, 'Asianisation' and 'multicultural ghettos'. The elections demonstrated that cultural transformation in society, especially among the working class, has been more extensive and more intensive than the conservative Anglocentric middle class 'experts' recognised when they so confidently claimed that Australians did not want it. It is doubtful whether many of them can see where and why they went so wrong. In a brief but very perceptive comment on the election results, Kalantzis and Cope asked how the Coalition and the pollsters in the media could have been so wrong in their predictions, and they wrote, *inter alia*:

> Both focused on what they thought the real issues were: the number games of economic management and taxation. But they failed to speak about and to women, immigrants, Aborigines and those who have a new vision for our national presence. Given that the economic numbers were so badly weighted against them, Labor won on culture. It won because it had a better intuitive feel for this country's developing sense of itself ... Keating won because he knew his electorate.   (1993)

Similar conclusions were reached by a Liberal Party member of the New South Wales state parliament (of non-English-speaking background) who analysed the voting patterns in one of the marginal electorates in Sydney and found that the highest percentages of votes for the Labor Party were in the areas of high concentration of NESB persons. From his analysis of the overall pattern of voting and of the comments in the ethnic press as well, as from his own experience of nine years in parliament, he concluded:

> The undisputed facts are that the ethnic communities in nearly every electorate leaned heavily towards Labor because they view the Coalition's vision as not reflecting contemporary Australia.   (Zammit 1993)

Immigrants from non-English-speaking countries have not been very visible in the field of politics, but this does not mean that they have not been involved in political activities. Involvement in politics may take a variety of forms, not all of which are of equal interest to political analysts. Political participation by NESB immigrants and their communities has been a field of social activity about which most political analysts, with some notable exceptions, know very little. Jupp *et al.* note that the 'academic literature on political participation by ethnic minorities in Australia is quite thin'; there are very few academics from ethnic minorities and 'the dominant intellectual traditions in Australia are assimilationist and there has been a historic reluctance to accept the validity of ethnic politics' (1989:11).

Similarly, in her study of ethnic organisations, Penny Anagnostou found an active political life in immigrant communities which academics in political science have failed to identify. Academic researchers' view that immigrants did not take an active interest in politics, Anagnostou says, has been due to the researchers' assumptions. In her observation:

> All studies appear to have assumed an assimilationist perspective. Implicit in them is the view that the political behaviour of migrants must follow the same pattern ... In line with the assimilationist perspective, researchers have also assumed a simple and naive view of migrants as people and the means by which they express their political beliefs and concerns.   (1982:28–9)

Anagnostou points out that political participation takes many forms and takes place at many levels – in political parties, in industrial organisations, in local communities – and immigrants have been active in all of these, especially in their own organisations which are 'intrinsically political'. Anagnostou also notes that for many years (until the 1970s) involvement in political activities by immigrants was not welcomed by Australian authorities, especially any activity in industrial matters. She records:

> In the selection of migrants those migrants with any known history of industrial involvement have generally not been allowed entry. In addition, various sanctions have been applied, including the taking away of Australian citizenship, to migrants who have become involved in industrial or other forms of political activity.   (1982:45)

Today, there is more involvement by immigrants in politics, more often in local government than in state or federal politics. On the other hand, all immigrant communities have a network of organisations pursuing a range of aims and interests – educational, artistic and cultural, religious, sporting, social-recreational, welfare – all of which are of a political nature, in the true sense of the term. In all states there are Ethnic Communities' Councils – joined together in the Federation of Ethnic Communities' Councils of Australia (FECCA) at the federal level – the so-called 'ethnic lobbies' which are often, quite wrongly, accused of being influential but not representative of their communities. Certainly, like all organisations, these committees tend to develop oligarchical characteristics, for a variety of reasons (such as personal skill, interest and availability of time for voluntary work). However, these bodies *are* representative of their communities and critics who say otherwise have very little knowledge of how they work. If Australia is to develop a new identity to reflect its social reality rather than its colonial inheritance, these ethnic multicultural organisations have an important role to play in the task.

The Colonial Inheritance

Throughout this book we have referred to the pervasive influence of the British (English) monocultural tradition on the thinking of Anglo-Australians and on their attitudes to other cultures. Nowhere is this inheritance more evident than in the attachment to the British Crown, to the members of the British royal family and to the British flag. The persistence of this attachment is astounding, evident not only in formal core institutions but in the pictures of the Queen adorning the walls of private homes and in the 'loyal toast' drunk at formal dinners and wedding receptions. Anyone who has had some experience of living in a country other than Australia, or anyone who takes even a limited interest in what happens in the world, finds it incomprehensible that a country which has obtained nominal and formal independence from a colonial power still clings to and worships that power nearly one hundred years later. It is incredible to the world at large that there are still people in this country who do not think that an Australian-born person would be good enough to be the head of state in a republic, or that citizens would be capable of electing their own head of state. These attitudes are one more example of the colonial baggage that is still carried by Australia, a heavy weight which prevents the country from establishing its own identity and deciding the direction of its destiny.

However, this attachment to the British monarchy is not only an attachment to the Anglo-Saxon inheritance; it is also an attachment to the inherited English class structure. The conservative forces still hold deep-seated beliefs that they are the people born to rule and that the Australian population has to be ruled, not simply governed. A twenty-three-year conservative Coalition government was 'normal' in their view; a ten-year Labor government a disaster.

The dilemma that traditional conservative Anglo-Australians face is how to develop an Australian identity without weakening the Anglo-British inheritance and without 'contamination' by non-English cultures. As long as the former continues to be regarded as superior to the latter, it will be an impossible task. It must be increasingly clear, even to the most committed Anglophile, that continuing subservience to the

British Crown is an anachronism which a country like Australia, calling itself an independent state rather than the 'self-governing colony' of the Constitution, cannot maintain for long. This kind of thinking is an example of cultural arrest, a phenomenon observed in societies which have become isolated from the outside world.

In discussing the dilemma the conservative forces face, we do not argue here for the rejection of the English, British, or Anglo-Celtic cultural inheritance, but against using that colonial inheritance as a means of maintaining the structure of class power and monocultural dominance. This inheritance is used to contain and suppress the evolutionary development of an Australian cultural identity, creating a gap between the society at large, which is changing in many of its aspects, and the institutionally based power structure which is rooted in the country's colonial history rather than in the reality of the present.

Australian society now has more than one cultural inheritance. With one in five persons being an immigrant from a non-English-speaking background and with the addition of the children of these immigrants, the proportion of people from a non-English-speaking background rises to four in ten; the cultural inheritance of Australian society can no longer be described as solely British or Anglo-Saxon or Anglo-Celtic. England is no longer the only 'home', because Australians now have many ancestral homes, and the society is much the richer for it. This is the social reality of contemporary Australia.

Immigration and Economic Reductionism

Another element which in recent years has exerted an inhibiting influence on Australia's development as a multicultural society with its own identity has been economic reductionism. As noted earlier (Chapter 4), from the beginning of the post-war immigration program the value of immigration in prevailing analyses has been perceived in narrow economic terms, immigrants being regarded mainly as a *supplementary labour force*, filling the immediate needs of industry. From that narrow perspective, which views immigrants as 'commodities', not only did other aspects of immigration receive little attention but the full potential economic value of immigration failed to be realised because much of the imported talent and skill was wasted. Unfortunately, lessons from years of experience with the immigration program have not been learned well, and in the 1980s the trend towards assessing the value of immigration by narrow economic criteria increased rather than decreased.

Economic reductionism may be appropriately regarded as the curse of the 1980s. This is not to reject the value of economics as such, but to point out that economists have claimed too much. They became the all-influential advisers to governments in every area of policy, extending from financial matters, employment, education, health, welfare and the environment, to political philosophy, immigration and multiculturalism. Economics became the dominant social science, and its disciples attempted to authoritatively translate and reduce all social issues to this one dimension, discrediting other perspectives and dimensions as 'soft'. Furthermore, it was not the overarching influence of economists as such but the ideas from the particular school of thought known as economic rationalism which promoted this one-dimensional approach to social issues. However, most economists during the 1980s followed the gospel of economic rationalism to varying degrees. It was economic reductionism that was the main damaging element: the 'one-dimensional' economic approach to social analysis resulted in a vulgarisation and devaluation of important social issues affecting directly the quality of life, in areas such as health, education, welfare, employment/unemployment: that is to say, the broad range of issues of varing degrees of tangibility which may be called culture.

In the narrow conceptual framework of economic reductionism there is no room for culture or cultural differences because those things do not fit easily into the concept of the 'rational economic man' who makes all decisions on the basis of economic self-interest: if there is no money-equivalence in a thing, the thing is not relevant or it does not exist. In applying such concepts to immigration, much research money has been spent and volumes of data have been published, but with little convincing results and little agreement among economists themselves. As Adele Horin comments:

> The fetish for measuring economic benefit omits the intangibles that calculators can't compute. Migrants have changed the social fabric of Australia, surely for the better, and enhanced the meaning of what it is to be an Australian. But it is impossible to put a figure on the benefits of cosmopolitanism and the pleasures of cultural diversity.   (1990)

The comment is apposite. The concept of economic rationality which guides the prevalent economic theories accepts only one kind of rationality, and abstract theories and simulated computer models do not always reflect social reality. Indeed, some economists who became committed disciples of simulated models have engaged in what amounts to a new version of medieval scholasticism. In such approaches to the analysis of social issues the theory becomes akin to an article of faith and social reality, which should after all provide the test for the theory, becomes irrelevant.

Where would Australia be today, we may ask, were it not for the immigration program? The question sounds rhetorical, but it is quite relevant in view of the arguments advanced against immigration and multiculturalism. Without the immigration program Australia would have by now become a small, insignificant and economically and culturally isolated country at the 'bottom of the globe'. There is no disagreement among commentators and analysts about the value of immigration in the economic development of the country in the earlier decades. Why, then, in their learned opinions, has immigration lost its value now?

Over the whole period of the post-war immigration program politicians, economists, employers and media commentators have emphasised the importance of bringing in skilled immigrants. The skills and educational levels of successive immigrant intakes have been rising and on all available data the levels of the imported labour force are above those of the Australian-born labour force (see Table 4.4). Particularly high educational and skill levels have been recorded among immigrants from Asian countries (Cook 1988, Hassan and Tan 1990, Jayasuriya and Sang 1990). It is also a well-documented fact that immigrant families place great emphasis on their children's education and their children's school performance is on the whole very good. By economic as well as social and cultural criteria these immigrants constitute not only a valuable addition of human resources but also an investment in human capital for the future. What, then, might be the reasons for concern? Are the arguments against immigration, especially against immigration from Asian countries, based on concerns about a different culture or 'race', or are they based on fears that '*they* will take *our* jobs away'?

Arguments against certain kinds of immigrants are not much different now from those of a hundred years ago. For example, the antagonism against Chinese people early this century was not based on the fear that they would become a burden on society but because they were industrious. When Reeves wrote about 'the swarming hives of Southern and Eastern Asia' who wanted to descend upon Australia he also wrote:

> Among Asiatics, much the most formidable migrating race are the Chinese, the tough people who can labour in almost any climate, who can shovel earth and outwit customers as imperturbably in the Alpine valleys of South New Zealand as on the scorched plains of the Darling, or the steaming flats that fringe the Queensland rivers.   (1902:328)

So is it fear of 'unfair competition'? Some decades ago W. K. Hancock observed that the concept of equality in Australia meant a state of mind which 'is properly anxious that everybody should run a fair race. It is improperly resentful if anybody runs a fast race' (1945:153). The fear of unfair competition from immigrants has been part of Australian history and the working class in the last century might have had legitimate grounds for such a fear because the colonial employers wanted the cheapest labour possible. Similar fears continue to be raised, as McCall *et al.* note, by analysts and commentators who see immigration as a significant factor in unemployment (1985:269–71). However, in the post-war immigration program it was mainly the middle-class professions that erected effective protective barriers against such competition. Anxiety among the new middle class about competition from educated and skilled professional immigrants is also rather strong. It is perhaps more than a coincidence that arguments against immigration have paralleled the rise of educational and occupational levels among more recent immigrants.

Multiculturalism and Resistance to Transformation

From the time the concept of multiculturalism was first mentioned (AEAC 1977) there was considerable debate about its meaning, its significance and its effect on Australian society. As noted in earlier chapters, the debate at first revolved around the difference between *cultural pluralism* and *structural pluralism*. The policy of multiculturalism adopted by the then conservative Coalition government was based on cultural pluralism, which critics saw as a mechanism for concealing the structural inequalities of Australian society with the ethnic communities located at the bottom of this structure. The succeeding Labor government attempted to overcome this problem in the 1980s by relating the concept of multiculturalism to the issues of *access and equity*, aiming to ensure that public services and related institutions provided non-discriminatory services to non-English-speaking immigrants. This policy meant that public institutions were to adapt their services to meet the ethnic diversity in Australian society. In effect, implementation of the policy at the operational level meant fairness and equality of treatment but at a more profound level it had a potential for *institutional change*.

The debate on immigration and multiculturalism which followed the CAAIP report and the release of the National Agenda for a Multicultural Australia was a debate conducted almost exclusively through the mass media. The opponents of multiculturalism came almost entirely from the political Right: not all of them explicitly opposed the concept itself, although they did by various inferences. For example, they would express concern about the economic effects of immigration (unemployment, cost, etc.), but on the issue of multiculturalism they adopted the '*on dit*' approach, that is, they claimed to reflect concerns of the public at large, as it were: 'We are saying only what people are saying and the government should take notice and respond to it'. Some critics, however, opposed the concept of multiculturalism directly, presenting it as a threat to what they called Australian values, traditions, the British or Anglo-Saxon or Anglo-Celtic inheritance, attachment to the monarchy, and a host of other real or mythical things (see Chapter 9).

On the other side, there have been many supporters of multiculturalism, although some of them might have disagreed with its interpretation and implementation in government policy. However, most supporters of the concept and 'friendly critics' have missed its real significance. To many of them, multiculturalism meant tolerance of ethnic or cultural diversity by the Anglo-Australian population. They spoke of the need to 'sensitise' service providers in public administration and community services to the 'special needs' of immigrants. In such 'welfare' perspectives, immigrant communities came to be seen as 'disadvantaged' or as 'dependent' populations, similar to other 'dependent' populations, or 'problem' populations, such as the unemployed, pensioners or 'the poor'. These attitudes, and services built on them, produced two negative outcomes: they led to the perception of immigration and multiculturalism as *costs* rather than benefits; and they focused attention on the immigrants and their problems in adjusting to the monocultural Anglo-Australian institutional structure rather than on the institutional structure itself. Multiculturalism thus remained an issue for 'the multiculturals', not for 'the Australians' and their institutions. Governments, both conservative and Labor, have been quite willing to provide funds for services which claimed to cater for the 'special needs' of immigrants, but such perceptions have kept public attention away from the structural inequalities in access to resources and from the core social institutions which continued their operations in time-honoured, unchanging ways. Marginal 'special provisions' in institutional operations and 'sensitisation' of service providers have, in fact, reinforced the stability of the institutional structure by claiming to be manifestations of flexibility and awareness of immigrants' 'special needs'. As noted earlier (Chapter 9), the evaluation of the 'access and equity' program (OMA 1993a) found that little change in the performance of the public service had actually taken place.

The conservative reaction against multiculturalism has not been against providing 'special' services to immigrants, as long as multiculturalism simply meant the tolerance of ethnic diversity by the mainstream organisations. The reaction rose to a crescendo of 'concerned' voices and '*on dit*' reports only when some people began to equate multiculturalism with institutional change. Reports such as those produced by ROMAMPAS (1986) and ACMA (1988) presented the path to a multicultural society as a two-way process, an essential part of which was an urgent need for institutional change. Implicitly, this meant that the institutions would need to become 'multicultural', a notion which the conservative Anglo-oriented middle class would not contemplate, and its spokespersons felt compelled to warn all 'Australians' about the potential danger of such notions.

In the political sphere, since the mid-1980s, both immigration and multiculturalism (but especially the latter) have become issues on which the major parties parted company. The end of a bi-partisan approach by the major political parties to policies on these two matters also signified a division on broad class lines. While both major parties look at immigration mainly in an economic perspective, the conservative Coalition now sees it as a threat to what it claims to be the Australian tradition and Australian values. What it means by these values are links with the British Crown and inherited privileges safeguarded through the maintenance of the class structure. The outcome of the 1993 elections was a rude shock to the conservatives and the awakening from it has not yet occurred.

What, then, have the policies of multiculturalism achieved, what is the current state of multiculturalism in Australia, and what are its prospects for the future? The best answers to these questions would be: the outcome, so far, has been variable, both in scope and degree; the current state is uncertain; and the future will depend on Australian society's perception of itself and on the will of the people in power.

In the field of the arts – or 'high' culture – there certainly has been progress towards multiculturalism, perhaps even transcending cultural diversity and developing into distinctive Australian multicultural art styles and forms. The visual arts and music have a universal appeal and speak a universal language, and some progress in these fields has been achieved. In drama, both in the theatre and on television, progress has been slow. As we noted earlier, television particularly, except for the Special Broadcasting Service, has remained rigidly monocultural, with the publicly-owned channel (Australian Broadcasting Corporation) presenting local and British programs, and the commercial channels aiming for the lowest common denominator of sex and violence, to maintain ratings. The widening of cultural perspectives in local film production is illustrated by the progression from a film like *Gallipoli*, which portrayed 'the birth of the Nation' on the battlefield, fighting and dying for the British Empire, to *Crocodile Dundee*, maintaining the myth of a 'typical Australian bush character', to *Strictly Ballroom*, where the sterile, culturally-empty tradition loses to multicultural creativity. The perspective has certainly broadened, but such examples are few. Nevertheless, with the participation of artists from other parts of the world in festivals of arts and the contributions of immigrant artists to music, painting, theatre and film, a widening of cultural vision has undeniably taken place.

In the broader spectrum, world culture is certainly influential, especially in the field of youth culture, as expressed in popular music, dress and social behaviour. However, youth culture, like much of the popular culture, from rock music to sporting activities, has been appropriated by the culture of the market. Increasingly, this culture advertises market products as being synonymous with national symbols. As pointed out by Davidson, 'McDonald's, in their television advertisements have not been backward in turning Ayers Rock [now Uluru] into a hamburger or the Twelve Apostles near Port Campbell [high rocks on the south coast, detached from the mainland] into French fries' (1990:38). Similarly, smiling blond children, young girls with white cream on the nose, truck drivers and cattle farmers are 'as Australian as Ampol'. One has to ask, who came to this country first: Australian Aborigines, white invaders, or Ampol petrol?

On the achievements of multiculturalism in a wider social and cultural sphere, opinions among academic teachers and researchers are widely divided, indicating clearly that people's attitudes, dispositions and prejudices colour their assessments. For example, Robert Holton (a sociologist) asserts that multiculturalism has been 'one of Australia's post-World War II successes'. Although the concept remains controversial and some people are confused about its meaning, 'multicultural policies have made a positive contribution not only to migrant welfare but also in the social well-being of Australian society'. Holton acknowledges there have been costs associated with the implementation of the concept, but, on the whole, 'Australian multiculturalism has much to teach the world about the simultaneous achievement of unity and diversity, of national identity and cultural pluralism' (1991:8–9). By contrast, another academic, Geoffrey Partington (a senior lecturer in education) sees the working of multiculturalism mainly as a 'grievance industry and part of a wider knocking campaign'. He sees the 'multicultural lobby' as spending much time 'in reviling Australian society for being ethnocentric, prejudiced and racist' and encouraging immigrants to complain and make constant demands on the government. He also questions some immigrants' loyalty to Australia, noting that during the Gulf War 'many Arab-Australians rallied to the cause of Saddam Hussein [Partington does not say what they actually did] and paid scant regard to what our elected government considered our national interests' (1991:89–91). Partington further argues, *inter alia*, that multiculturalists 'overplay the importance of ethnic languages' and children of ethnic families who take up ethnic languages at school 'gain very high marks just for being able to speak the language'. By contrast, 'native English-speakers' learning English find the task much harder because they have to show more than fluency in the language.

As to the current state of multiculturalism, Jupp expresses the view that the policy of multiculturalism started as a 'euphoric phase' (1973–78), followed by a phase of 'consensual consolidation' (1978–83), then by a phase of 'disillusion and retreat' (1983–88), and it was now in a phase of a 'total abandonment' or 'total confusion' (1990b:123–35). Other scholars writing on this issue such as Foster and Stockley (1988) and Jayasuriya (1990, 1991), consider that Australia has now reached a post-multiculturalist stage and the issues of ethnic diversity would be more appropriately viewed under the concept of democratic pluralism.

It is evident that multiculturalism remains a contested concept. For example, Leonie Kramer (1990) argues that 'the word multiculturalism is strictly meaningless. There is no such thing as "multiculture". There is an Australian culture, which changes with the expansion and diversification of the society from which it grows'. In a somewhat different perspective, Lauchlan Chipman (1985) sees Australia as a 'poly-ethnic society' which has not yet resolved the problems and tensions which are associated with mixed communities. The kind of multiculturalism which is influencing state educational administrations in particular is of a 'hard' quality, which is 'of doubtful theoretical validity, is confused and confusing in application, is backward-looking, and could well be itself a source of new tensions as it rides into influence through denigration and de-legitimation of what there is of a "mainstream" Australian culture'.

In certain aspects of social life, especially among the lower class strata, negative attitudes to cultural change persist but cultural diversity has become reasonably well accepted. However, in the upper strata and in the core institutions cultural diversity is still regarded as something foreign to Australian society. To date, despite the policy rhetoric, institutional change has remained minimal. As Foster and Stockley note, any change in the working of public administration, health, education, and welfare – has been marginal. They comment:

> This effect essentially is *confined to situations of crisis* rather than underpinning normal practices in the various institutions. Indeed, in a number of institutions, multiculturalism has remained marginalised and has had virtually no effect on the attitudes and practices of the dominant groups in Australian society.   (1988:7) (emphasis in the original)

Important social institutions have remained monocultural in the composition of their personnel, especially at the higher echelons of organisational hierarchy, and correspondingly in attitudes and social orientation. For example, in discussing the cultural orientation of

Australian universities, Milner concludes that '... Australian university English departments have remained one of the last important British garrisons east of Suez' (1991:32). Looking at a wider field of social institutions, Manfred Jurgensen observes:

> As far as I can see, almost all social institutions, representing the legislature, the judiciary and the executive, are firmly in the hands of Anglo-Australians. The same applies to institutions of cultural power, such as publishers, distributors, the print and the electronic media.   (1991:25)

This is certainly the situation in the bureaucracy of public administration. Overall, the percentage of employees born in non-English-speaking countries working in the public service is lower than in most sectors of industry, and at the higher levels of the hierarchy it is extremely small. For example, in his study of the Senior Executive Service (SES) in Canberra, Pusey found that only four per cent of personnel at that level were of non-English-speaking background (1991:49). A similar situation would certainly be found at that level of the bureaucratic hierarchy in all states.

The monoculturalism entrenched in these institutions means that while at the level of everyday life Australia may appropriately be regarded as a society of cultural diversity, at the institutional level it remains monocultural and is identified as such. This is clearly evident in the opinions of those analysts and media commentators who authoritatively distingish between 'Australian Australians' and 'ethnics' who live in 'cultural ghettos'. As Jurgensen sees it, the question of cultural identification 'is not merely who owns the power of cultural definition, but who is in control of the process of arriving at social identities'. Many of those in power resist cultural transformation for Australia because they 'know better'. In Jurgensen's words:

> The conservative forces resist a redefinition of Australia; they already know what it means to be Australian. A new assessment of the Australian character is perceived as a threat, for it would no longer superimpose a cultural assumption based on power politics, but interpret social history from below – it would relate not so much to the land as to the people, a people of migrants.
> (1991:26)

The future of multiculturalism in Australia is uncertain. In our view, for the concept of multiculturalism to become a social reality, the cultural transformation would need to be a bilateral process. The cultural heritage of the various ethnic communities will need to be maintained, cultivated in the host social environment, and progressively integrated with the dominant Anglo-Celtic heritage. Organisations of ethnic communities also need to broaden the orientation of their activities so as to include the mainstream Anglo-Australian organisations and influence them towards receptiveness to new cultural inputs and to progressive cultural transformation. In sum, if multiculturalism is to become a social reality in Australia in all aspects of social, political and cultural life, then ethnic communities will need to integrate their own cultural heritage with the Anglo-Celtic heritage and, reciprocally, the Anglo-Celtic inheritance will need to be 'diluted' with the inflow of the new cultures. In essence, the aim would need to be the disappearance of the division between 'Australians' on one side and 'the multiculturals' on the other. The concept of an overarching umbrella of values drawn from the core values of various ethnic communities, as suggested by Smolicz (1985, see Chapter 5), appears to be a promising and feasible concept to pursue.

The search for a new identity which would reflect the social reality of contemporary Australia will need to focus on the essential necessity of transforming the core social institutions which continue to present a monocultural image of society. Unless a cultural transformation takes place at all levels of Australia's social structure and becomes accepted by the core social and political institutions, Australian society will suffer internal divisions and tensions, social and economic decline and a loss of the relatively high place in international standing currently held by Australia. In particular, its relations with the neighbouring countries of the Asian-Pacific region will become increasingly difficult.

Australia and its Neighbours

In addition to the search for identity in its internal make-up, Australia also faces the task of finding an identity in relation to its neighbouring countries and in the world as a whole. The internal and external identities are closely related: Australia is not, and cannot become, a closed system insulated from the outside world. Internal events – policies, attitudes, economic activities – are of interest to neighbouring countries, in the same way and for the same reasons as events in those countries are of interest to Australia. The inevitability of this two-way process appears to elude the thinking of some people who freely express their views on events in neighbouring countries but maintain that 'what we do in our country is our business'. It is very difficult, it seems, for some people to see that the British Empire is there no longer.

Denis Kenny sees this issue in a wider framework, differentiating between what he calls regional 'cultural ecologies'. He argues that Australian thinking and view of the world has been solidly grounded in the cultural ecology of the Atlantic, not noticing that the 'cultural ecology of the Pacific ... is already establishing its ascendancy over the cultural ecology of the Atlantic'. In particular, he notes:

> Our universities, especially, have tended to remain citadels of the central beliefs, assumptions, attitudes and values of the European Enlightenment, and far-flung outposts of the cultural ecology of the Atlantic.   (1990)

Such a view is certainly not universally shared. Some see closer relationships with neighbouring countries as a necessity, but maintain that such a development would not necessarily mean that Australia would have to discard its European or British cultural inheritance. Others see closer cultural links with the countries of the region as a path towards exchanging one kind of dependency for another. Others go further, arguing that Australia can never become a part of Asia and that thinking along these lines was a 'pipedream' (Blainey 1993).

Australia's attitude to its neighbours is in some way similar to Britain's attitude to Europe. Both countries realise that their survival depends on close co-operation and the integration of economies and trade, even politics, with their neighbours; but in both countries there is fear that such integration would mean a loss of independence and national identity. In both societies the attitudes seem to indicate a certain degree of insecurity and lack of confidence in the strength of their own cultures.

In Australia, in the political sphere there is no longer the bi-partisanship of the two major politial parties on the future direction of Australia's relations with its neighbours. There is a broad bi-partisan acceptance of the necessity to maintain friendly links with neighbouring countries for the purpose of trade, but seeking cultural links in a reciprocal manner is perceived in conservative circles as a threat to the implicitly 'superior' Australian culture.

Commercial links between Australia and South-East Asian countries have been developing and growing for some years, as Australian investors and manufacturers have been taking advantage of cheap labour costs and an acquiescing workforce in these countries. Imports of goods and capital from these countries have grown to high levels, successfully competing with local products and capital. Neighbouring countries have been the favourite destination of Australian tourists, and tourism in the reverse direction, mainly but not exclusively from Japan, has become a major source of foreign exchange. Education has now become an important income earner, as students from neighbouring countries study at Australian universities and high schools, paying full fees. In 1992, an estimated 18 500 overseas students, mainly from Hong Kong, Malaysia, Singapore, Indonesia and China, were enrolled at Australian universities (Jones 1992). By comparison, the number of

Australian students studying in South-East Asian countries has been insignificant.

With such developments the caution and even open resistance to closer cultural links with neighbouring countries would seem surprising. Yet such resistance is certainly there, as shown by the critical comments from some commentators and politicians about the Prime Minister's open declaration on the future of Australia being with Asia. An example of such a cautious attitude is the following comment by a well known university professor who, while stating that 'our links with Asian economies have become absolutely crucial', nevertheless expresses concern:

> And yet ... and yet: it is one thing to reconstruct economic links, even to begin redefining our diplomacy ... But it is actually another thing to call on an entire new nation to think differently about itself.   (Schreuder 1992)

The tenor of such comments is 'yes, perhaps ... but not yet, not so fast'. Indeed, Schreuder points out, quite appropriately, that there is no such country as 'Asia' but a multitude of different countries, each with a different language, culture and social system. To develop closer links with these countries, he argues, Australians will need to learn to know these societies, learn to know what they think of Australia, and learn to interact with them. Nor should closer links become another form of dependence.

Australia does not have to become 'Asian' to be accepted as a neighbour by Asian or Pacific societies. In its search for identity, Australia does not need to jettison its Anglo-Celtic or Anglo-Saxon heritage, any more than it has to jettison that heritage to become a multicultural society. What it needs to jettison is what we have called the colonial baggage so jealously preserved and nurtured in conservative circles of power and in the core institutions. It needs to jettison what is still, in effect, subservience to the British Crown: symbolic as this subservience might be, it still maintains the myth of the Empire. Above all, the country needs to jettison the mimicking of the English class structure. It needs to resolve the conflict with the original inhabitants of the land by acknowledging that the right to possession by conquest is legally and morally wrong. It needs to cease being a 'self-governing colony' and become a 'self-governing multicultural society': give itself a chance of a rebirth in cultural diversity. It needs to maintain links with Britain, as it needs to do also with other countries, but it needs to cease acting, and being perceived as, the remnant of the Empire in a part of the world where the past is viewed as colonial oppression. As long as Australia continues to identify with that past, it will be seen as part of that oppression. This does not mean that Australia should forget its past; it means, however, that the myth of the past, cultivated by the people who benefit from the myth, needs to be replaced by the history which more truthfully reflects the past, including the recent past. One common feature of social change of many contemporary societies has been a rediscovery of the past in new perspectives. In that process, many myths have turned to dust, many gods have fallen, and by rediscovering their past many communities have created their own new identity. To create its own new identity and maintain its place and respect in the world of free societies, Australia needs to have the courage to do the same.

The post-war immigration program and the opportunity this program has created for Australia to become a multicultural society has been beneficial economically, socially, and culturally, even if the value of this opportunity has not always been recognised and human resources wasted. Immigration has also created benefits for Australia in its external relations, in trade, cultural exchanges and international politics through the United Nations and its agencies.

Future policies on immigration are likely to have a greater significance for Australia's place in the world than they had in the past. Irrespective of the views that people and their government might have on the internal effects of continued immigration, Australia will find it increasingly difficult to resist international pressures to accept more immigrants, be they 'voluntary' economic immigrants or 'involuntary' political or economic refugees. It will be increasingly untenable for Australia to justify its relatively small population inhabiting a vast continent, in a world of great population pressures, especially in neighbouring countries. To many people in the outside world Australia is undoubtedly seen as a *terra semi-nullius*, presenting challenging opportunities for starting a new life for themselves and their children. Those who have already arrived have certainly demonstrated their willingness and ability to contribute to their new society as good and productive citizens. The options for Australia seem to be either to continue with a reasonably high level immigration program and modify economic activities to make such a program economically sustainable, or to adopt a 'Fortress Australia' policy and become internationally isolated as an insignificant country 'down under'. The first option will be challenging; the second will most likely be illusory and would end in failure, in the way that the internal cultural 'Fortress Australia' pursued through assimilationist policies proved to be a failure.

Jerzy Zubrzycki, the Chairman of the Australian Ethnic Affairs Council in the 1970s, expressed Australia's options and hope for the future in the following words:

> I look forward to the day when history books will tell us that Australia became freely accepted by the nations of Asia as one of us; that Australia became a

multi-racial society and that the nation's resources were used for the first time
to make possible the reign of justice and compassion in our part of the world.
(1977:141)

This is certainly the time for Australia to consider its future, both in
terms of its internal political structure and culture, and its relations with
other societies. Its geographical position is fixed: it is not 'far away' from
anywhere; it is where it always was and always will be – a large country in
a dynamic multicultural region of the globe. With the cultural diversity
of its population and roots mainly in the different countries of Europe,
but with growing roots in the nearby region, Australia may be seen as a
cultural bridge between the 'old' world and the 'new', but it should not
act as a 'messenger' of European power or as a 'launch pad' for British
or other European business into South-East Asia, as some people seem to
see it. It should establish its new identity in its own autonomous and
completely independent right.

The Search for Identity and the New Middle Class

In the search for a new identity of Australian society the role of the new
middle class will be crucial. The reason for this lies in the societal
function this class performs as a collectivity. It is members of this class
who engage in what is known as mental production, that is, the production, dissemination and reproduction of knowledge and information. This production consists of activities such as research and
publication of research findings, writing books and journal articles,
presenting papers at conferences and seminars, and participating in
public debate through the mass media – the press, radio and television.
It also includes the application of this knowledge and information to
various activities carried out authoritatively with societal sanctions:
advice to governments, public and private administration, teaching,
healing, counselling, consulting, socialising, controlling. It is through
this diversity of activities that the new middle class collectively defines
and interprets the nature of social reality. In other words, this class plays
an important, if not entirely exclusive, role in *defining the society's identity*.
The wide-ranging polemic on the issues of immigration and multiculturalism in which academic researchers, media commentators,
politicians and others have engaged in recent years needs to be seen in
this light.

On the issue of immigration and multiculturalism the new middle
class displays a variety of attitudes. As shown in various chapters of this
book (see also Figure 4.1), the diversity of conflicting arguments on

these issues indicates clearly a high degree of normative content in the authoritative opinions, ostensibly formulated on the basis of evidence claimed to be irrefutable and obtained through 'scientific' methods of inquiry and analysis of relevant data. This does not mean that some researchers or commentators engage in deception; it means, however, that empirical evidence may be valid in a particular context and be used selectively to support a value position or personal or group preference or interest. However, it needs to be noted that some arguments against immigration, or against the immigration of particular ethnic groups, have been substantiated by empirical evidence of dubious validity, relying on arbitrarily selective data or untested assumptions; or attempting to substantiate certain attitudes or prejudices. For example, some economic analysts and commentators have argued with great authority that allowing immigration to continue in times of recession contributes to the growth of unemployment (and the government has followed their advice, substantially reducing the intake in the early 1990s); but equally convincing arguments have been advanced to show that immigration is a stimulus to the growth of employment.

Various individuals and sections of the new middle class have played an important role in the formulation of policy on immigration and multiculturalism and in the formation of public attitudes to these issues. Many have been and continue to be active in professional and community organisations which act as lobbies or pressure groups, aiming to influence government decisions in a particular direction. More often than not, such activities are claimed to be 'in the interests of the community' but are really aimed to protect or enhance the self-interest of the group. Professional organisations which have consistently maintained the barriers to the admission of persons with professional credentials from non-English-speaking countries to their membership and practice are an example of such actions.

It needs to be acknowledged that individual and collective interests of the new middle class are vested in the core social institutions from which the members of the class derive their income, life-time occupational careers, social status and political influence. It is these institutions that have been the guardians of the British or Anglo-Saxon colonial inheritance and have proved to be extremely resistant to change. Collectively therefore, and irrespective of the diversity of views and attitudes held by its individual members, the new middle class has been an important force of resistance to the cultural transformation of Australian society.

Immigrant communities also rely on their own new middle class to protect or advance their interests. In her study of the political aspects of ethnic organisations, Penny Anagnostou emphasises the significance of social networks and ethnic professionals. 'Both appear to be the key to understanding ethnic politics'. She observes:

> The characteristics which are common to the ethnic leaders include high level of education, association with tertiary institutions, second and third generation migrants and overlapping membership. (1982:89)

The outcome of the search for an Australian identity is therefore likely to depend to a significant extent on the growth of the new middle class among the non-English-speaking communities, in the first, second or third generation of immigrants. It will further depend on the extent to which this class will find a place in the core institutions and, having found such a place, be able to resist the monocultural indoctrination and work for the cultural transformation of these institutions. It is not going to be easy, but it will be the successful completion of this task that will provide the foundation for a truly multicultural Australian society.

CHAPTER 11

Culture, Change and Social Life

Australia is certainly not the only society in the world today that has been undergoing processes of social change and cultural transformation. There are, however, certain features of these processes in the Australian context that may be perceived as somewhat unique, although any such uniqueness depends on the perspective in which the Australian experience of social change and cultural transformation is perceived. As we have made abundantly clear in the previous chapters, this experience has not been perceived uniformly by Australian observers, and it is even less likely that it would be so perceived by observers from other countries.

This chapter sums up the analysis of social change and cultural transformation in Australia by discussing some of the causal links and relationships between the economy, culture and social life, which became apparent in the analysis presented in earlier chapters. The chapter brings together our empirical observations and interpretations of the Australian experience of social change and cultural transformation and discusses these processes in a broad theoretical framework. Whether one can generalise from the Australian experience to other societies in which cultural diversity has become (or is likely to become) an issue will be discovered only in the future.

Class, Culture and Social Change

In examining the processes of social change and cultural transformation, we have looked at Australian society as a class society. We have defined a class society as a society whose characteristic feature is social, economic and political inequality, or structural inequality in the 'command over resources through time'. We have examined this society in a perspective of close to 50 years, from the start of the post-war immigration program in 1947 to the 1990s, but with references to earlier periods. The longer time perspective has led us to the conclusion that some recent and current issues go back to the time of Federation and to the colonial times of the previous century. Indeed, it seems that the embeddedness of the colonial inheritance in Australia's core social institutions militates against transforming those institutions so that they can reflect the current social reality.

The immigration program has undoubtedly been one of the most important factors in changing the nature of Australian society over a relatively short period of time: from a numerically rather small society, with its economy based essentially on agriculture and related primary industry, to one of twice the population with a diversified economy. This now includes not only agriculture and mining but also a developing high-technology manufacturing industry and a growing diversity of service industries. Thus, apart from population size, important changes have also occurred over these years in economic production.

Economic change and social change are causally linked, and change in the economy which is always manifest, first and foremost, by change in the means of production, always leads to change in the social structure. In Australia, as in the other industrialised societies, the feature of change has been a shift of industrial activity from material production to service and management industries, with a corresponding decrease in manual occupations and a growth of professional and related white-collar occupations. This growing social stratum, which is also increasingly diverse occupationally, has acquired the characteristics of a class and become known as the new middle class. The class has become economically and politically significant, not only because of its growth in numbers but especially because of its key role in the generation, control and dissemination of knowledge and information (Gouldner 1979, Jamrozik 1991a). In performing this role, the new middle class effectively defines the social reality of society and its culture.

In the currently prevailing analyses of social issues theoretical perspectives embodying the concept of class are very few and the new middle class is rarely mentioned. Reluctance to examine current social, political, economic and cultural issues in the framework of class theory and neglecting to look at the new middle class, as a class, amounts to an analysis of society in concealed class terms. There seems to be a fear that such an approach would turn the spotlight on the new middle class, that is on the class to which the analysts – the definers of social reality – belong. Charity may begin at home, but not social analysis. It is indeed interesting that the largest identifiable social stratum with common characteristics tends to be omitted from social analyses. Conceptually, this neglect constitutes a serious flaw, as it omits from the analysis one of the key elements in contemporary social structure – it omits most of the core and focuses instead on the periphery (Kreckel 1989).

In examining the concept of cultural transformation, we have focused on the transformation in the 'culture of everyday life', that is, the way people act towards one another as individuals and groups, the way they express attitudes and values, the way they work and play, the way they perceive and express themselves as individuals and communities, and the way they perceive other individuals and communities. Bearing in mind the class nature of Australian society, we aimed to ascertain whether any cultural transformation that might have occurred had occurred to the same extent and in the same direction in all social classes and social strata, or whether the extent and nature of such transformation differed from one class to another or from one social stratum to another.

The role of the new middle class in the definition of social reality has figured prominently in this study, as social reality exists only as it is perceived and experienced. It is perhaps less important to hear what people say or think about certain issues than to know how public opinion is formed, that is, who initiates and propagates certain views; the latter knowledge leads to a better understanding of society, its power structure and class interests. As we have demonstrated in the previous chapters, perceptions of social change and cultural transformation, of immigration and ethnic diversity have differed widely among observers, analysts and commentators; perceptions and interpretations have also changed considerably over time. Furthermore, certain recent events (for example, the 1993 election) indicate that significant differences have arisen between the authoritative perceptions and interpretations of social change and cultural transformation by analysts and commentators, and those by the people who have been the actors in these processes through their own experience of everyday life. The conclusion that may be drawn from this discrepancy is that perceptions and authoritative interpretations of social reality by researchers, analysts and commentators are mediated through their position in the class structure and their perceptions of their own class interests.

Society and Economic Reductionism

In the analysis of perceptions and interpretations of events we have raised the issue of economic reductionism and economic rationalism. Our critique is that, first, the prevailing economic analyses have been based on abstract models which have become dogmas rather than scientific theories testable in the empirical world of social reality. Second, the economists' influence has extended to social issues which by their very nature are 'non-economic', yet they have been subjugated to economic analyses and converted into economic indices. Important social issues have thus been either vulgarised or have been discarded as irrelevant. Governments have accepted such analyses because economists have offered 'neat economic models' rather than data which would reflect the complexity of society, with its many intangible aspects and values which do not easily translate into tidy economic equations (Hirsch *et al.* 1987).

There are also profound normative and ideological issues embedded in economic reductionism. It is important to keep in mind, as Therborn has observed, that the prevailing position in economics is to examine social issues from the perspective of the accepted theoretical and value position of the capitalist system (1976:143). The 'rational economic man' is essentially a capitalist. For this reason, it is difficult for an economist who follows the prevailing theories to examine such issues as social inequality without imposing the capitalist normative element of inequality on the analysis. Indeed, the normative element of inequality has been built into some of the methods of economic analyses in, for example, the use of the concept of 'incidence' (allocation of public funds calculated as a percentage of the recipient's income) rather than 'distribution' (allocation expressed in actual terms). This method allows government allocations of resources favouring the affluent classes to be presented as a redistribution to lower income populations. A number of economic analyses of social policies in Australia emanating from government-funded research institutes have been of that nature (for example, see Economic Planning Advisory Council 1987).

In the 1980s and the early 1990s the social dimension in analyses of social issues in Australia was displaced by economic indices. Economic reductionism also became more and more detached from social reality as analysts developed increasingly abstract models, which were to serve as simulations of the real world but in time acquired a life of their own. The reification of such heuristic devices led to the elevation of economic theory to the status of dogma and unchallenged 'scientific' truth. The more 'scientific' the theory became, the more detached it became from the social reality of the everyday life which originally it was supposed to explain. In this new form of medieval scholasticism the ideologically-based conceptual models became the 'real' world which was authoritatively presented as such, even if those uninitiated to that superior wisdom failed to see the emperor's clothes. As Pusey so appropriately observed:

... the economists ... set the wrong answers into models that are no longer recognisable as *metaphors* and therefore as *social* constructions. They are instead 'invested' with a nature-like facticity that would raise a blush on the face of any self-respecting Azande witchdoctor.   (1991:226)

In the prevailing economic analyses of immigration, which became prominent during the late 1980s, the value of immigrants was again reduced to a single dimension, by treating people not even as a labour force as such, but as a *supplementary* labour force to meet the immediate needs of industry. Issues of family reunion, long-term social implications, and the policy of multiculturalism were presented as additional costs burdening the economy. Social and cultural aspects of immigration were thus reduced to narrow economic values, but with inferences which raised fears of a threat to social cohesion and Anglo-Australian cultural hegemony.

The leaders of the conservative Coalition saw the economic reductionist arguments as a useful vehicle for raising the traditional fears of immigration as a threat to the Anglo-Australian heritage and thereby gaining support to win power. This ploy failed in the federal election of 1990, but was tried again in 1993. It failed again, this time convincingly. The results of the 1993 election were a rude awakening for many people: politicians, economic advisers, the press gallery, the pollsters. The experts saw society in the image they themselves had created; in reality people thought and acted otherwise. The omniscient, so vocal during the campaign, became silent for a while, but soon were back with claims that the voters 'did not understand' and it was only a matter of time before they would see the light. The 'born to rule' and the 'born to know the truth' could not see why things should be otherwise.

Were the elections a sign of a significant change in people's thinking about social issues and about the kind of society they wanted? Only time will tell, but it appears certain that the social and cultural dimensions in such issues as immigration and multiculturalism may be given a place again in future public debates and policy-making considerations.

Methodologies, Mythologies and Social Reality

Analysts applying economic reductionism to social science research have tended to reify their heuristic concepts and begun to believe their own myths. However, the problem has become much wider. With the growth of the social and behavioural sciences and related professions the knowledge generated by some researchers and practitioners in these areas has become more normative in orientation and content, although accepted by their disciples as 'scientific' and 'objective', and disseminated as such.

Increasingly too, the ideas and concepts developed in the social and behavioural sciences have become class-based, that is, society and social issues are perceived and interpreted from the vantage point of the new middle class and reflect the interests of that class. This class-based culture is reinforced among the members of the new middle class, and class-based norms and values are then used to authoritatively judge the life-styles and values of the people 'out there', that is, the culture of the other classes. The upper class of the super-rich can and does ignore such judgements, but the lower classes are subjugated to these judgements because they do not have the means to propagate their own perceptions and judgements beyond their own communities. Because of differences in access to the means of communication, such as the mass media, books, journals, the arts, teaching, and so on, the culture propagated by the new middle class becomes the dominant culture.

Such a class-based dominant culture is also, by definition, a culture of inequality. This problem is not confined to Australia. As Eder observes, contemporary theories of social inequality tend to present the class structure of the industrialised societies 'as being legitimate forms of social inequality', aiming to 'legitimate social inequality and at the same time uphold the idea of equality'. The effect is that 'the more modern society advances the more the forms of representing the class structure within theories of legitimate social inequality gain importance' (1989:127). This trend has been reinforced by a departure in the education and practice of the 'helping professions' from an orientation based on social explanations to one based on individual explanations. Social inequalities tend to be perceived in terms of individual 'personality characteristics', inferred from personal achievement, or personal failure, thus explaining structural advantage or disadvantage in individual terms and validating inequality accordingly. This process of individualisation serves to conceal 'clusters' of characteristics which, when revealed, show the 'hidden class structure' (Eder 1989: 127). Furthermore, as shown in the study of urban distribution of population characteristics (Jamrozik and Boland 1993, see Chapter 6), there is a cumulative and compound effect of such distribution, which reveals not simply a spatial distribution of socio-economic stratification but a class structure in terms of a differential 'command over resources through time'. By individualising the class characteristics of the population the class nature of society can be denied and the myth of equality of opportunity can be maintained.

Similarly, cultural differences also tend to be interpreted as personality characteristics: immigrants are perceived as being either 'overly ambitious' (if they do well economically), or 'maladjusted' if they do not do so well. They are perceived as either unfairly competitive in exploiting opportunities in the market to their own advantage, or, if they cannot find employment, as a burden on society. The 'successes' become a threat, and the 'failures' have to be assisted through 'counselling' or 'treatment' by welfare or mental health personnel. This attitude is the same as that which is displayed towards working-class persons. Cultural differences thus become class differences.

In the debates on immigration and multiculturalism in Australia some arguments have been based on empirical evidence, some on subjective values and prejudices, some on self-interest, and some on a multitude of mixed reasons. However, many arguments against immigration or against immigration from particular countries and against multi-culturalism have been based on nothing more than myths. Myths are created and maintained not only in folklore, conventional wisdom and common beliefs. Myths are also created and maintained in social analyses and research, in turn included in text books and disseminated to teachers and students. Some myths are created through a mistaken belief in a so-called scientific discovery which later proves to be false, but tends still to become part of the conventional wisdom. For example, theories about the shape of the human cranium as an indicator of intelligence or a criminal mind, the 'YY' chromosome as an indication of aggression, lower intelligence in black populations: all these myths were at first 'scientific truths'. Among the Anglo-Australian middle class and its professional members myths about immigrants have been created, ranging from beliefs in extensive malingering and claiming workers' compensation payments so as to 'retire in comfort back home in Greece', to 'untrustworthy and disloyal Arabs' undermining Australia's war efforts against Saddam Hussein. Images of extremely authoritarian patriarchal family structures, maltreatment of women and exploitation of children; all such assertions add to the mythology of an 'un-Australian' culture among immigrants.

Cultural Transformation from Below

Authoritative middle-class perceptions and mythologies of ethnic and cultural diversity rarely reflect the social reality of Australia's multi-cultural society. The Australian experience with immigration and the shift from assimilation to multiculturalism provides strong empirical evidence that cultural transformation is a process which is embedded in the experience of everyday life. It is through the activities of everyday life – work, play, social encounters – that people experience, modify and create their culture (Thompson 1968). In other words, cultural trans-formation is a process which starts from below.

The post-war immigration program had two basic aims: to increase the size of the population ('populate or perish'); and to provide a labour force for heavy construction and development work. However, there was fear in ruling circles that mass immigration would threaten the Anglo-Saxon character of society, and to overcome this threat there was a plan for a ratio of immigrants of ten to one in favour of immigrants from Britain. The British immigrants and selected immigrants from northern Europe (the 'Teutonic' people with 'flaxen hair and light blue eyes', as Reeves would have called them, see Chapter 3) were recruited for all occupations; the others only for labouring and domestic jobs. The program did not work out as planned: the demand for labour was greater than Britain was able to supply, despite the costly 'Bring out a Briton' campaigns and ten pound fares (which many people used as cheap travel for a short working holiday in what they saw as a British colony), special assistance on arrival, guaranteed employment and housing, and full citizenship rights. The northern European countries did not provide many immigrants, either. Not long after the start of the program the balance of the intake changed in favour of non-English-speaking immigrants, first from central and eastern Europe and then from southern Europe, the Middle East and eventually from South-East Asia.

The outcome of this 'dual immigration policy' has been that the working class in Australia has become much more multicultural than the middle class because the middle class ('old' and 'new') remained isolated from direct contact with immigrants in their everyday life. This difference in the cultural composition of the two classes has been exacerbated by the defensive practices of the professions in accepting the newcomers' educational and professional qualificatons. Hence class division became also a cultural division.

The cultural or racial conflict prophesied did not occur. As the demand for labour was high and the non-English-speaking immigrants were confined to labouring jobs, local workers generally did not object, especially as the arrival of newcomers with rigidly restricted employment choices provided unprecedented opportunities of upward occupational mobility for the locals. Furthermore, despite initial apprehensions, local workers found that the newcomers fitted reasonably well into the workplace (except that too many of them might have worked too hard, which spelled danger to the established norms) and also into the social life of the neighbourhood. It was through the direct experience of the workplace and social life that cultural integration began. In the working-class suburbs the locals found that the newcomers were good neighbours and, far from the predicted lowering of the value of real estate, they contributed to the improvement of the neighbourhood character. Integration of cultures might have proceeded slowly but it was nevertheless taking place.

The situation was different in middle-class suburbs. The population living in those suburbs, largely consisting of professionals and other white-collar workers very rarely had direct experience of meeting the non-English-speaking immigrants, either in the workplace or in their localities. Non-English-speaking immigrants rarely moved into those suburbs for a host of reasons: the high cost, the desire to live close to their own communities, and discouraging, negative attitudes on the part of real estate agents who seemed to work in tacit agreement with local government bodies and residents towards ensuring that real estate values would not fall through any 'contamination' of the Anglo-Saxon purity of these middle-class suburbs. Any acceptance of cultural diversity among the middle classes has been acceptance *within* the dominant Anglo-Saxon or Anglo-Celtic culture, while among the working classes cultural transformation has occurred as a *two-way process*, as a form of a dialectic process resulting in a multicultural synthesis.

The change in policy from assimilation to integration did not arise until the occupational composition of immigrants began to change. As various ethnic communities grew in numbers, leaders emerged and such communities became more organised and visible as identifiable communities. Through their organisations and later through joint peak representative bodies, such as Ethnic Communities' Councils, they also acquired a public voice. The assimilation policy had clearly failed and in due course the legitimacy of ethnic identities was acknowledged in the policy of multiculturalism. The notions of integration and cultural pluralism was an acknowledgement of the cultural transformation which was taking place in everyday life among increasing sections of Australian society. The policy of multiculturalism which followed was a conceptualisation of what was already present in Australian society, at least in large parts of it.

Initially, the notion of a multicultural society did not raise much criticism, except from social analysts on the Left who saw the policy of cultural pluralism as a means of concealing the class disadvantage of ethnic communities by creating an illusion of equality based on acceptance of ethnic diversity. For the middle classes and core institutions, as long as the 'multiculturals' were seen to be distinct from 'Australian Australians' and separated from the Anglo-Australian middle class in the workplace and in the urban environment, cultural pluralism could be tolerated. Tolerance of diversity became difficult when more immigrants, and then the children of immigrants, began to compete for middle-class professional and technical jobs. The immigration policy had thus created a dilemma: changing structures of industry and occupations called for more highly skilled labour, but the more skilled the imported labour became the more threatening the immigration

program became to the middle-class professions. Cultural diversity
began to be seen as a threat to the privileged position of Anglo-
Australians in the class structure. It was not the 'ordinary' working-class
Australians, 'Anglo' or 'ethnic', who in the 1980s raised ethnocentric or
implied racist arguments against further immigration and multiculturalism: those arguments were raised by the middle-class analysts, commentators and politicians: some of the working class might have
accepted those views, although the results of the 1993 elections indicate
that not many did so.

Reactions against immigration and multiculturalism reached new
heights when it became increasingly apparent that the changing social
and cultural composition of immigrant intake might threaten the Anglo-
Saxon, or Anglo-Celtic, hegemony of the core social institutions. Over
time the pressure for change built up, reaching closer to these institutions: education, professions, the law, established Christian religions.
Invoking the fear of 'Asianisation', the threat to Christianity from Islam,
or lack of 'commitment to Australia' represents efforts to distract
attention from the real nature of the threat to class privilege, which has
been presented to the public as a threat to Anglo-Australian cultural
homogeneity, to historical links with England and the British Crown.
Certainly, the increase in the population with no historical links with
Britain and no 'colonial inheritance' in views and attitudes has
weakened the 'double loyalty' of the Anglo-Australian population, and
at the same time it has become a threat to class privilege built on that
'double loyalty'.

Cultural Transformation and Identity

Australia today presents a situation *par excellence* of a society in which
cultural transformation is of utmost importance for its future, but such
transformation is resisted by the dominant power structure for reasons
of tradition, cultural prejudice and, above all, monocultural class
privilege. A certain degree of cultural transformation has occurred in
some aspects of social life, to a much higher degree in the lower class
strata of the population than in the middle classes, old or new. As a
result, Australian society is a society with an institutionalised monocultural core surrounded by a developing multicultural 'periphery'. The
longer that difference persists the more difficult it will be for Australia to
define its true identity and establish itself as a society and a nation in its
own right, among neighbouring societies in the region from which it
cannot escape.

Whether Australia will make the necessary step towards complete
autonomy by jettisoning its 'colonial inheritance' and accepting its

position in the part of the world where it is geographically located is not yet certain. There is in the Anglo-Australian psyche a certain kind of inertia, and also a certain kind of expectation inherited from the colonial times that complete autonomy is not important because some powerful protector will always look after Australia. It is a kind of dependence and a fear of autonomy that seems to have been developed through years of socialisation by the British-oriented bourgeois middle class. Someone, somewhere, will 'look after our interests'. This colonial socialisation has proved to be remarkably strong. In writing about this in the *Death of the Lucky Country*, Donald Horne observes:

> ... we have never 'earned' our democracy. We simply went along with some British habits, amending them as little as possible. We have never seriously bothered even to teach the forms of our democratic government, such as it is, in schools. We have never put the ideals of democracy into the written Constitution or into the rituals and symbols of the state.   (1976:96)

Why bother to change, is the conservative attitude, if the country has done well until now? 'If it ain't broke, don't fix it'; or 'The situation is not very good at present, but if immigration of non-English-speaking people were slowed down, or stopped altogether, and if the dangerous notion of multiculturalism were abandoned, things will come good again'. The myth creation industry continues its work. Why search for a new Australian identity?

Australian identity will emerge, not so much by deliberate design as by abandoning some of the inherited myths we have discussed and acknowledging the present internal and external social reality. In discovering this identity, the new middle class will have an important role to play. We reiterate that it is this class that collectively defines social reality, and will continue to do so in the future. However, the definers need to ensure that what they define is the social reality of everyday life, not the colonial myths of the past or a mythical world of their own creation. The new middle class has the knowledge and skills to lead the search for an Australian identity, provided its members resist the seduction of the conservative forces and the pursuit of their own class interests by supporting the status quo in the institutions which have so far resisted the cultural transformation of Australian society.

Whether the new middle class will take up that challenge is an open question. Each year thousands of enthusiastic and idealistically-minded young people enter universities and hope that they will contribute to making this society a better place to live in and one more open to cultural transformation. By the time they complete their courses of study, which have increasingly become normatively prescriptive rather than intellectually enlightening, they are no longer so hopeful, and when they take up positions in the core institutions they soon become socialised into the organisational culture, the monoculture which resists change. They are made aware of their superior class position in relation to the people 'out there', and their potential as a force of enlightenment is converted into a force of social control, repressing change. Those who do not submit to the conversion process pay the penalty of exclusion or living an unhappy professional life.

Acknowledging this problem is, however, not to offer a counsel of despair, for there is always hope that the future will be different from the past. This hope applies to the new middle class as well, especially to its potential as an agent of social change and cultural transformation. In his theory of the new middle class, or the New Class as he called it, the late Alvin Gouldner saw this class as 'the most progressive force in modern society and a centre of whatever emancipation is possible in the foreseeable future' (1979:6–8, 83–4). He did not have complete confidence that the new middle class would fulfil that role because he saw it as being 'both emancipating and elitist, ... morally ambivalent, embodying the collective interest but partially and transiently, while simultaneously cultivating its own advantage'. Despite these contradictions, he thought that this class 'may also be the best card that history has presently given us to play'.

We think that the Australian new middle class, like the new middle class in other countries of the world today, has the potential to take up the challenge and fulfil this promise. To a significant extent it is on the fulfilment of this promise that the successful outcome of the Australian · multicultural experiment depends, an experiment which serves not only as a vehicle for the cultural transformation through which Australian society will find its true identity, but also as a model for other countries in the world to follow. Time will tell.

Bibliography

Abbott, T. (1990) 'The real issue is the changing face of our society', *Australian*, 31 May

Abercrombie, N. and Urry, J. (1983) *Capital, Labour and the New Middle Class*, London: Allen and Unwin

Adams, P. (1993) 'Challenging choice on the smell of an oily rag', *Australian*, 6–7 March

Advisory Council on Multicultural Affairs (1988) *Towards a National Agenda for a Multicultural Australia* (discussion paper), Canberra: Australian Government Publishing Service

Alcorso, C. (1989) 'Migrants and the workers' compensation system: the basis of an ideology', *Australian and New Zealand Journal of Sociology*, 25(1): 46–65

———(1991) *Non-English speaking background immigrant women in the workforce*, Canberra: Office of Multicultural Affairs

Alexander, J. C. and Seidman, S. (eds) (1990) *Culture and Society: Contemporary Debates*, Cambridge: Cambridge University Press

Alford, R. R. (1969) 'Religion and politics', in R. Robertson (ed.), 321–30

Allison, C. (1991) 'Mosque battle may be won in court', *Sydney Morning Herald*, 23 February

Anagnostou, P. (1982) *Ethnic Politics: Migrants and Ethnic Organisations*, unpublished honours thesis, School of Social Sciences, Adelaide: Flinders University of South Australia

Anderson, B. (1983) *Imagined Communities: Reflections on the Origin and Spread of Nationalism*, London: Verso

Anderson, D. S. (1988) 'Education and the social order', in J. M. Najman and J. S. Western (eds), 214–38

———(1991) 'Is the privatisation of Australian schooling inevitable?', in F. G. Castles (ed.), 140–67

Aronowitz, S. (1992) *The Politics of Identity: Class, Culture Social Movements*, New York: Routledge

Ashbolt, A. (1985) 'Radio and television services for migrants: problems and prospects', in I. Burnley, S. Encel and G. McCall (eds), 104–10

Atkinson, M. (ed.) (1920) *Australia: Economic and Political Studies*, Melbourne: Macmillan

243

Australia Council (1986) *Multiculturalism and the Arts*, Sydney: Australia Council
Australian Ethnic Affairs Council (1977) *Australia as a Multicultural Society*, Canberra: Australian Government Publishing Service
Australian Population and Immigration Council (1976) *A Decade of Migrant Settlement: Report on the 1973 Immigration Survey*, Canberra: Australian Government Publishing Service
Australian Bureau of Statistics (1989) *Australia's Children, 1989*, Catalogue No. 4119.0
——(1989) *Cafes and Restaurants Industry, Australia, 1986–87*, Cat. No. 8655.0
——(1991) *Australian Demographic Statistics*, June Quarter 1991, Cat. No. 3101.0
——(1991) *Multicultural Australia*, Cat. No. 2505.0
——(1992) *Transition from Education to Work, Australia, 1992*, Cat. No. 6227.0
——(1992) *Labour Force Status and Educational Attainment, Australia, February 1992*, Cat. No. 6235.0
——(1992) *The Labour Force, Australia, August 1992*, Cat. No. 6203.0
——(1992) *Schools, Australia, 1991*, Cat. No. 4221.0
——(1992) *Fertility in Australia*, Cat. No. 2514.0
—— (1992) *1990 Survey of Income and Housing Costs and Amenities: Persons with Earned Incomes, Australia*, Cat. No. 6546
——(1993) *The Labour Force, Australia, August 1993*, Cat. No. 6203.0
Australian Financial Review (1988) 'Howard takes a dangerous road', editorial, 5 August
Barnett, D. (1990) 'What the government ignored', *Bulletin*, 29 May, 36–42
Bauman, Z. (1987) *Legislators and Interpreters: on Modernity, Post-modernity and Intellectuals*, Cambridge: Polity Press
——(1992) *Intimations of Postmodernity*, London: Routledge
Beckett, R. (1984) *Convicted Tastes*, Sydney: Allen and Unwin
Beilharz, P., Considine, M. and Watts, R. (1992) *Arguing about the Welfare State: Australian Experience*, Sydney: Allen and Unwin
Bennett, T., Martin, G., Mercer, C. and Woollacott, J. (eds) (1981) *Culture, Ideology and Social Process: a Reader*, London: B. T. Batsford/Open University Press
Bennoun, P., Bennoun, R. and Kelly, P. (1984) *The Peoples from Indo-China*, Melbourne: Hodja Educational Resources Cooperative
Berger, P. and Luckmann, T. (1971) *The Social Construction of Reality*, Harmondsworth: Penguin
Bills, K. (1988) 'CAAIP in context: an economic-demographic critique', *Journal of Australian Population Association*, 5(2): 146–63
Birrell, R. (1990) 'It's time Australia's ship came in – without another load of migrants', *Sydney Morning Herald*, 13 November
Birrell, R. and Hay, C. (eds) (1978) *The Immigration Issue in Australia: a Sociological Symposium*, Melbourne: Globe Press
Blainey, G. (1988a) 'Australian Australians must begin to shout loudly', *Australian*, 2 July
——(1988b) 'Racist: a word hijacking the immigration debate', *Australian*, 20–21 August
——(1989) 'Too few true blue', *Australian*, 27–28 May
——(1990) 'The conflict of self-interest', *Australian*, 2–3 June
——(1993) 'Joining Asia a pipedream', *Australian*, 13–14 February
Boland, C. (1989) *A Comparative Study of Home and Hospital Births: Scientific and Normative Variables and Their Effects*, SWRC Discussion Papers No. 12, Kensington: University of New South Wales

————(1991) 'The social organisation of birth services: are class variables relevant?', *New Doctor*, 55: 17–19

Borowski, A. and Shu, J. (1992) *Australia's Population Trends and Prospects*, Melbourne: Bureau of Immigration Research

Bottomley, G. and de Lepervanche, M. (eds) (1984) *Ethnicity, Class and Gender in Australia*, Sydney: Allen and Unwin

Bourdieu, P. (1984) *Distinction: a Social Critique of the Judgement of Taste*, London: Routledge and Kegan Paul

Bourdieu, P. and Passeron, J-C. (1990) *Reproduction in Education, Society and Culture*, London: Sage

Bowen, M. (ed.) (1977) *Australia 2000: the Ethnic Impact*, Armidale: University of New England Publishing Unit

Bringmann, L. P. (1988) *The Hospitality Industry in Australia: Yesterday-Today-Tomorrow: Food to Eat and Food for Thought*, unpublished monograph with author

Bunk, S. (1992) 'The long wait', *Australian Magazine*, 12–13 December, 38–45

Burnley, I. (ed.) (1974) *Urbanisation in Australia: the Post-war Experience*, Cambridge: Cambridge University Press

————(1974) 'Urbanisation and social segregation in Australian cities', in I. Burnley (ed.)

————(1975) 'Ethnic factors in social segregation and residential stratification in Australian large cities', *Australian and New Zealand Journal of Sociology*, 11(1): 12–20

————(1985) 'Neighbourhood communal structure and acculturation in ethnic concentration in Sydney, 1978', in I. Burnley, S. Encel and G. McCall (eds), 167–97

————(1986) 'Convergence or occupational and residential segmentation? Immigrants and their Australian-born children in metropolitan Sydney, 1981', *Australian and New Zealand Journal of Sociology*, 22(1): 65–83

Burnley, I., Encel, S. and McCall, G. (eds) (1985) *Immigration and Ethnicity in the 1980s*, Melbourne: Cheshire

CAAIP, see Committee to Advise on Australia's Immigration Policies

Campbell, I., Fincher, R. and Webber, M. (1991) 'Occupational mobility in segmented labour markets: the experience of immigrant workers in Melbourne', *Australian and New Zealand Journal of Sociology*, 27(2): 172–94

Castles, F. G. (1985) *The Working Class and Welfare: Reflections on the Political Development of the Welfare State in Australia and New Zealand, 1890–1980*, Sydney: Allen and Unwin

————(ed.) (1991) *Australia Compared: People, Policies and Politics*, Sydney: Allen and Unwin

Castles, S. (1984) *Here for Good: Western Europe's New Ethnic Minorities*, London: Pluto Press

Castles, S. and Kosack, G. (1985) I*mmigrant Workers and Class Structure in Western Europe*, second ed., Oxford: Oxford University Press

Castles, S., Kalantzis, M., Cope, B. and Morrissey, M. (1988a) *Mistaken Identity: Multiculturalism and the Demise of Nationalism in Australia*, Sydney: Pluto Press

Castles, S., Morrissey, M. and Pinkstone, B. (1988b) *Migrant Employment and Training and Industry Restructuring*, Canberra: Office of Multicultural Affairs

Castles, S., Mitchell, S., Morrissey, M. and Alcorso, C. (1989) *The Recognition of Overseas Trade Qualifications*, Canberra: Australian Government Publishing Service

Castles, S., Collins, J., Gibson, K., Tait, D. and Alcorso, C. (1991) *The Global Milkbar and the Local Sweatshop: Ethnic Small Business and the Economic Restructuring of Sydney*, Canberra: Office of Multicultural Affairs

Chipman, L. (1985) 'Ethnicity and national culture', in M. E. Poole, P. R. de Lacey and R. Randhawa (eds), 260–5

Clegg, S. R. (ed.) (1989) *Organisation Theory and Class Analysis: New Approaches and New Issues*, Berlin: de Gruyter

Clyne, M. (1991) *Community Languages: the Australian Experience*, Cambridge: Cambridge University Press

Collins, J. (1988) *Migrant Hands in a Distant Land: Australia's Post-war Immigration*, Sydney: Pluto Press

Committee for Stage 1 of the Review of Migrant and Multicultural Programs and Services (1986) *Don't Settle for Less*, Canberra: Australian Government Publishing Service

Committee of Inquiry into the Recognition of Overseas Qualifications (1983) *The Recognition of Overseas Qualifications in Australia*, Canberra: Australian Government Publishing Service

Committee of Review of the Australian Institute of Multicultural Affairs (1983) *Report*, Canberra: Australian Government Publishing Service

Committee to Advise on Australia's Immigration Policies (1988) *Immigration: a Commitment to Australia*, Canberra: Australian Government Publishing Service

Commonwealth of Australia, *The Commonwealth of Australia Constitution Act 1900 and the Statute of Westminster Adoption Act 1942*, Canberra: Commonwealth Government Printer

Connell, J. (1993) 'Soul searching', *Sydney Morning Herald*, 1 April

Cook, B. (1988) 'More business migrants, fewer Asians – common sense or contradiction?', *Migration*, October/November, 14–16

Cope, B., Castles, S. and Kalantzis, M. (1991) *Immigration, Ethnic Conflict and Social Cohesion*, Canberra: Australian Government Publishing Service

Crisp, L. (1990) 'The underclass: Australia's social time bomb', *Bulletin*, 3 April, 48–56

Dahrendorf, R. (1959) *Class and Class Conflict in Industrial Society*, London: Routledge and Kegan Paul

Davies, A. F. and Encel, S. (eds) (1970) *Australian Society: a Sociological Introduction*, second ed., Melbourne: Cheshire

Davies, A. F., Encel, S. and M. J. Berry (eds) (1977) *Australian Society: a Sociological Introduction*, third ed., Melbourne: Longman Cheshire

Davidson, J. (1990) 'The manufacture of Australian culture', in B. Hocking (ed.), 24–45

Dennis, A. (1991) 'Between a wok and a hard place', *Good Weekend, Sydney Morning Herald* magazine, 13 July, 22–8

Department for Community Welfare (1987) *The Next Five Years: Discussion Paper*, Adelaide: Department for Community Welfare

Department of Employment, Education and Training (1987) *Meeting Australia's Skill Needs*, Canberra: Department of Employment, Education and Training

——(1989) *The National Office of Overseas Skills Recognition: Information Kit*, Canberra: Australian Government Publishing Service

Department of Health and Community Services (1987) *Towards Better Nutrition for Australians*, Canberra: Australian Government Publishing Service

Department of Immigration, Local Government and Ethnic Affairs (1987) *Australia's Population Trends and Prospects 1987*, Canberra: Australian Government Publishing Service

Dickey, B. (1987) *No Charity There*, Sydney: Allen and Unwin

Eccleston, R. (1991) 'Religious teachings spell division for Queensland classrooms', *Australian*, 24 December

Economic Planning Advisory Council (1987) *Aspects of the Social Wage: Social Expenditures and Redistribution*, Council Paper No. 27, Canberra: Economic Planning Advisory Council

Eddy, J. (1991) 'What are the origins of Australia's identity?', in F. G. Castles (ed.), 17–37

Eder, K. (1989) 'The cognitive representations of social inequality: a sociological account of the cultural basis of modern class society', in H. Haferkamp (ed.), 125–46

Edgar, D. (ed.) (1974) *Social Change in Australia: Readings in Sociology*, Melbourne: Cheshire

Ehrenreich, B. and J. (1979) 'The professional–managerial class', in P. Walker (ed.), 5–45 and 313–34

Ellis, E. (1992) 'Utzon: my orange peel opera house', *Good Weekend, Sydney Morning Herald* magazine, 31 October, 12–19

Encel, S. (1970) *Equality and Authority: a Study of Class, Status and Power in Australia*, Melbourne: Cheshire

Encel, S. and Bryson, L. (eds) *Australian Society*, fourth ed., Melbourne, Longman, Cheshire

Esping-Andersen, G. (1985) *Politics against Markets: the Social Democratic Road to Power*, Princeton: Princeton University Press

Ethnic Affairs Commission of New South Wales (1987) *Review of Ethnic Affairs Policy Statements (E.A.P.S.) Program in New South Wales*, Sydney: Ethnic Affairs Commission, NSW

Ethnos (1990) 'Planning for religious development in NSW', September, 74–8

Family and Children Services Agency (1981) *Who is 'Unresponsive'? Negative Assessment of Aboriginal Children*, Sydney: NSW Government Printer

Featherstone, M. (1989) 'Towards a sociology of postmodern culture', in H. Haferkamp (ed.) 147–72

——(ed.) (1990) *Global Culture: Nationalism, Globalisation and Modernity*, London: Sage

——(ed.) (1992) *Cultural Theory and Cultural Change*, London: Sage

——(1992) 'The heroic life and everyday life', in M. Featherstone (ed.), 159–82

Federation of Ethnic Communities' Council of Australia (1988) *1988 FECCA Congress Report: Multiculturalism: a Commitment for Australia*, Sydney: FECCA

Ford, G. W. (1970) 'Work', in A. F. Davies and S. Encel (eds) 84–119

Foster, L. and Stockley, D. (1988) ' The rise and decline of Australian multiculturalism, 1973–1988, *Politics*, 23(2): 1–10

Galbally Report, see Review of Post-Arrival Programs

Galbally, F. E. (1985) 'Multiculturalism in the 1980s: progress and prospects', in I. Burnley, S. Encel and G. McCall (eds), 113–18

Geertz, C.(1975) *The Interpretation of Cultures*, London: Hutchinson

Gellner, E. (1969) 'A pendulum swing theory of Islam', in R. Robertson (ed.), 127–38

Gerth, H. H. and Mills, C. Wright (eds) (1948) *From Max Weber: Essays in Sociology*, London: Routledge and Kegan Paul

Giddens, A. (1987) *Social Theory and Modern Sociology*, Cambridge: Polity Press

Gill, F. (1992) 'Inequality and the wheel of fortune: systemic causes of economic deprivation', in P. Saunders and D. Encel (eds), 35–50

Glezer, L. (1988) 'Business and commerce', in J. Jupp (ed.), 860–64

Goodman, D., O'Hearn, D. J. and Wallace-Crabbe, C. (eds) (1991) *Multicultural Australia: the Challenges of Change*, Melbourne: Scribe

Gouldner, A. W. (1979) *The Future of Intellectuals and the Rise of the New Class*, London: Macmillan

——(1990) 'Ideology, the cultural apparatus and the new consciousness industry', in J. C. Alexander and S. Seidman (eds), 306–16

Grassby, A. J. (1984) 'National identity: cohesion or fragmentation', in D. J. Phillips and J. Houston (eds) 155–60

Graycar, A. (1979) *Welfare Politics in Australia*, Melbourne: Macmillan

Graycar A. and Jamrozik, A. (1993) *How Australians Live: Social Policy in Theory and Practice*, second ed., Melbourne: Macmillan

Greenfield, H., Martlew, M. A., Balmer, N. and Wills, R. B. H. (1980) 'Composition of Australian foods: Lebanese foods and meals' *Food Technology in Australia*, 32(11): 578–81

Greenfield, H., Makinson, J. H., Weyrauch, A. and Wills, R. B. H. (1984) 'Composition of Australian foods: Italian foods', *Food Technology in Australia*, 36(10): 469–71

Gunew, S. (1990) 'Multiculturalism is for everyone: "Australians" and "ethnic" others', in B. Hocking (ed.), 100–13

Haferkamp, H. (ed.) (1989) *Social Structure and Culture*, Berlin: de Gruyter

Halligan, J. and Paris, C. (eds) (1984) *Australian Urban Politics: Critical Perspectives*, Melbourne: Longman Cheshire

Hancock, K. (ed.) (1989) *Australian Society*, Cambridge: Cambridge University Press

Hancock, W. K. (1945) *Australia*, Sydney: Australasian Publishing Company

Hassan, R. and Tan, G. (1990) *Asian Migrants in Australia: a Socio-Economic Study*, Adelaide: Flinders University of South Australia, unpublished monograph

Hay, C. G. (1978) 'Immigrants, cities and the environment, in R. Birrell and C. Hay (eds), 103–14

Henderson, G. (1991) 'Careless talk all grist to the racist's mill', *Sydney Morning Herald*, 12 March

Henderson, R. F., Harcourt, A. and Harper, R. J. A. (1970) *People in Poverty: a Melbourne Survey*, Melbourne: Cheshire

Hewson, J. (1990) *Australians Speak: Australia 2000*, Canberra: Parliament House, Leader of the Opposition

Hickman, D. C. (1977) 'Religion', in A. F. Davies, S. Encel and M. J. Berry (eds), 234–67

Hill, S. (1988) 'Work and technological change in Australia', in J. N. Najman and J. S. Western (eds), 239–92

Hirsch, P., Michaels, S. and Friedman, R. (1987) '"Dirty hands" versus "clean models": is sociology in danger of being seduced by economics?', *Theory and Society*, 16: 317–36

Hocking, B. (ed.) (1990) *Australia towards 2000*, London: Macmillan

Hoffman, J. E. (1984) 'Historical and geopolitical considerations of an immigrant nation in Asia', in D. J. Phillips and J. Houston (eds), 58–66

Hoggett, P. (1990) *Modernisation, Political Strategy and the Welfare State: an Organisational Perspective*, Bristol: University of Bristol

Holton, R. (1991) 'A lesson in social well-being', *Bulletin*, 27 August, 88–9

Horin, A. (1990) 'Quality of life that they can't measure', *Sydney Morning Herald*, 23 October

——(1992a) 'Why middle-class men no longer marry down', *Sydney Morning Herald*, 17 November

——(1992b) 'New servant class a sign of inequality gap', *Sydney Morning Herald*, 24 November

Horne, D. (1968) *The Lucky Country: Australia in the Sixties*, second ed., Sydney: Angus and Robertson

——(1976) *Death of the Lucky Country*, Ringwood: Penguin

——(1983) *The Perils of Multiculturalism as a National Ideal*, Melbourne: Australian Institute of Multicultural Affairs

H.R.H. The Duke of Edinburgh's Third Commonwealth Study Conference (1968) *Anatomy of Australia*, Melbourne: Sun Books

Howard, J. (1989) 'Address to 1988 Congress of the Federation of Ethnic Communities' Council, *Congress Proceedings*, Sydney: FECCA, 122–9

Humphrey, M. (1984) 'Religion, law and family disputes in a Lebanese community in Sydney', in G. Bottomley and M. de Lepervanche (eds), 183–97

Inglis, K. S. (1970) 'Religious behaviour', in A. F. Davies, and S. Encel (eds), 437–75

Inglis, P. and Strombach, T. (1984) *A Descriptive Analysis of Migrants' Labour Market Experience*, Working Paper No. 38, Canberra: Bureau of Labour Market Research

Iredale, R. R. (1987) *Wasted Skills: Barriers to Migrant Entry to Occupations in Australia*, Sydney: Ethnic Affairs Commission of NSW

——(1989) 'Barriers to migrant entry to occupations in Australia', *International Migration*, 27(1): 87–106

Ironmonger, D. (ed.) (1989) *Households Work*, Sydney: Allen and Unwin

Jakubowicz, A. (1974) 'The city game: urban ideology and social conflict, or who gets the goodies and who pays the cost', in D. Edgar (ed.), 329–43

——(1981) 'State and ethnicity: multiculturalism as ideology', *Australian and New Zealand Journal of Sociology*, 17(3): 4–13

——(1984) 'Ethnicity, multiculturalism and neo-conservatism', in G. Bottomley and M. de Lepervanche (eds), 28–48

Jamrozik, A. (1982) *Empowerment and Welfare: the Issue of Power Relationships in Services to Aborigines*, Occasional Paper No. 2, Sydney: NSW Ministry for Aboriginal Affairs

——(1989) 'The household economy and social class', in D. Ironmonger (ed.), 64–78

——(1991a) *Class, Inequality and the State: Social Change, Social Policy and the New Middle Class*, Melbourne: Macmillan

——(1991b) 'The roots of unemployment', *Ethnic Spotlight*, Issue 23: 12–14

——(1991c) 'Immigrants and the recession: an expendable labour force?', *Migration Action*, November, 22–8

Jamrozik, A. and Boland, C. (1988) *Social Welfare Policy for a Multicultural Society*, Canberra: Office of Multicultural Affairs

——(1993) *Human Resources in Community Services: Conceptual Issues and Empirical Evidence*, SPRC Reports and Proceedings No.104, Kensington: University of New South Wales

Jamrozik, A., Boland, C. and Stewart, D. (1991) *Immigrants and Occupational Welfare: Industry Restructuring and its Effects on the Occupational Welfare of*

Immigrants from Non-English Speaking Countries, Canberra: Office of Multicultural Affairs

Jamrozik, A. and Hoey. M. (1982) *Dynamic Labour Market or Work on the Wane? Trends in the Australian Labour Force 1966–1981*, SWRC Reports and Proceedings No. 27, Kensington: University of New South Wales

Jamrozik, A., Urquhart, R. and Wearing, M. (1990) *Contribution of Immigration to Skills Development and Occupational Structure*, Melbourne: Bureau of Immigration Research

Jayasuriya, L. (1985) 'Multiculturalism: fact, policy and rhetoric', in M. E. Poole, P. de Lacey and R. Randhawa (eds), 23–34

——(1990) 'Rethinking Australian multiculturalism: towards a new paradigm'. *Australian Quarterly*, Autumn, 50-63

——(1991) 'State, nation and diversity in Australia', *Current Affairs Bulletin*, 67(11): 21-6

Jayasuriya, L. and Sang, D. (1990) 'Asian immigration: past and current trends', *Current Affairs Bulletin*, 66(11): 5–11

Jenkins, D. (1993) 'Quarter-Asian Australia: why it's coming soon', *Sydney Morning Herald*, 4 December

Jones, B. (1983) 'Technology, development and employment', *Sixth National Conference of Labor Economists: Proceedings*, Sydney, 29–30 October

Jones, C. (1992) 'Learning to exchange ideas', *Australian*, 25 November

Jones, F. L. (1987) 'Marriage patterns and the stratification system: trends in educational homogamy since the 1930s', *Australian and New Zealand Journal of Sociology*, 23(2): 185–98

Jordan, A. (1989) *Of Good Character and Deserving a Pension: Moral and Racial Provisions in Australian Social Security*, SWRC Reports and Proceedings No. 77, Kensington: University of New South Wales

Jupp, J. (ed.) (1984) *Ethnic Politics in Australia*, Sydney: Allen and Unwin

——(1984a) 'The politics of "ethnic" areas of Melbourne, Sydney and Adelaide', in J. Halligan and C. Paris (eds), 110–28

——(1984b) 'Ethnic politics in Australia: a research perspective', in J. Jupp (ed.), 4–13

——(ed.) (1988) *The Australian People: an Encyclopedia of the Nation, its People and their Origins*, Sydney: Angus and Robertson

——(1988a) 'The response of Australian institutions to multiculturalism', in Federation of Ethnic Communities' Council (1989), 65–71

——(1988b) 'Immigration and ethnicity', in J. M. Najman and J. S. Western (eds), 162–81

——(ed.) (1989) *The Challenge of Diversity: Policy Options for Multicultural Australia*, Canberra: Office of Multicultural Affairs

——(1990) 'Upwards, downwards or just round and round: multicultural public policy in Australia', in B. Hocking (ed.), 123–35

——(1991) 'From free entry to tight control: the entry of immigrants to Australia since 1788', in G. Withers (ed.) 11–29

Jupp, J., York, B. and McRobbie A. (1989) *The Political Participation of Ethnic Minorities in Australia*, Canberra: Australian Government Publishing Service

Jurgensen, M. (1991) 'The politics of imagination', in D. Goodman, D. J. O'Hearn and C. Wallace-Crabbe (eds), 21–30

Kalantzis, M. and Cope, B. (1993) 'Cultural victory for Labor', *Sydney Morning Herald*, 18 March

Kendig, H. (1979) *New Life for Old Suburbs: Post-War Land Use and Housing in the Australian Inner City*, Sydney: Allen and Unwin

Kenny, D. (1992) 'Australia teeters on rim of the Pacific', *Sydney Morning Herald*, 22 December

Kewley, T. H. (1973) *Social Security in Australia, 1900–72*, Sydney: Sydney University Press

Knight, S. (1990) *The Selling of the Australian Mind: from First Fleet to Third Mercedes*, Melbourne: Heinemann

Kondos, A. (1992) 'The politics of ethnic identity: "conspirators" against the state or institutional racism?', *Australian and New Zealand Journal of Sociology*, 28(1): 5–28

Konrad, G. and Szelenyi, I. (1979) *The Intellectuals on the Road to Class Power*, New York: Harcourt Brace Jovanovich

Kramer, L. (1990) 'Aunty and the road to one culture', *Australian*, 11 June

Kreckel, R. (1989) '"New" social inequalities and the renewal of the theory of social inequalities', in S. R. Clegg (ed.), 137–55

Kunz, E. (1988) *Displaced Persons: Calwell's New Australians*, Canberra: Australian National University Press

de Lepervanche, M. (1980) 'From race to ethnicity', *Australian and New Zealand Journal of Sociology*, 16(1): 24–37

——— (1984) 'Immigrants and ethnic groups', in S. Encel and L. Bryson (eds), 170–228

Lewins, F. (1976) 'Ethnic diversity within Australian Catholicism: a comparative and theoretical analysis', *Australian and New Zealand Journal of Sociology*, 12(2): 126–35

Liffman, M. (1981) *Immigrant Welfare: a Research Perspective*, SWRC Reports and Proceedings No. 6, Kensington: University of New South Wales

McCall, G., Burnley, I., and Encel, S. (1985) 'Introduction: issues, ideas and ideology', in I. Burnley, S. Encel and G. McCall (eds), 1–39

McCallum, J. (1988) 'Religion and social cohesion', in J. Jupp (ed.), 938–42

Magnet, M. (1987) 'America's underclass: what to do?', *Fortune*, 11 May, 80–90

Marginson, S. (1992) 'Implications of the emerging educational markets', in P. Saunders and D. Encel (eds), 121–31

Martin, J. I. (1981) *The Ethnic Dimension*, Sydney: Allen and Unwin

Menadue, J. (1983) 'Immigration and Australia's development: with particular reference to the labour market', *Australian Bulletin of Labour*, 9(2): 93–101

Millett, M. (1990) 'Sydney 2021: standing room only', *Sydney Morning Herald*, 10 November

——— (1992a) 'Decision on Chinese may lead to 300 000 blow-out' and 'Govt to lop 31 000 off migrant intake', *Sydney Morning Herald*, 13 May

——— (1992b) 'Lib plan: no English, no vote', *Sydney Morning Herald*, 12 November

Mills, C. Wright (1956) *White Collar: the American Middle Classes*, New York: Oxford University Press

Miller, J. D. B. (1989) 'Australia in the world', in K. Hancock (ed.), 228–43

Milner, A. (1991) *Contemporary Cultural Theory: an Introduction*, Sydney: Allen and Unwin

Moeller, S. (1991) '"Whites only" policy persists', *Australian*, 30 November

Mol, J. J. (1970) 'Church schools and religious belief', in A. F. Davies and S. Encel (eds), 476–93

Murray, J. (1993) 'Unwise allegiance in attack on pledge' *Australian*, 16–17 January

Najman, J. M. and Western, J. S. (eds) (1988) *A Sociology of Australian Society*, Melbourne: Macmillan

Nathan, R. P. (1987) 'Will the underclass be with us?', *Society*, 24(3): 57–62

National Advisory and Co-ordinating Committee on Multicultural Education (1987) *Education in and for a Multicultural Society: Issues and Strategies for Policy Making*, Canberra: Department of Education

Neales, S. (1990) 'Immigration plot thickens', *Australian Financial Review*, 25 May

New South Wales Committee of Inquiry into Overseas Qualifications (1989) *Recognition of Overseas Qualifications*, Sydney: NSW Government Printer

Nicolaou, L. (1991) *Australian Unions and Immigrant Workers*, Sydney: Allen and Unwin

Office of Multicultural Affairs (1989a) *National Agenda for a Multicultural Australia: Sharing Our Future*, Canberra: Australian Government Publishing Service

——(1989b) *Issues in Multicultural Australia: Frequency Tables*, Canberra: Office of Multicultural Affairs

——(1990) *National Agenda for a Multicultural Australia: the Year in Review*, Canberra: Australian Government Publishing Service

——(1993a) *Access and Equity: Evaluation Summary*, Canberra: Australian Government Publishing Service

——(1993b) *Focus*, February

O'Malley, P. (1978) 'Australian immigration policies and the dirty-worker syndrome', in B. Birrell and C. Hay (eds), 47–59

Ossowski, S. (1963) *Class Structure in the Social Consciousness*, London: Routledge and Kegan Paul

Partington, G. (1991) 'Grievance industry at work' *Bulletin*, 27 August, 89–91

Pascoe, R. (1990) *Open for Business: Immigrant and Aboriginal Entrepreneurs Tell Their Stories*, Canberra: Australian Government Publishing Service

Phillips, D. J. and Houston, J. (eds) (1984) *Australian Multicultural Society: Identity, Communication, Decision Making*, Blackburn, Victoria: Drummond

Pittarello, A. (1990) 'The religiousness of the Italians', *Migration Monitor*, 5(17–18): 6–10

Polish Task Force (1983) *The New Polish Immigrants: a Quest for Normal Life*, Sydney: NSW Government Printer

Poole, M. E., de Lacey, P. R. and Randhawa, R. (eds) (1985) *Australia in Transition: Culture and Life Possibilities*, Sydney: Harcourt Brace Jovanovich

Price, C. A. (1968) 'Migrants in Australian society', in H.R.H. The Duke of Edinburgh's Third Commonwealth Study Conference, 95–112

——(1985) 'The ethnic composition of the Australian population', in I. Burnley, S. Encel and G. McCall (eds), 43–57

—— (1988) 'The ethnic composition of the Australian population', in J. Jupp (ed.), 119–28

Przeworski, A. (1977) 'Proletariat into a class: the process of class formation from Karl Kautsky's *The Class Struggle* to recent controversies', *Politics and Society*, 7: 343–401

Pusey, M. (1991) *Economic Rationalism in Canberra: a Nation Building State Changes Its Mind*, Cambridge: Cambridge University Press

Read, P. (1982) *The Stolen Generations: the Removal of Aboriginal Children in New South Wales 1883 to 1969*, Occasional Paper No. 1, Sydney: NSW Ministry of Aboriginal Affairs

Reeves, W. P. (1902) *State Experiments in Australia and New Zealand*, London: Grant Richards

Reid, J. and Trompf, P. (eds) (1990) *The Health of Immigrant Australia: a Social Perspective*, Sydney: Harcourt Brace Jovanovich

Review of Post-Arrival Programs and Services for Migrants (1978) *Migrant Services and Programs*, Canberra: Australian Government Publishing Service

Rizvi, F. (1986) *Ethnicity, Class and Multicultural Education*, Geelong: Deakin University Press

Robertson, R. (ed.) (1969) *Sociology of Religion: Selected Readings*, Harmondsworth: Penguin

ROMAMPAS, see Committee for Stage I

Saunders, P. (1993) *Economic Adjustment and Distributional Change: Income Inequality in Australia in the Eighties*, SPRC Discussion Papers No. 47, Kensington: University of New South Wales

Saunders, P. and Encel, D. (eds) (1992) *Social Policy in Australia: Options for the 1990s*, Volume 2, SPRC Reports and Proceedings No. 97, Kensington: University of New South Wales

Sawer, M. (1990) *Public Perceptions of Multiculturalism*, Canberra: Australian National University

Schreuder, D. (1992) 'Born free: the advent of a new Australia', *Australian*, 25 November

Seitz, A, and Foster, L. (1985) 'Dilemmas of immigration – Australian expectations, migrant responses', *Australian and New Zealand Journal of Sociology*, 21(3): 414–30

Sheaves, R. (1988) 'Building on ethnic influences', *Migration*, August/September, 29

Sheridan, G. (1988) 'Howard's prejudice shames us all', *Australian*, 20–21 August
———(1990) 'Migrants offer benefits for cities', *Australian*, 15 November

Signy, H. (1993) 'The future looks mixed for marriage', *Sydney Morning Herald*, 10 March

Sivanandan, A. (1988) 'The new racism', *New Statesman and Society*, 4 November, 8–9

Smith, A. (1976) *Social Change: Social Theory and Historical Processes*, London: Longman
———(1981) *The Ethnic Revival*, Cambridge: Cambridge University Press

Smith, B. (1990) 'Lemontey's prophecy', in B. Hocking (ed.), 11–23

Smith, D. (1993) 'Slave trade: the new servant class', *Sydney Morning Herald*, 8 March

Smolicz, J. (1985) 'Multiculturalism and an overarching framework of values', in M. E. Poole, P. R. de Lacey and R. Randhawa (eds), 76–87

Storer, D. (1978) 'The legacy of post-war migration policies', in R. Birrell and C. Hay (eds), 75–102

Strahan, K. W. and Williams, A. J. (1988) *Immigrant Entrepreneurs in Australia*, Canberra: Office of Multicultural Affairs

Stubbs, J. (1966) *The Hidden People*, Melbourne: Cheshire

Tatham, P. (1993) 'All in the clan', *Australian Magazine*, 9–10 January, 18–24

Taylor, L. (1992) 'Hand denies racism on refugees', *Australian*, 14–15 November

Tenbruck, F. H. (1989) 'The cultural foundation of society', in H. Haferkamp (ed.), 15–35

Therborn, G. (1976) *Science, Class and Society: on the Formulation of Sociology and Historical Materialism*, London: New Left Books

Thompson. E. P. (1968) *The Making of the English Working Class*, Harmondsworth: Penguin

Titmuss, R. M. (1963) *Essays on the 'Welfare State'*, second ed., London: Allen and Unwin

Trevitt, L. and Rish, G. (1989) 'Why is Ramsay Street full of Anglos?', *Newswit*, Sydney, 20 September, 11

Tucker, R. C. (ed.) *The Marx–Engels Reader*, second ed., New York: W. W. Norton

Vanderber, A. and Dow, G. (1991) 'Farewell to the Swedish model', *Australian Left Review*, 126, March, 26–30

Visontay, M. (1989) 'The unwanted ones', *Sydney Morning Herald*, 31 March

Viviani, N. (1990) 'The Asian equation: how many is too many?', *Australian*, 29 May

Waldinger, R., Aldrich, H. and Ward, R. (1990) *Ethnic Entrepreneurs: Immigrant Business in Industrial Societies*, Newbury Park, CA: Sage

Walker, P. (ed.) *Between Labour and Capital*, Hassocks: Harvester Press

Walsh, M. (1988) 'Exploiting the politics of paranoia', *Sydney Morning Herald*, 22 August

Walsh, P. (1990) 'High immigration at our economic peril', *Australian Financial Review*, 8 May

——(1991) 'Immigrating more deeply into recession', *Australian Financial Review*, 30 April

Ward, R. (1966) *The Australian Legend*, second ed., Melbourne: Oxford University Press

Webb, K. and Manderson, L. (1990) 'Food habits and their influence on health', in J. Reid and P. Trompf (eds), 184–205

Weber, M. (1968) *Economy and Society: an Outline of Interpretive Sociology*, Berkeley: University of California Press

Whelan, J. (1989) 'Who is taking the oath for Australia?', *Sydney Morning Herald*, 7 April

White, R. (1981) *Inventing Australia: Images of Identity 1788–1980*, Sydney: Allen and Unwin

Whiteford, P. (1991) *Immigrants and the Social Security System*, Melbourne: Bureau of Immigration Research

Williams, L. (1992) 'Bosses prefer Aussie culture over skills', *Sydney Morning Herald*, 6 October

Williams, R. (1981) 'The analysis of culture', in T. Bennett, G. Martin, C. Mercer and J. Woollacott (eds), 43–52

——(1983) *Towards 2000*, London: Chatto & Windus

Withers, G. (1989) 'Living and working in Australia', in K. Hancock (ed.), 1–22

——(1990) 'Controlled intake could aid economic recovery', *Australian*, 30 May

——(ed.) *Commonality and Difference: Australia and the United States*, Sydney: Allen and Unwin

——(1991) 'The great immigration debate: immigration and national identity', in G. Withers (ed.), 49–60

Wood, A. (1990a) 'Australia's population puzzle', *Australian*, 28 April

——(1990b) 'Setting a population target the key to proper planning', *Australian*, 29 May

Wright, E. O. (1985) *Classes*, London: Verso Edition

Young, M.(1991) 'Our immigration policy challenges', in D. Goodman, D. J. O'Hearn and C. Wallace-Crabbe (eds) 69–79

Zammit, P. (1993) 'Libs need a healthy dose of culture', *Sydney Morning Herald*, 29 March

Zubrzycki, J. (1977) 'Toward a multicultural society in Australia', in M. Bowen (ed.), 130–41

Index